Second Lieutenant and Army Air Corps
Fighter Pilot Richard P. Cooley

# Level Best

## A MEMOIR ABOUT FAMILY, CAREER, AND GRATITUDE

## By Dick Cooley

*With* Mary Beth Abel *and* Ann Boreson

Foreword by Bill Ayer

Documentary Media
Seattle, Washington

*This book is dedicated to Sean Murray Cooley.*

*Level Best*

A MEMOIR ABOUT FAMILY, CAREER, AND GRATITUDE

Published by Documentary Media
3250 41st Ave SW
Seattle, WA 98116
(206) 935-9292
books@docbooks.com
www.documentarymedia.com

Expanded Edition, 2017
(Original Edition: *Searching Through My Prayer List*, 2010)
Printed in Canada

Author: Dick Cooley, with Mary Beth Abel and Ann Boreson
Editor: Chris Boutée
Book Designer: Paul Langland
Editorial Director: Petyr Beck

*Bridget Cooley would like to thank Jill Smith for her assistance in writing "Atlantic Adventure." Additional thanks for their contributions to the memoir go to Naveena Ponnusamy of the RAND Corporation, Will Guyman, and Father Michael Ryan.*

ISBN: 978-1-933245-44-7

*Photos on pages 8 and 208, courtesy of the University of Washington Foster School of Business.*

*Photos on pages 111, 112, 131, 136, 152, and 174, courtesy of Wells Fargo.*

# Contents

Dick Cooley and Bill Ayer co-teaching "The CEO and the Board"
at the University of Washington Foster School of Business,
May 16, 2016.

# Foreword

I have had the pleasure of knowing Dick Cooley for over 10 years, but have known of him for much longer. I feel truly lucky and blessed because of our friendship and the time we spent together teaching at the University of Washington Foster School of Business.

Years before we met, my colleagues often asked me if I knew Dick Cooley. His large group of fans were in awe of his banking prowess as CEO of Wells Fargo. Most importantly for those of us in the Northwest, he was known as the person who was brought in to work his magic to turn around the troubled Seafirst Bank. For years I continued to hear about this terrific guy who was involved in everything worthwhile in Seattle. He was, and still is, a giant in the community.

I first met Dick vicariously in the book *Good to Great*, where author and researcher Jim Collins called him a rare "Level 5 Leader." I invited Collins to be the keynote speaker at an Alaska Airlines leadership conference in 2004, where we heard a lot about Dick Cooley's principles and leadership in discussing Wells Fargo's amazing long-term performance.

I knew I needed to get to know him and finally had the opportunity when he invited me to speak to his Executive MBA class at the University of Washington. It was a fun experience, and I saw in Dick not only a highly competent leader, but also a passionate teacher. A couple of years later, he asked me to take over teaching his class. I agreed, but was smart enough to ask him to stick around and do it with me.

Teaching with Dick was enlightening, and I learned from him how to make the class as valuable as possible for our students. I also benefited greatly from Dick's mentorship and wisdom as we discussed some of my challenges as CEO of Alaska during a crazy and tumultuous time in the airline industry.

When Dick is passionate about something, nothing gets in his way. How he came to teach at the business school after retiring from the bank is a case in point. He has a strong (and, in my opinion, correct) belief that an MBA program that lacks exposure to leaders and their real-world issues is shortchanging students. His offer to the school was to create a class that would fill in the gaps that come from a purely academic course of study, though he received some pushback from his initial overtures. Thankfully, he persisted, and Dick's class, now called The CEO and the Board, has become one of the most popular in the nationally ranked two-year EMBA program. Several thousand students (and the companies they've worked for) have benefited. I've been lucky to now be leading this course and am happy to have had Dick make an occasional appearance. His presence at Foster has been appreciated by students and faculty alike, and his always-astute comments often get a round of applause at the end of the class period.

The memoir you're about to read provides fascinating insights into this remarkable human being. You'll follow him through his many dreams, successes, and celebrations, as well as through the tough times that were sometimes filled with angst and regret. Dick shares his joys and sorrows in a way that will allow you to reflect on your own life and perhaps find some new meaning in your journey.

Every person, every organization, and every community
Dick has touched is better because of him. He is rightfully proud
of his family and his wife, Bridget (who loves to fly as much as
anyone I know). Dick Cooley is the real deal and he has lived an
extraordinarily full life.

Here's your chance to get to know Dick. As you spend time
with him through his story, you, too, will be inspired to give your
"Level Best" to all that you do.

BILL AYER

*Retired Chairman and CEO Alaska Air Group and*
*currently a Regent at the University of Washington April, 2016*

SEAN COOLEY AND JEAN KAYSER AT STINSON BEACH, CALIFORNIA.

# Preface

Sean was my middle son, who many people said resembled me more than his two brothers do. He was a delight and a friend to all who knew him. On the day of his memorial service, more than 400 people came to say goodbye and share their thoughts and memories of him. Many of these diverse mourners knew Sean well and were able to present an incredible picture of who he was and what he did with his short life. He died of pancreatic cancer on April 30, 2015, after battling it for sixteen months.

There was so much love and respect, and many tears, as different aspects of his life were finely laid before us. His six closest friends, including his son, Sean Jr., let us see what an outstanding person he was.

Not well known, but clearly memorable, was Sean's reputation as a polo player during his college years at the University of California, Davis, where he captained the team to four national collegiate championships in a row. His mother was a fine equestrian and so was he.

After college Sean got started in the commercial real estate business and made for himself a successful career. He worked hard at it, finding help from many friends and mentors. Within our family, he became an expert at accommodating our individual needs for finding the best options to eat and sleep as we traveled around the world. In addition, we all have benefited financially from doing what he has suggested. And on that subject, I think he has made more money than anyone else in the family, including his dad.

An exceptional quality, which came out of the various talks at Sean's memorial, was the depth of his kindness and care for others. If he could help you, he tried hard and always went the extra mile to solve your problem, which he was good at doing.

As a father it was easy to be more than pardonably proud of how he lived his life and shared it generously with so many people. He had friends everywhere and was trustworthy, smart, and creative.

Although Sean's first marriage did not work out, he and his first wife, Brenda, had two fine children, Bridget and Sean Jr. Later, Sean met Jean Kayser and married her in Sun Valley more than twelve years ago. Jean graduated from the Wharton School of Business but decided she wanted to become a doctor rather than a businesswoman. She turned around, went back to school, and eight years later became a licensed OB/GYN working for the Kaiser Foundation in Oakland, California.

Jean, Bridget, and Sean Jr. were always at the top of Sean's list. Their activities dominated his calendar, and they skied and golfed whenever they could. With his brother, Mark, they bought a lovely pink stucco home in Carmel and called it the Pink Palace. Situated on a hill above the Carmel Mission, it became their favorite place to spend extra time when they could get away from their home in suburban Lafayette, California. The Pink Palace turned into the center of a large number of extended-family activities.

We all miss Sean and his lightness, sense of fun, and all the personal gifts he brought to us. At times he struggled, but in spite of the ups and downs, which each of us faces, he put his family first and was a joy to all.

With Sean's passing to the next world, I feel grief and sadness, but also hope that he is with God and happy for all eternity. How wonderful to have had a child like him to dedicate this story to.

Gratitude for the life I have been given underlies my memoir. My appreciation for my children, their children and spouses, and for all the love that has come with them is paramount.

——————

Thank you, Lord.
Dick Cooley

DICK AND SEAN ON THE FAIRWAY AT
AUGUSTA NATIONAL GOLF CLUB.

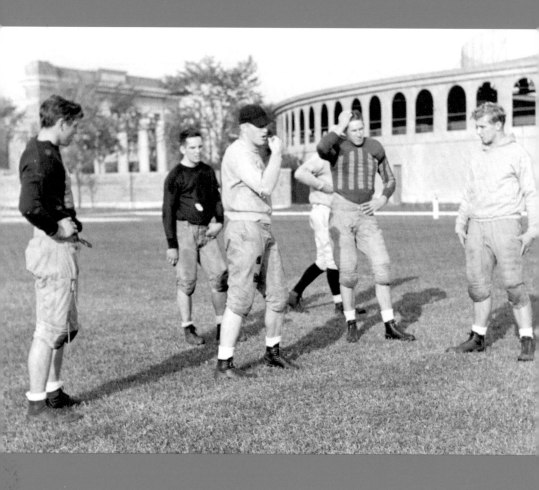

DICK (FAR RIGHT) AS A FRESHMAN FOOTBALL PLAYER AT YALE, 1940.

# Prologue

I was considered an experienced pilot when a brand-new Lockheed P-38 Lightning was delivered to our squadron based in Florennes, Belgium, on December 11, 1944, just 16 days after my 21st birthday. I requested permission to test-fly the plane. My selection came with a firm lecture from my commanding officer. While flying, I was to take notes concerning temperatures, pressures, speeds, and anything pertaining to the plane's performance. As it was a test flight, I was able to head west and away from German lines toward France. D-day had happened June 6, Paris was liberated in August, and by December 1944 much of France was occupied by the Allies.

The idea of flying out of formation and not being shot at was exciting. After all, I had just turned 21, I was flying a brand new plane, and I was on my own. I'm having the time of my life, I thought, as I dutifully went through the checklist I balanced in my lap.

Once I completed all the checks and with all systems performing perfectly, I took the plane up to 20,000 ft.— enough altitude, I figured, to test the P-38's new dive flaps. One of the joys of flying is letting a wing drop and feeling the plane fall away. With the plane purring across the sky with precision and ease, I dipped a wing and swooped down to 10,000 ft. It was then that I pushed the dive flap button to give the plane what it needed to resist gravity and swoop back up to 20,000 ft. But nothing happened. I pushed the button over and over again, but it would not engage. The electrical system was not working for this part of the plane. I watched the altimeter go around and around, knowing that I was in terrible trouble. That is the last thing I remember.

What happened next I have to leave to hearsay, as I was not in any condition to recall the events that followed. I was told that a Frenchman saw the plane spiraling toward the ground, saw a parachute open, and found and carried me to a nearby hospital in

Chambray in northern France. I was never able to thank him. The only detail I have about him was that he was black.

My right arm was dangling by threads of skin. The hospital staff cleaned me up and wrapped me tight in hospital blankets. I do not remember much about the next few days, except to faintly recall an ambulance ride that involved serious pain and seemed to last forever. When I eventually regained consciousness a few days later, the pain had eased, but I didn't know what had happened or where I was. I felt groggy and I was hurting, but I had no idea that I had lost my arm.

---

The Battle of the Bulge began on the morning of December 16, 1944. The attack on the Western Front by German forces caught the Allies by surprise and German troops were advancing toward our location. I'd received my last sacraments of the church in a hospital ward lined with soldiers, all of us in the same miserable state. We remained on the top floor of the hospital, while the staff and all transportable patients were evacuated to the basement. Being immobile, we looked up at the ceiling, wondering when the bombs were going to come through the roof or when the German paratroopers would break in and shoot us. As the battles raged, all we could do was lie there in the dark and listen. Fortunately, the Germans never got that far into France.

It took a while for my base to find me because in those days there was no instant communication. When the plane did not return, questions were asked, but there was no way of knowing I was 100 miles away in France, fighting for my life.

A few days later, my squadron received word that I was in a U.S. Army hospital in Reims. My roommate, Bob Anderson, packed my personal items and, along with a few other men, drove down from Florennes to see what was left of me. They told me that our squadron's P-38s were being replaced with P-51 Mustangs. That was welcome news for them. The single-engine P-51 was more reliable than the P-38, which suffered from engine failures.

Just before Christmas it was decided that the mortal danger from shock and wounds had passed and I was moved to a tent hospital between Paris and Le Havre. Being west of Paris and even farther from the German lines and battle in eastern France, it was safer and quieter. It was there that I faced the fact that I had lost my arm, and many diverse thoughts began running through my mind. Coping with the amputation of a limb is a mental process and I realized that I needed to overcome my profound feeling of loss. It may sound odd, but even though I was faced with a life-altering debilitation, I knew I would survive and would be okay without the arm. I would make a living. I would find a wife. I would be happy. But I would probably never play football again. The challenge of football, particularly those years I spent playing at Yale, had been huge. I had not been brave as a young-ster. So it meant a lot to me to get over the fear of being knocked around and be able to truly enjoy the game, learn my positions, and become a skilled player. Sometimes during my recovery I found myself dreaming about returning to Yale and playing varsity football. When I realized that I was no longer physically able to accomplish my goal, I cried and cried. There was no consoling me. It was one of the first times in my life that some-thing I desperately wanted was taken away.

I had to learn how to let go and accept, to understand that when dreams are gone, you have to rise above the pain and self-pity and go on with life.

Although it was a difficult time, that lesson has served me well over the years.

# Part One

*What a lucky person I am! How many people get to experience
something full circle like that? The fact that I could
walk on a field that had meant so much to me as a teenager
and experience it once more this many decades later was truly
satisfying. It reminds me again how God has kept me going.
When He decides it is over, well, that will be it.
But in the meantime, I am thankful for all the people
who have helped me.*

Dick after fishing on the Rogue River, Oregon.

# Meeting Babe Ruth

In 1929, when I was about six years old, my mother and father moved our family from Albany to Rye, New York. My father had been promoted and was now head of PR for the New York Bell Telephone Company.

Rye was a fine suburban community, conveniently located to everything in the New York area. Not long after our move, my family joined the Apawamis Club. It was not far from our home and, as a teenager, I could play golf, tennis, and squash there as a junior member. The locker room for juniors and guests was smaller than the senior members' facility, but it had three wonderful showers with huge circular heads that resembled sunflowers, each producing a magnificent waterfall-like spray.

I was taking a shower after playing tennis when one of the guests for the day entered. He was an enormous man with a hairy chest and large belly. In those days, we didn't wear bath-robes. If you were a man, you walked around the locker room as God made you and no one thought anything of it.

As this man came toward me, there was no denying that he was solid and strong. I was in the last shower stall and he took his place in the space beside me.

After showering and once we were dried off and dressed, he finally spoke to me, "Hi kid, how're ya doing?"

"Fine, sir. Thank you. How are you?"

We talked for a while and I learned he had just finished a round of golf.

Later on my way home, I finally got it through my thick head who the man was — Babe Ruth! Someone had mentioned that he was practicing at the club. His career with the Red Sox, Yankees, and Braves had ended in 1935, and now he was trying to translate his home run ability into a PGA golf swing. He ended up doing that fairly well. On May 10, 1939, for example, Ruth was a member of a Long Island Golf Association team that beat the New Jersey State Golf Association team for the Stoddard Trophy. The match was played at the Apawamis Club.

I have never forgotten that meeting. It happened around 1937, when I was about 14. Babe Ruth's presence and that experience left an indelible impression on me. It was my first indication that all men are essentially the same. Even as a young boy standing next to a great historical figure, I recognized that he and I were basically built the same way. He was bigger, stronger, older, and more experienced, but no matter how famous and idolized he was or anyone is — be it a president, a pope, a star athlete, or a movie star in Hollywood — the needs, desires, and potential for greatness are the same.

That day changed the way I view relationships, or perhaps it formulated a new outlook that has lasted all my life. I learned that people may wear different clothes or have a different color of skin or have more fame, titles, or money, but basically God made us all the same.

He gave us our human bodies and no one should ever feel they are put together better or worse than anyone else, because we are all created equal, just like it says in our Constitution. There are infinite variations in all of us that make each individual unique. That is why every one of us is our own special work of art. It is a good thing to remember when you worry about meeting someone important. You should not feel intimidated. You can respect someone for what they do or who they are, which I certainly do, but it is important to remember that we all belong to the human race.

Meeting Babe Ruth was my first clue that what makes a difference in life is how you use your God-given talents. Babe Ruth was famous and a star, but he was also a regular man. Meeting him gave me confidence that I could achieve whatever I set my mind to.

DICK AS A SMALL CHILD.

# *Lessons from Early School Days*

My first years at school were spent at Rye Country Day School. I do not remember much about those early years, but there was one memorable event that took place in the third grade. My teacher at the time was Mrs. Foshay, a smart, accomplished woman.

One day Mrs. Foshay passed out math workbooks. We were to do multiplication problems, making sure that we showed all of our calculations. I have always had a tendency to search for ways of beating the system, and this time was no exception. I soon discovered that the answers to the problems we were working on were at the bottom of the next page. I could not believe my luck. Of course we were not to show the answers without the necessary calculations, but that did not stop me. I was moving ahead feverishly, jotting down those answers, when Mrs. Foshay tapped me on the shoulder and said loudly, "Dick, you are cheating. You cannot solve the problem without doing the work. You are two pages ahead of the class and into double multiplication. We have not done that yet. It takes two lines of figures that have to be added together to get the answer. Your page is full of one-line answers, which shows you are copying them from the answer sheet." Then she gave me and the whole class a lecture on cheating and how I was hurting myself by trying to take a shortcut. She was right, and I was mortified. She taught me a lesson that has never left me. And I learned the right way to do multiplication.

Throughout my life, Mrs. Foshay's words have come back to me: You cannot solve the problem without doing the work.

---

Later, around the time I met Babe Ruth, I attended Iona School in New Rochelle, New York. It was an old, conservative school run by the Irish Christian Brothers. The method of teaching followed the doom-and-gloom, fire-and-brimstone philosophy that seemed to be favored by the Catholic Church at the time. We learned to think about our behavior as it related to God's law and to understand the consequences of doing sinful things and ending up in hell.

While at Iona School I became acquainted with Brother Finch. I felt that he knew me better than I knew myself. The phrase that comes to mind is that he could see straight through me and I know many other students felt the same way. Even though he knew I had strong athletic ability, he also recognized that I was timid. The idea of being considered cowardly was horrifying to me. I had the body and the skills, but not the attitude to go with them. In my early years, as well as later in life, I had to learn to overcome my social anxieties.

Brother Finch asked me one day, "Why do you always back up before you go forward?" It seemed to me that he was onto my fears. I had something to overcome, and I worked at it for a long time before it ceased to be a problem. One day when Brother Finch was coaching, I finally began to take his message to heart. I chased a football full-speed ahead and forgot all about the grandstand in my way. I ran smack into it and broke my nose. My nose endured two more breaks on the football field, so it's not surprising that it does not rest on my face as it was designed.

Just before my 14th birthday, the Iona School coaches discovered that I was a good kicker. One afternoon they took me out on a field and asked me to attempt as many points-after-touchdown kicks as I could, and I kicked 19 in a row before I missed. No one had done that before, not to mention a ninth grader who weighed only 125 pounds.

I had been playing on the junior varsity team, not with all the gigantic upperclassmen on varsity, but after that kicking exhibition they suited me up for the big varsity Thanksgiving Day game against All Hallows, our traditional rival. I was called to kick a point after touchdown and I missed. It was devastating. Back in the locker room at halftime, the coach was saying something about that kick and he turned to me and said, "How old are you, Dick?" I told him I was 14, and he said, "Oh, I thought you were 13," at which point I muttered something about having had a birthday recently. Suddenly pure terror overcame me, because that very day was my birthday and I did not want anyone to know it for fear of what they might do to me. Probably those big guys would have done nothing, but I could imagine their deep, cracking voices taunting me. That was one of the first times I can remember being one of the youngest and involved in something that was over my head. In many ways it struck me as a disaster. Now that I am older than everyone else, it is easier to look back and be amused at my younger self.

Being in over your head isn't a disaster unless you don't find a way to cope. In time, I learned how to do that and, trust me, it gets easier the older you get.

Dick's parents, Victor E. and Helen Pierce Cooley,
in Yosemite National Park, circa 1950.

# Learning from My Parents

I was born on November 25, 1923. My childhood was idyllic in many ways. I was the oldest and the only boy in the family. My twin sisters, Kay and Ann, were born four years later, and Helen came five years after the twins. We were a close family, but being so much older than my sisters, I sometimes felt like an only child. My interaction with my younger sisters was limited, and like many older brothers, I teased them unmercifully. Today I regret not having been a better brother and nicer to them. Fortunately, with the passage of time, we have all become much closer.

My mother was a conventional Catholic, well indoctrinated in her faith. She was extremely concerned about doing the right thing at all times, not only as it related to the church but socially and in everything else. She worried about what other people would think, a trait that rubbed off on all of us children.

When she married my father, he agreed that if there were any children they would be raised Catholic. Pop was not a Catholic, but he was not opposed to it either. My mother always wanted him to join the church and asked all of her children to pray for his conversion, but it never happened. He would attend Mass with us on Christmas and Easter, and we were told that he prayed on his knees every night before going to bed. We interpreted his absence from the church as part of how he expressed his personal form of religion.

Along with teaching us etiquette, manners, and culture, my mother took it upon herself — very matter-of-factly — to teach me about sex. One day she sat down next to me on the piano bench while I was practicing. She literally had a book about the birds and the bees in her hands. I will never understand why she picked that particular moment to spring the mechanics of human reproduction on me, but she went through the whole process and in retrospect, left little to the imagination. She began with a woman's period and continued on with exactly how an egg is fertilized. I think I was nine or 10 at the time and could not have cared less. The whole thing sounded disgusting to me. But her talk served me well and much sooner than you might expect.

My neighborhood was bicycle territory. I could go anywhere on my bike with my friends. We rode back and forth to our various meeting places, never lost steam, and covered a large area daily. Not long after my mother's talk, I was with the bicycle gang and able to impress the older boys in the group. They were convinced they knew all about sex. They thought I was a goody-goody, but one day as they were talking about girls, which the gang innocently did from time to time, I said, "I know how it works." At that moment, I knew I had knowledge they didn't have and I felt superior. My mother had already taught me, but no one had talked to them. Most of the parents hoped their children would simply learn from peers at school, which meant, of course, that their kids didn't understand the subject at all.

Unlike my mother, my father circled around the subject of sex. Off of our living room was a den, which is where he liked to sit. It was a wonderful space with a working fireplace and two big easy chairs with a chessboard set between them where we would play. One night Pop broached the subject of women, specifically the temptations of sex. His talk was not educational like Mother's, but I could tell that he wanted to add a male perspective. He said,

"Dick, I never messed around sexually with women for two reasons. First, I did not want to get them pregnant, and second, I didn't want to catch a disease."

With that pronouncement, I got the distinct impression that my father's policy was to avoid certain activities if he didn't want to suffer the consequences. I know he liked women and women liked him, but he was never one to play around. He knew that life comes with responsibilities. No one stands alone; each of us affects others by our actions. Pop's speech played right into my fear of not doing the right thing and incurring horrible lifelong consequences. I did not want to fail. I never thought about it concretely as if something awful would happen, but I definitely tried to avoid any behavior that would disappoint my family or cause me to turn out poorly.

---

My father ran the public relations division of the New York Bell Telephone Company. He was promoted to this position and had accepted a 10 percent cut in pay before we moved to Rye, but this was the extent of the Great Depression's effect on our family. Because the phone company was both a utility and a monopoly, the public was the customer and more important than the shareholders. This meant that my father had to get along with absolutely everyone, regardless of religion, political leanings, or what have you. He could never choose sides or show favoritism because everyone had to be considered and listened to. Consensus was his thing, though he never lost sight of his principles or honesty in the process. He was upright and square, and his ethics were impeccable. In retrospect, I do not know how my father's overall job performance was evaluated, but I do know that he was a fine man who was well respected and ran his business and family life with dignity. That was the way I was brought up, and in turn I was always trying to find consensus for courses of action and do the right thing. I could make decisions if I had to, but I always tried to make people feel included and involved as quickly as possible.

Much later, I got over my accommodating way of thinking. What I have learned through the years is that no one can make everyone happy, nor is it a good thing to even try. If your goal is to please the masses, inevitably you do not do some of the things you should. Sometimes you have to respect the fact that you cannot make two opposite sides coalesce. What's important is to do the right thing, and that can sometimes force a tough decision.

Dad instilled in me a positive attitude. He presented me with many opportunities, but he rarely pushed me according to his own bias. Instead, he would listen and remain neutral as I navigated my choices. Inheriting that ability to listen, I was known as "heart-to-heart Cooley" when I was a boy.

I mostly got along well with girls and had lengthy conversations with them when the other boys would not. Over time it backfired somewhat, as the young women I was attracted to tended to think of me as a friend or brother as opposed to a boyfriend. This, however, was not always the case. I must have been around 11 years old when the Rye bicycle group was in full cycle mode. One day we were hanging out in front of my house with all the bikes scattered on the lawn like a yard sale. It was a larger group than normal, and it included a girl about my age and size by the name of Betty Ayer. Somehow Betty and I exchanged some words, and the next thing I knew we were in a fight. To this day I will never understand why she jumped on me and beat me with both fists. There she was, knocking the stuffing out of me, and I felt paralyzed, unable to do anything about it. I was reluctant to hit a girl because I had been taught that they were off-limits. It seemed unfair that I could not defend myself. With each blow I felt increasingly mortified that I had lost face and appeared weak in front of my friends.

It was not that she hurt me, although there is no denying that her blows carried a sting. It was the fact that she could do whatever she wanted while I had to keep my hands at my sides. Betty could haul off and hit me as long as she liked, which she did for quite some time, and I was supposed to take the higher ground because she was a female. Afterward I went upstairs into my room and cried. A short time later a few friends came up the stairs and knocked on my door. "Hey, come on, Dick, it's alright," they said. But I hardly heard them. I was humiliated. It felt like Betty had kicked my ego from Rye to Hoboken.

Betty's battering was cataclysmic. In time I got over it because that's what I tend to do. I know I probably would not have felt good about myself if I had gotten mad and connected with a few hard swings, but the fact remains that I was afraid to act in a way that might have stopped what was happening. It was a confusing time. I knew I wanted to be both confident and strong, yet I was painfully aware that I wasn't.

———————

Summers were a time for trips. Early on, my sisters were considered too young to go, so they would stay home with a sitter. They may have felt left out, but it seemed perfectly natural to me, since I was well on my way to being spoiled. In my defense, taking those excursions alone with my parents was one of the true joys of my childhood and part of the tremendous privilege of being the oldest child.

Eventually, my mother would take all the kids to Santa Clara, California, to visit her mother and our relatives. We had lots of family in the area, and it was always a good time. I also looked forward to our family trips west by rail, as I have always had an affinity for trains. On one such excursion, the train had stopped to refuel in Laramie, Wyoming. In those days, trains were powered by steam engines that required regular replenishment of coal and water. Mother was trying to organize the four of us children, as a stop like this usually involved getting off the train and stretching our legs. When the train started up again, Mother could not find me. Frantic, she begged the conductor to wait, but after five minutes he said there could be no more delays. He convinced her that I would be put on the next train and said that was the best he could offer. Soon after, the train pulled away from the station and headed down the tracks.

I had no idea that I had become a missing person, having wandered into the observation car and become completely mesmerized watching the coupling of the freight cars, the movement of the switch engines, and all the things that went on in an old railroad yard. It had not occurred to me to tell Mother where I was going, and she never thought to look for me on the train. When she did come across me, she was furious. If Pop had been there, I am sure she would have made him spank me. Fortunately, he was not on board, so I received a verbal lashing instead.

One of Pop's many benefits working with the telephone company was that he received four weeks of vacation each year, which he spent in California in August. During this time my parents would sometimes take me fishing with them. One trip that comes to mind was on the Rogue River in Oregon. My mother was not crazy about fishing, but she was a good sport and threw her line into the water with the rest of us.

It was during the long summer trips to California that I became close to my cousin, Jack, who was the son of my mother's oldest brother and four years older than I. Jack (John) Pierce and I had free rein to bicycle anywhere, and we were granted access to the old family tennis court at my grandmother's house and the neighbor's pool across the street. (The neighbor was a distant cousin.) We seemed to find enough trouble to occupy our days, including setting off fireworks in the tennis court and shooting birds out of trees. Jack was the perfect companion. He was a fisherman, a smart but humble sort. Without Jack those summers would have been deadly; we did everything together and became fast friends. He served in the Navy and went to Stanford for his college and graduate school degrees. Eventually, he became a professor at the UCLA School of Medicine in the Department of Biochemistry, serving from 1953 to 1984.

One of the last summer trips we took to California happened in the mid-1930s, when I was 12. As the time neared to return to New York, I had an idea that I wanted to cross the country alone. I do not recall if there was a debate on the subject, though I know Mother was concerned, but my parents finally came to the conclusion that I could take my first solo trip. Before I stepped on board the train, my father gave me safety advice and money to cover my expenses.

I had a berth in a regular Pullman car, and fortunately, it was a lower berth. You needed to climb a ladder to get to the upper berth, which didn't have a window like the lower one. In those days there was a long hammock-like holder that the porter would assemble across the windows when he made up the bed at night. You could put your things in there and it was said to be secure. Dad showed me how to wrap my wallet in the hip pocket of my pants and then roll my pants up and put them in the holder. He explained that if I followed his instructions, no one would steal my money and I would not lose anything. That turned out to be good advice. The cross-country trip happened without incident. I did not lose my money and I had enough to cover my expenses.

Before World War II there were no coast-to-coast trains. We traveled across the country on the Overland Limited, from San Francisco to Chicago, and then changed trains and stations and boarded the New York Central bound for New York. The switch-over in Chicago was the only issue. I had to change stations, trains, and railroads, and that required I navigate my way from the West Side of Chicago to the East Side. Somehow the techni-calities of the transfer took place and I got on a green Parmelee

Transportation System vehicle. It was like one of today's shuttles that you might take from an airport to a hotel, but we didn't called them "shuttles" back then.

My days were spent on the outside deck of the observation car looking forward into the wind, watching what seemed to be endless country pass by. It was such an exhilarating experience as a young man to lean out the side of the train and feel the cars take corners and curves while watching billowing clouds of smoke rise high into the sky. On big curves I could look ahead and count the cars on the train beginning with the engine. When I was not occupied with the landscape, I had conversations with the conductors and brakemen and anyone else who would talk to me. I do not recall ever feeling alone or scared, because there was always something to fill my thoughts. By the time I arrived in Harmon, New York, I had a taste of independence and a love of travel that has endured for a lifetime. That trip across the country is one of my fondest childhood memories. Later, when I was in the army, I found out that not all train travel was as pleasant as my summer trips.

DICK AS A YOUNGSTER.

Dick as a young man before he joined the Army Air Corps.

# Chapter 4

# Portsmouth Priory and Yale

Through his job at the telephone company, my father became acquainted with Bruce Barton. Mr. Barton was a partner in a New York advertising firm, BBDO (Batten, Barton, Durstine & Osborn). Mr. Barton had been elected to Congress, representing the so-called Silk Stocking District of Manhattan's Upper East Side. One day Pop came home after listening to one of Mr. Barton's addresses that included the phrase: "The Greatest Adventure in Life Is Doing One's Level Best." My father had the words printed in bold font, framed, and hung over my desk. He drew inspiration from the adage and hoped that I would never settle for mediocrity. Pop often told me that everything would work out fine as long as in my heart I knew I had done my best.

I'm not sure if this event was the deciding factor for my departure to boarding school, or if my father had taken issue with my pastime of listening to Jack Benny and Fred Allen skits on the radio instead of devoting time to homework. In the ninth grade my school marks had fallen slightly, and he blamed the airwaves for my movement in the wrong direction. He was also thinking about college, whereas I had not even considered it. Although it must have been a financial hardship for my family, my father decided that I should go to Portsmouth Priory, a boarding school that housed about 95 boys and was built on a 500-acre site on the idyllic shores of Narragansett Bay in Rhode Island. He felt that at Portsmouth, which was known for its superior education, strong supervision, and discipline, I would have plenty of time to focus on my studies and ultimately increase my chances of getting into a good college.

Portsmouth Priory (now Portsmouth Abbey School), founded in 1926, is a school in the English Benedictine tradition. The Benedictine Order began over 1,500 years ago with what Saint Benedict called "the Rule" and which later became the basic outline of the monastic principles of love and work. The Benedictines are credited with carefully having copied books by hand and preserving Western culture during the Dark Ages. Through their dedication and perseverance, they were able to protect the intellectual and cultural history for generations to come. Committed to higher education and reverence for God, the Benedictines at Portsmouth Priory translated these values to students by teaching that if you work hard and love God, then everything else falls into place.

The curriculum provided for a six-day-a-week class schedule with athletics at the end of each day. Academics were demanding, but we were encouraged to stay physically fit and play sports. We learned about teamwork: how to win and lose, the importance of good sportsmanship, and the kind of effort it takes to excel. At such a small school, students were able to join almost any team if they showed reasonable talent. You might not become an expert at any one sport, but at least you were given the opportunity to play. I had considerable natural athletic ability, so I successfully joined the football, soccer, basketball, baseball, tennis, and golf teams — basically anything that was offered, with one exception.

One night I tried out for boxing. I did not know anything about it, but I thought I should give it a try. Bob Glennen, the star of the program, was bigger than I and one year older. I got in the ring with him and he basically just knocked me all over the place, from one side of the ropes to the other. Bob understood a lot about boxing. I learned that you should never go into the ring if you do not know what you are doing. That probably applies to a lot of things. I can honestly say that this particular lesson did not have to be repeated. Boxing was off my list.

Life at Portsmouth Priory boarding school felt confining and dreary. Aside from athletics, there was little to do besides study and that did not suit my personality at all. I felt isolated and a long way from home. The freedom that I had experienced in Rye was gone, and I was anxious to get it back. I knew that Portsmouth was a first-rate school, but I was too young and immature to understand the nature of the opportunity. All I wanted to do was rush through my high school years and move on to college.

Looking back, I realize that all the things that Pop expected to happen to me while I was away at school did happen. I received an excellent education, and I became more religious. I learned to love God and began to understand what love meant in the religious sense. I could see that there was more to it than the fear of the Irish Catholic church. In hindsight, it was a fine place to spend two years. I met some great friends, both on the faculty and in the student body, but I regret that I did not enjoy the experience to its fullest. Instead I pushed ahead, reading various college brochures. Though only a junior, I wanted to get on with life.

My lifelong friends from Portsmouth include Peter Flanigan, Jerry Dwyer, and Gordon McShane. When I left school a year early, Peter stayed on and graduated before attending Princeton. While we never lost our closeness in a general sense, our lives went in different directions. Peter was busy. He went to work in the investment banking business, and after World War II he worked for the Marshall Plan in London. He had a great experience there, finding out how things worked in England. During his career, Peter went in and out of government jobs in Washington, D.C. In between times he was an investment banker. He always did very well.

The Flanigans were affluent, as Mrs. Flanigan was from the Anheuser-Busch family, and all the kids had inherited large

amounts of money. I think Peter handled his wealth professionally and increased his family's financial well-being. I am sure
none of them had to work if they did not want to, but Peter
always worked. He was eager to improve himself, and he continued that drive for success his whole life. After Peter's wife, Brigid,
died, he remained lonesome until 2007, when he married an
Austrian woman named Dorothea whom I have yet to meet. She
is Catholic and has five children. Peter also has five children and
16 grandchildren. I look forward to meeting Dorothea one day
and hearing the story of how they met and married when he was
84 and she was 68. Peter passed away in 2013 at the age of 90.

Peter's older brother, John, was also a good friend of mine. He
worked for Anheuser-Busch for a while both as a distributor and
in the company. He married his first cousin, Lotsie Busch, right
off the bat, soon after high school. Peter and I were both in that
wedding. Then John got tired of the family business and went
other ways. He and Lotsie moved to Southern California but after
a while that marriage broke up. John married again, to Nancy, and
they were together for over 30 years. John and Peter were both
members of the Bohemian Club, a private men's club based in the
San Francisco Bay area. The club has annual two-week-long
retreats that meet at the Bohemian Grove in Sonoma County.
There, the club is divided into camps. John and Peter joined
the same camp that I did, Mandalay. I would see John in the
summertime, but our paths rarely crossed otherwise.

Jerry Dwyer remains one of my oldest and best friends. At
Portsmouth, I roomed with Peter Flanigan, and I played tennis
with Jerry. We were number one and number two on the tennis
team. I won the Rhode Island State Singles Championship, and I
am sure Jerry and I won the doubles championship because we
played so well together and didn't have much competition in that
small state. Jerry was an only child and lived in Newport, Rhode
Island. We maintained a close friendship until he passed away a
few years ago.

In our older age, I became closer friends with Gordon McShane, but he has since passed away as well.

For years, the four of us — Peter, Jerry, Gordon, and me — would gather to play golf, even though we lived in different states. I was in California, Peter was in New York or Washington D.C., Jerry was in Rhode Island, and Gordon moved around but was mostly in Florida.

---

Even when I was young, Rye was considered a New York City commuter town, and many of the boys in the area went away to boarding school. If they had gone to private school for the first eight grades, then the only options to continue would be boarding school or transferring to a public school. In Rye, most of the people who went away to school attended Ivy League colleges, and specifically Yale, but from Portsmouth Priory the majority of boys were accepted at Harvard. (Both Robert and Ted Kennedy attended Portsmouth before entering Harvard.) Naturally I looked at the entrance requirements for both colleges, and there was one thing in particular that caught my attention. Yale required the standard 15 solid credits in addition to passing the college boards, but no high school diploma. That was music to my ears!

By the time I was a junior at Portsmouth, I had earned only 10 credits, so I continued to search for the last five credits needed to fulfill Yale's requirements. I had to go back to my ninth-grade work at Iona School, where there were four solid subjects — English, mathematics, science, and German — plus a fifth class called Civics. I was afraid it might not meet Yale requirements even though it was a good course. The class taught how the U.S. government worked, how smaller and larger districts functioned, how Congress was composed, and what differences existed between the executive, judicial, and legislative branches. This information has served me well throughout my life. I don't think my children ever took such a comprehensive class on the inner workings of the government. To my way of thinking, that is a shame because it is the sort of practical knowledge that would generate more interest and participation in the political system. At least Yale recognized its value.

Portsmouth Priory had an excellent English department, and I was able to get a score of 620 on my college boards. It was an honors-level score, but not earthshaking, though I think for a high school junior it showed the Yale acceptance committee that I was able to read, write, and comprehend. It may have helped offset my language boards, which did not turn out as favorably. In preparation for my German boards, I studied words and vocabulary all spring, and although I received a score of only 450, apparently it was enough for Yale to give me credit and accept me a year early into their freshman class.

When the acceptance letter arrived at the end of my junior year at Portsmouth, I was elated. It was at this time that my father discussed another scenario. Since Yale had given me the option to defer enrollment for a year, he proposed a trip around the world. My uncle, who ran a steamship company, graciously offered me the owner's cabin and the privilege of bringing a friend on what would have been a remarkable adventure. Unfortunately, the timing of the trip coincided with the outbreak of World War II in Europe, shelving all plans to travel.

With the trip on hold, I had another discussion with my father. It was the fall of 1940 and everyone suspected that eventually the U.S. would join the war, which meant that I would be drafted. In the heartless way that kids do sometimes, I said to him, "Okay, if I'm going to get killed in the war anyway, I might as well go to Yale and get as much done as I can beforehand." It was a terrible thing to say to my father, but of course I did not know it at the time. I was a difficult child in a lot of ways, spoiled and headstrong. I did not mean to push and insult him by telling him I was going to be killed, as if he would not care. Of course he cared and he was worried, but he did not show it. He knew that I had to accept going into the army and I had to accept that I might lose my life. That was a fact that most young men had to live with at the time.

———————

I arrived in New Haven in the fall of 1940 at the age of 16. Out of the thousand students who were enrolled in Yale's freshman class, I was the second youngest. The youngest happened to be a 14-year-old genius, something I was not. Although no one knew that I was underage, I was keenly aware of it. As I walked through the campus amidst a sea of unfamiliar faces, all my insecurities might as well have been written on my forehead.

I applied for a Catholic roommate and by a stroke of good fortune, I was assigned Jim Buckley. He came from Sharon, Connecticut, and like me had attended a small boarding school, one called Millbrook. Although Jim and I were quite different in our pursuits, a lifelong friendship ensued. He was much more intellectual than I. If I was able to get by with what we called "gentleman's Cs," that suited me fine. Serious-minded and bright, Jim became a member of the *Yale Daily News* staff and was chosen on "Tap Day" to join the Skull & Bones, the hardest-to-get-into and most exclusive secret senior society. Jim remains an immense talent, and my deep regard for him has lasted through the years, as our paths have continued to cross with his marriage to my sister, Ann.

The first year Jim and I roomed together in Wright Hall, a five-story Gothic brownstone on the northwest corner of the old campus. Our dorm room had two bedrooms separated by a sitting area. Each student had his own room, which was just big enough for a bed and a small desk. We shared a john with the two students across the hall. I remember sitting on the brick bulkhead outside Wright Hall dangling my feet off the ledge while watching a swarm of campus activity all around me. There were students flocking in and out of wonderful old buildings, stacks of books in their arms, inspired by newfound knowledge and an undeniable determination to succeed.

For me, Yale had an intellectual, physical, and emotional energy that flowed like the Mississippi River. Anyone who thinks they can change its course or its mission, or wants to for that matter, is seriously mistaken. For more than three hundred years, Yale has proven to be an institution where geniuses and scholars share their knowledge in classrooms and research labs, and coaches inspire and motivate athletes to achieve their highest potential. That day it dawned on me that no matter what I did personally during my college years, it would never leave an indelible mark on this grand, well-oiled machine. I had to decide how I wanted to spend my time there and what I wanted to get out of the experience.

Sixty-seven years passed between the time I first stepped onto that campus and returned in 2007. Although there have been a lot of structural changes, my initial reaction to the place is the same. The momentum lives on. There's a feeling of excellence, a feeling that all of life is about putting forth one's finest effort. Yale's goal remains the same — to give each and every student the opportunity to become a full and contributing individual instilled with the knowledge that it is an honor and a responsibility to help others.

Yale was challenging. I have always been a curious type, and in my freshman year I felt as if I were being pulled in all new directions. There did not seem to be enough hours in the day to dedicate to all the interests that lay in wait. Although I was settling into the routine of classrooms and homework, sports and practice schedules, there was one subject I knew would be my downfall: German.

It should not have come as a big surprise to me because I had struggled with it at Portsmouth, but there did not seem to be a way to get around the fact that all Yale freshmen were required to take a foreign language. Naturally, I signed up for the only language of which I had some working knowledge. As I sat in the back of the class the first three weeks, I realized that I was never going to pass. I was not up to the level of performance and, sadly, it was the lowest course level offered. I began to explore the requirements for graduation and found that there was only one course of study that did not require a language to earn a degree: Industrial Administration and Engineering. Fortunately, it was early enough in the year that I could apply for a transfer into the scientific school.

Although my initial reason for becoming an industrial engineer was to escape the language requirement, it turned out to be the perfect major. It was designed for industrial management, but it offered a broad range of knowledge about a lot of different fields. Years later when I entered the banking world, I found that banks lend money to all types of commerce and in order to be a good loan officer, you have to understand how different businesses work. You may lend money to a farmer to harvest his wheat crop, or to someone who is starting a chain of drive-in movies, or someone who wants to build an automobile dealership. Bankers must have diverse knowledge of the community they serve, and understanding a little bit about everything makes it easier to relate to clients' specific needs.

Industrial Administration and Engineering required that I take classes such as chemistry, physics, and calculus, with one allowed elective per year. My first exposure to Shakespeare was in English 101, taught by Professor Whimset, a tall, imposing man who instilled a love of this great master from his classroom in the basement of Strathcona Hall. I learned about art history and psychology ("Sex 67," as we referred to it; the main topic was how to meet and talk to people, and we college guys, of course, applied all we learned to our attempts at getting dates). Looking back, my only regret is that I was not allowed to take more classes outside my engineering curriculum, as there were so many subjects that interested me. There was only one elective that my mother forbade me to take, and that was not to be disputed.

Before I entered Yale, my mother made a deal with my father. If I attended Catholic school until college, then I could attend any university I wanted. When I selected Yale, she agreed on the grounds that I did not enroll in any philosophy courses. Mother had built into me the idea that I had to fight for my faith. She did not want the materialism of Yale to make my religion seem unimportant or falsify it in some way. Her belief was that I might become distracted from my faith, and Nietzsche and other philosophers might challenge my Catholic belief. As it was, I was not drawn to their ideals at the time. Instead, I started to go to daily Mass.

I attended Mass not because I was holy, but because I felt I needed it. I was young and impressionable and did not think I could argue with my classmates about my beliefs. If they were going to make fun of my religion, which they might have, I needed to be able to stand up for my convictions, because I knew that sometimes you find yourself in an adversarial climate. There were a lot of people at Yale who did not believe in God, people who said it could not be so that God existed. I had to be grounded in my faith and actively living it. It started out as a protective device, but to keep my faith as the core of my principles, I had to work at it. Listening to God's word and talking to Him every morning became a lifelong ritual, one that I have no desire to ever forgo. Daily Mass continues to give me structure and guidance in how to serve God and others better.

I suppose it was a stroke of luck that I was diverted to engineering. The course requirements had nothing to do with God or challenging my belief system. By accident I got into a nonconfrontational environment, all the while building up my defenses so I could clearly be a Catholic without having to worry if I was right or wrong in my faith.

While my roommate, Jim, favored more intellectual pursuits, I was drawn to athletics and playing on the Yale football team was one of the biggest highlights of my college years. It all began in September of 1940, when I tried out for the freshman team and made the second string. I do not recall much of that year, except that I played both as a defensive linebacker and offensive blocking back in the old-fashioned single-wing formation. I was playing behind Jim Whitemore, who was a fine athlete and well regarded by the coaching staff. I spent enough time on the field that season to make friends with the other players and realize that I wanted nothing more than to work my way up to the starting varsity team.

Sophomore year I tried out for the varsity squad and made the fourth team. One of the jobs for the third and fourth teams was to learn the basic plays of the coming week's varsity opponent and run them against the first string so they would have an idea of what they would be facing the next Saturday. During early training we were doing a lot of changing around, and at the end of each practice we had to sprint 100 yards down the field as fast as we could. Invariably, I was the second fastest on the squad. Nelson Talbot consistently beat me. He was not as big as I was, but he was a wingback and he could run. After witnessing our head-to-head sprints, the coaches decided that I would be better off playing end, where speed was more important. The switch was made, and I began new and different training.

After the U.S. joined World War II in December of 1941, Yale established a year-round academic schedule which had three semesters instead of two. That meant I became a junior in June of 1942 and was able to play football that summer. I had reached a playing weight of 195 pounds, had a bull neck, and trained rigorously for the end position, eagerly practicing the steps and moves that the coach taught us. The principal action consisted of charging forward two or three yards, remaining strong on your legs, with your hands out and ready to ward off anyone who came at you while you pushed the play back into the middle of the line. Above all, you were never to allow anyone to get around you. That summer I put on my football pants and practiced running sideways, back and forth, and throwing myself on the ground over and over again in the warm Connecticut dust. It was conditioning as well as technique training.

By the time September rolled around, I was on the second varsity team and for the most part I was backing up a fellow fraternity brother named George Green. The coaches would play me at different positions because in those days football players needed to understand and cover both defense and offense.

The first game went well. I got to play almost the whole last quarter, as they put in the second string since we were beating our opponents handily. The second game was different. We played Navy at Franklin Field in Philadelphia. The kickoff went to George Green, who got knocked out cold and went out of the game. The coaches sent me in and I played almost the whole game. I don't know how I did it, but at least I held the position. George returned for the rest of the season and even though I was behind him and on the second team, I began to play more and more.

At one point in the Cornell game I was playing the defensive right-end position. Cornell was using a single-wing attack, which meant there was a wingback outside their end; a blocking back behind the guard or the tackle; then the fullback, who was back a few yards; and the tailback, who was four or five yards back. Usually the ball went to the tailback, sometimes to the fullback. For example, if they started an end run and I was playing right end, they would try to run around me the conventional way. To do that, they would pull a guard, who would go out and lead the attack, followed by the blocking back or the fullback, then the tailback with the ball, who would try to skirt the end.

Cornell would attempt to knock our end over and then get around the corner so the ball carrier could run and hopefully get around fast enough to make a large gain down the field. That was how it happened in this particular case, and I remember it as clearly as if it happened yesterday instead of over 70 years ago.

I charged in just the way they told me to — hands out, legs firm — and I rammed the first guy who came around. I do not know if he was a guard or the blocking back, but I hit him with everything I had. The world was beautiful at that moment because the whole Cornell backfield was lined up one behind the other, like stars in the heavens. They should never have been lined up in that formation, but there they were. When I hit the first man, I knocked him off his feet and backwards hard enough that he bumped into the player behind him, who then hit the man behind him. It was like dominoes falling. I got two or three of them all at once and suddenly the ball carrier was out there all by himself and was soon swarmed. It was such a big play for me. Although no one ever commented on it, it was very satisfying because that play was exactly what I had been practicing all summer.

The experience taught me that if you are told what to do and it makes sense, then work at it until you become competent and someday it will really pay off.

It's a great lesson on life. I wish I could watch film clips and see if it really happened the way I remember. Regardless, I got to play more in the Cornell game, and as the year went on, the coaches thought I was doing well enough to bump me up to the first team. I was playing on the left side of the line as an end with two sophomores, Cottie Davidson, a guard, and Bolt Ellwell, who was the tackle. Bolt became a Marine and died in the war, but that year he edged me out as best athlete of the year. The three of us started the Princeton and Harvard games, which was a big deal for us.

Being on the first string and starting both of those big games that year was the greatest thing that happened to me at Yale. A lot of wonderful things took place during those years, but playing football at that time in my life meant everything.

On many levels, working my way up to varsity was a major accomplishment. I learned how to play for the sheer pleasure of the sport, for the fun of winning and even the disappointment of losing. I discovered the importance of teamwork and working together to achieve a common goal. Maybe more important, I learned to overcome my physical fear of the game and compete for the pure joy of it. Conquering that fear early on in my life helped me face some of the challenges and obstacles that came later.

When I was not playing football, I played tennis most summers and squash in the winter. Growing up in Rye, I entered a lot of tennis tournaments, and while at Portsmouth Priory, I became the State Champion of Rhode Island, which is the smallest state and so the smallest champion you can be. Tennis and squash came easier to me than football. I had grown up playing tennis and it felt natural to pick up a racket. At Yale, I played on the freshman tennis team and then on the varsity team starting my sophomore year. We were a good group and even better friends. We were probably not the best players that Yale produced, but we were not bad. I was number one most of the time, though once in a while I would lose a challenge and drop a notch.

At the end of my sophomore year we had a tennis banquet. It was held in one of the fraternities by some of the players on the team. They were older and more sophisticated than I, having experimented with various degrees of success in drinking, smoking, women, and New York stuff. I had never had a drink or a cigarette, and I was a virgin to boot. All those were things on which they were planning to shed some light. They gave me a drink that tasted like lemonade, and I do not remember if I knew what it was, but it tasted pretty damn good. It turned out that on this particular night they were drinking Tom Collinses. I had one and then another, and pretty soon I was high as a kite. All I can recall about the rest of the night was that my doubles partner, Bobby McKenna, who is unfortunately no longer with us, took me home. We must have been a sight! I was probably six inches taller than he was and heavier. I was sort of wrapped around him while he struggled to maneuver me back to Timothy Dwight College, the residential college.

We got back to my room and I got into bed, but immediately after I lay down, I felt sick. There was no time to get to a bathroom so I rushed to the window, opened it wide, and let go. That should have been the end of the problem, but as luck would have it, the screens were on. What a mess! I cannot tell you how I got through the night, let alone cleaned it up in my sorry state, but when I went home to Rye the next day I was feeling lousy. That hungover feeling lasted for three days. It gave me a lot of respect for alcohol as I tried to work it out on the golf course. I kept walking around, inhaling fresh air in hopes that it would revive me, but to no avail. The whole experience slowed my attack on alcohol considerably. I learned more about it later when I went into the army and further in life, but I have never been able to drink a Tom Collins since.

In the winter of 1941, I made it to the National Intercollegiate Squash Finals at Yale. Princeton had the best player at the time, Charlie Brinton. I played him in the finals and he beat me decisively. Then, at the end of the winter season in 1942, right before the National Intercollegiate Tournament, which was again at Yale, I got the measles. I was released from the infirmary just in time to watch my teammate win it. Sometimes things work out that way, and I was happy for him.

The following March, in 1943, I was called up for active duty. Life was about to change.

Three proud warriors in 1944. Shown from left are U.S. Army
Air Corps Second Lieutenant Richard P. Cooley, U.S. Navy Reserve
Midshipman James L. Buckley, and U.S. Marine Corps Cadet
Francis G. Dwyer. The photograph was taken at Mrs. Harris's in
Rye, New York, when Dick and his friends were over for
lunch one Sunday.

# Learning to Fly

My senior year at Yale was already underway when I was called up. Because I enlisted and didn't wait to be drafted, I could choose where I wanted to go. I tried to get into the navy, but I had a bad knee and was rejected. The navy was referred to as the "white shoe group," which meant that more well-off people tended to be accepted. The army, more of a place for common folk, did accept me, bad knee and all.

Along with five Yale classmates, I left for basic training in Nashville, Tennessee, by way of a miserable train ride. We traveled coach with three people sitting in a space that was designed for two, en route to army indoctrination. The first and most important things I learned in basic training were the three acceptable answers to every comment or question directed at you by a senior officer: "YES, SIR," "NO, SIR," and "NO EXCUSE, SIR." Those answers were all inclusive.

After six weeks of training in Nashville, we were sent to Santa Ana, California, for basic training in the Air Corps cadet program. Those same three answers were very much in use there as well.

———————

In the service there was little variance in what you could do. There were rules and a regimen that had to be followed. Every soldier was assigned to a specific unit in alphabetical order by last name. We did not have smart bombs or precision-directed artillery, but we did have discipline. It is a quality that I still feel strongly about and hope will always be in the forefront of my mind. In my opinion, discipline is important for our country's well-being and for the survival of human nature.

The direction that comes from discipline not only applied to the military during WWII, it applied to the civilian population as well. We experienced shortages and strict rationing of gas and household items such as butter, sugar, coffee, and beef. Travel plans were limited, and we found that we could not do everything we wanted to do. The discipline to endure that kind of privation has not been required of the general population since that war. The fact that we had to sacrifice together as a nation and as a world pulled us closer. Today while the military, their families, and the government in Washington, D.C., fight all our battles, we give lip service to the need for patriotism and supporting the military. We attach bumper stickers to our cars, but it is not the same as being involved together as a country in the way we were during World War II. Today, individuals can escape the sacrifice that others are making for the whole.

Looking back on that period of history, World War II is from a bygone era. That time period may be hard to relate to today. You had to be there, and if you were, you could never forget the experience. The things we saw and did during that period of history will remain with my generation forever.

World War II was also a time of camaraderie. We entered the war together in pursuit of a common goal. There was the drudgery of the army and a lot of waiting around, but we came to appreciate one another. We found commonalities and ways to connect. Sometimes during recreation breaks we would play basketball. It was fun and I looked forward to those pick-up games a great deal. I learned so much and in the process started to mature. I had spent my youth in a nice suburb, where I attended the "right" schools and had the "right" friends. But the army prepared me for life. I learned how to get along with people from different backgrounds, with different opinions and ideals and their own ways of doing things. Serving in the military solidified what I had realized when I met Babe Ruth — that God and our Constitution gave every one of us the same rights.

We each have as much claim to live on this planet as anyone else. Being in the army helped me see that everyone is equal and everyone is needed to accomplish common goals without lines being drawn.

———————

After two months in Santa Ana, spent mostly on classwork and physical training, we moved on to Hemet, California, where I received my basic air training and soloed as a pilot. Fortunately, my instructor did not give up on me, as it took me 14 hours to solo. That was a lot of hours to get that little PT-19 off the ground and back in one piece. I was close to washing out. After two and a half months, the next stop was basic training in Hanford, California, where the planes grew in size and the flight instruction became considerably more detailed and demanding.

In Hanford, groups came together from many of the smaller primary training fields and the cadets were divided into platoons. The officers did not know much about us and we did not know each other. There was much more marching and military activity, and for this they needed to have platoon leaders who were selected in an interesting way. Cadets were allowed to volunteer for the position, and I decided to try for it at the tender age of 19. There were several of us competing for the job. Whatever else they used as determinants, it seemed to me that the principal thing they were looking for was the ability to command with a loud voice and march the platoon from place to place on schedule. I was one of the last to try out for the job. By then I had observed that the platoon responded better to orders that were shouted loudly and clearly; weak-voiced cadets could not keep the platoon in line and in step. The best cadets performed like the proverbial drill sergeants we had encountered during our basic training. So when it was my turn, I let the platoon have it, shouting my commands as if I had been in the army all my life. It must have been okay because they made me platoon leader, even though I did not have a clue about how to run things in the army, and it showed over the next two months. Today I see that this experience was important to my early leadership training.

However, the seasoned cadets who had been in the army longer knew better than to volunteer for a job that involved extra work. But, for me, volunteering was all part of the "army experience" and I wanted to try out each new opportunity. Being in charge as platoon leader sounded interesting.

Advanced flight training took place in Chandler, Arizona. There we were introduced to the AT-6, with retractable wheels and a variable-pitch prop. That was my first experience with night flying and long cross-country trips. After almost a year in the army, in February 1944, we graduated, got our wings, became second lieutenants, and received our assignments. Some in our class headed for Bomber training. I joined the Fighter group and was sent to Portland Army Air Base. I was there for three months, which was the longest time I spent in any training location. We attempted to complete our flight time requirements, but the weather was so awful that we spent most of our time on the ground waiting for a clearing. In order to log our hours, we were finally sent across the Cascade Mountains to Redmond, Oregon, and for 10 days we flew all the time and got caught up with the program. I remember that occasion with great satisfaction. It was an exhilarating time.

After Portland I was sent to Santa Rosa, California, where I learned to fly the P-38. I flew all the time, practiced gunnery, and learned about formation flying. It was serious combat training. We were officers by then and when we were not flying or going to classes, our time was our own. We found that San Francisco was only 80 miles away and quite accessible. With my newly purchased secondhand Ford, I made that trip many times. I had family and friends there who made the time very enjoyable and a good break from army life.

Three friends stand out from my army days. Rodney P. Colton was a farmer from Eastern Oregon. The two of us did everything together, including being sent to Fighter training in Portland after we graduated from flight school. During one of the lulls in our training due to bad weather, Rodney met a young girl in a dance hall. They married and I was his best man. I didn't have any personal knowledge of sex, but it turned out that Rodney knew even less about how things worked than I did. Before his wedding I gave him the facts-of-life speech that my mother had given me years earlier. Rodney became an auditor for Portland Gas and Electric and fathered six children, so he must have figured it out.

Seymour Crofts was a bright Jewish man from Chicago. I saw a lot of him during the war, but our paths have not crossed since. Seymour introduced me to handball, which was similar to squash. I enjoyed the sport and his company.

Bob Anderson was my roommate when we were stationed in Belgium. His father was a well-known Hawaiian entertainer and the family played in his band. Bob was a nervous type, moody at times, but he was always there when I needed him. He brought my things to Reims after my crash.

After we completed our training, our group was ready to go overseas as replacement pilots. Instead of sending us out to the Pacific, they put us on another train bound for the East Coast. For six days we slept two in a bunk until we arrived in Jersey City to board the SS *Île de France*, a classy old French ocean liner. At the time almost every large passenger ship had been taken over for military use. The *Île de France* could not be used by the French because the country's ports were occupied by the Germans, so in 1941 she was turned over to the British as a troop-transporter. The ship made many crossings before being decommissioned in 1945 and handed back to the French in 1947.

Along with 4,000 others, we sailed from Jersey City to the port of Southampton, England. From there we were transported by truck to a training facility close to Sheffield. It was soon clear why additional flight time in Europe was needed. We could fly, but we found navigation challenging. Because the topography was flat and unchanging, it was easy to lose your bearings. From the air, the ground looked like one little farmhouse after another placed on a checkerboard of different-colored fields.

Four weeks later, in August or September of 1944, we took a boat to France and were driven to Paris for our final assignments. I was then loaded onto a truck with a dozen other soldiers and driven to a town in Belgium called Florennes. Our base was located at an old airstrip that the U.S. had taken over from the Germans. After settling in, I somehow got ahold of a bike to check out the countryside around Florennes. There were three or four very large homes that were owned by wealthy Belgians and royalty, but the army had appropriated everything for military housing. Our particular unit stayed in a château owned by a count and his family. They were moved to the basement and our squadron took over the second floor. The count did not like the fact that we had moved in, but he had little choice. He had a pretty 14-year-old daughter and her presence among all of us soldiers might have caused him concern.

Although they were inconvenienced by our arrival, the count seemed to take a liking to me. He learned that I had been a Benedictine schoolboy, so he took me on a bike ride of about 10 miles to a Benedictine monastery. It had a magnificent church, a breathtaking setting, and the monks were warm and welcoming. After our bike ride, the count and countess invited me to dinner in their basement. The night turned out to be quite stiff because no one could speak English except the countess. I often wonder how I communicated with the count during that long bike ride, but we got along fine.

AFTER HIS ACCIDENT, DICK RECEIVED THIS WOODEN STATUE OF THE VIRGIN
MARY FROM THE COUNTESS HE MET IN BELGIUM. HE WAS TOUCHED BY HER
GIFT AND CONSIDERED IT ONE OF HIS DEAREST POSSESSIONS.

THIS P-38 LIGHTNING IS THE TYPE OF PLANE DICK WAS FLYING
WHEN HE HAD HIS ACCIDENT.

# Life's Unexpected Turn

In the fall of 1944, I was a fighter pilot, a second lieutenant, and serving as a replacement pilot assigned to the Ninth Air Force. Our squadron was flying P-38s out of a newly established base next to an airfield we had recently taken from the Germans near Florennes. It was toward the end of World War II, only a few months after D-day.

The Lockheed P-38 Lightning was a large twin-engine aircraft designed to fly long-range bomber support missions at high altitudes. Our squadron's initial assignment was to defend the Eighth Air Force bombers as they flew in and out of Germany. We would rendezvous with them at various locations and escort them deep into enemy territory. In all, I flew 17 missions, enough to be shot at and to crack up the plane a couple of times. One time, I overran the runway. I was too close to our formation leader as we all came in for a landing and I was worried about using my brakes because the P-38's tires could easily blow out. Unfortunately, I did not fly enough missions to know what to do in unusual situations. Additionally, I had flown only one escort mission for the Eighth Air Force because by the time I arrived, the Army Air Force command had started to transition the use of P-38s from bomber defense to dive-bomber. The P-38 pilots did not focus on fighting at the front line or protecting foot soldiers because this particular aircraft was too big and fast for that. Instead, we were there to break up the German supply chain.

For extended range, the original P-38 design included two auxiliary fuel tanks, one under each wing that could be jettisoned when empty. When it was reconfigured into a dive-bomber, the fuel tanks were replaced with thousand-pound bombs, which we dropped onto railroad tracks, marshaling yards, supply depots, bridges, roads, and basically anything that would ultimately dismantle the German war effort. The only hitch in the plan was the P-38's limitations. It was not designed to be a dive-bomber. It was nose-heavy, and when a pilot put the aircraft into a dive and dumped its bomb load, the plane tended to invert, with sometimes tragic consequences. In addition to the P-38's aerodynamic failings, we had been trained as fighter pilots, not bombardiers.

I turned 21 on November 25, 1944. Sixteen days later, a brand-new P-38 was delivered to our squadron. I really wanted to fly that plane so I asked to do the test flight. I was considered a knowledgeable pilot. It spite of my age, it wasn't a big deal to be that young and granted permission to do so. Besides, the older, more experienced guys were not eager to go and no one else had volunteered.

But it ended up being a big deal. In fact, December 11, 1944, the day of my test flight, changed my life forever.

I flew away from my Belgian base young and spirited with hopes of returning to Yale to play football. Instead, I never returned. I ended up in an army hospital with severe injuries from a crash that included the loss of my right arm. As a result of the events of that day, my daily prayers include a man I never met. He picked me out of my parachute shrouds and carried me to a field hospital in Chambray, France, saving my life.

While I was recovering from my injuries and during moments of lucidity, I tried to reconstruct the sequence of the crash and speculate how my arm was torn off. I came up with only two scenarios. The first was impact with the plane's horizontal stabilizer. The P-38 was powered by two huge engines mounted on the wings and with counter-rotating props that kept the plane from pulling to one side or the other. Instead of regular fuselage, this airplane had two long booms behind the engines that joined at the tail, with open space between the tail's horizontal stabilizer and the cockpit. Many pilots were injured, and some lost their limbs, when they were forced to bail out of the P-38. It's easy to imagine, going down at 300 miles an hour, opening the canopy, and having the full force of the wind suck you from the cockpit and into the knife-edged stabilizer. My second theory was that my arm hit the armor plate located directly behind the seat, which protects pilots from getting shot in the back. All I know for certain is that there is still a part of me somewhere in France.

I have lived the events of that day over and over in my head, wondering what I could have done to prevent the crash. It all comes down to a life-altering assumption. When you are a replacement pilot and waiting for your turn to fly real missions, it sometimes feels as if you are just going through the motions. I am a much more knowledgeable pilot today. Back then, the main focus was on how to follow orders. Our instruction had less to do with the mechanics of a plane than the instructions of a mission. We were told that when flying into Germany, keep your plane next to the captain and be his wingman. As long as he did not get into trouble, you were fine. The day I went out for the test flight, the captain told me to be careful, but he did not tell me to do something I should have done: check the dive flaps in level flight before using them in a 300-mile-an-hour drop to 10,000 ft. I just assumed they would work, since everything else did. The lesson I learned was to never take action, big or small, on assumptions when it is not necessary.

I had been raised and educated as a Catholic, but my faith had not been tested until the crash. One thing remains a mystery I have since credited to divine intervention. Every Army Air Corps pilot wore a parachute, and we were drilled in how to use it. It buckled around your legs and shoulders and had a red handle on the left side that you pulled tight across your chest to open the chute. Amid episodes of pain and pity afterward, I tried to figure out how my parachute deployed. I lost my right arm, the arm I would have used to pull the red handle, and it seemed highly unlikely that, under duress and with limited seconds, I could have pulled the handle across my body with my left arm. My crash, I have since concluded, was totally in the hands of God. The parachute opened only a few hundred feet above the ground and just before my plane exploded into a ball of searing heat and shrapnel. God saved me for some reason, and all these years later, I still don't know why. I am working on that one. It has been 72 years since the crash that should have left me dead.

Eventually, I was put on a boat bound for England and sent to a medical facility between Southampton and London. It was the time of the V-1 flying bomb (also known as the buzz bomb). The Germans were firing V-1s at London and we were on the flyway. They were aiming for densely populated areas, but we nevertheless held our breath each time a buzz bomb passed overhead. There was little else we could do besides pray that the buzzing sound of those motors did not stop.

In February I was considered well enough to head back to the States by ship. We landed in New Jersey after a long trip. My mother and father were there to meet me. Joe Louis, the world heavyweight champion, was there to greet all the vets. I remember seeing him and then taking advantage of the free long-distance phone call the army granted returning soldiers. I called a girlfriend in Portland, Oregon.

I spent a little over a year in the hospital. Along with the amputation of my arm and dealing with a concussion and shock, there was a big slice out of my lower right leg and much discussion about how to patch it. At a facility that specialized in plastic surgery, doctors removed skin from the inside of one of my legs to cover the wound. In those days, the process wasn't as advanced as it is now, and sometimes such skin grafts did not take, which was the case with me. After the first operation, the doctors determined that they had not gone deep enough with the initial graft, so I needed another. This time a thicker skin graft was taken from the inside of my other leg. Eventually my leg mended, and the doctors focused on my arm.

I was experiencing severe phantom pain. It's a fairly common occurrence among those who have lost a limb because the nerve endings are still alive. For some people this pain never goes away, but I was fortunate. Mine lasted for only a few years. There were many surgeries. They tried to pull the nerve out of my spine or from my neck or inject Novocain into the nerve, but nothing seemed to work. That was bothersome in the sense that it was an odd sensation, that feeling and pain in my arm even though it was not there. When I retired from the military, we had another go at it. My father knew a specialist in St. Louis who was able to operate under my arm and pull the nerve down in such a way that he deadened it. After that, things improved. The war was over and it was time to look ahead.

# Living as an Amputee

Once you become an amputee, you enter a different world. You have problems that other people do not have. They are not any worse or any better, they are just different. From the beginning, the important thing is your attitude.

The first thing an amputee has to do is learn to accept it. If you cry about it and feel sad for your luck, it does not solve your problem. You have to deal with it and learn to live with what you have.

An amputee who loses an arm quickly realizes that one arm does most of the things you need done. The other arm usually is a holder. You put a piece of paper down to write your name and the other arm holds it still. Or you try to thread a needle, and one hand holds the needle and the other pushes the thread through. So one arm keeps the object secure while the other arm takes on the active role. I was right-handed, so losing that arm was more of an obstacle. I had to learn how to write with my left hand, throw, shake hands, and everything else. I still think of myself as right-handed, so I continue to write the same way as I did with my right hand. I do not curve my hand across the pen the way "lefties" do. Though the slant is slightly different, my handwriting is much the same as it was before the accident. Basically, you have to learn to do everything again in your own way. You are always thinking about it.

Getting dressed. Putting on socks. Tying shoes or a tie. Tucking a shirt in behind you. These can be hard things to do unless you have systems in place. You can get by without two hands if you learn new ways of doing things. For instance, charging a cell phone. If I hold the phone between my knees then I can put the charging cord into the phone with my left hand; then I just plug in the charger. Does not sound like much, but it is. You have to learn to constantly adjust. Your brain realizes that the normal function is gone, and it looks for a new way to tackle the issue. One great substitute "holder" is your teeth. I use mine as a replacement for my arm all the time. It can sometimes look a little funny, but it works and saves me an infinite amount of time. Imagine going to Starbucks to get a latte and a scone on the way to the office. The little bag holding the scone is clamped tightly between your teeth and you pick up the latte with your hand. You walk out and nobody cares.

You have to analyze each activity, and because many things involve two hands, you have to get a holder in order to create a system. For example, a thing as simple as pulling up your pants: I stand in a doorway, reach across and pull up the right side of my pants and then lean hard against the right side of the door jamb, which serves as a holder in this case. The door jamb holds up the right side up and I reach down and pull up the left side of the pants, which I then press hard against the left side of the door jamb. It takes two or three times going back and forth until the pants are up enough. Still leaning against the right side, you can pull up the zipper and fasten the clip at your waistline. After that you put the buckle end of the belt in your teeth and start threading the front end through the loops in your pants. I know this sounds laborious (often it is) but it works and I can dress myself.

Sometimes people will say, "do this" or "do that" when they have forgotten that you cannot do some things. This is success from the amputee's point of view. For instance, you cannot row a boat with one hand, but you can paddle a canoe with great care. Tennis is not a problem. You have to throw the ball up to serve, so you place the ball on the racket and toss it up. Everything you do has to be analyzed and modified.

The amputee does not want to appear different. You want to do whatever the task is and be a part of the group. I will admit that it is hard to play baseball. Catching the ball in a mitt and then throwing it is difficult. You might learn to throw again with your left hand, but how do you get rid of the mitt?

There are certain things you cannot do as an amputee, and you want to accept that and not dwell on it.

Golf takes patience. Most golfers will tell you that it is a left-handed game anyway. With practice, you can hit the ball quite well. The majority of golfers are right-handed, but you can learn how to hit with the left hand because of the way the wrist cocks and does not snap like the right hand wants to do. When I was a kid playing at the Apawamis Club course, I remember playing 18 holes with a score of 82, but the best round I ever played was at Pebble Beach on Cypress Point when I was 35 years old. I scored 80, and if I had not ringed the cup on the 18th hole, I would have broken 80 for the only time in my life. For a while I managed to play tough courses and maintained a handicap of 18. With patience and practice you can gradually do most everything.

If you are an amputee, you have to get used to people staring at you. I do not look at peoples' curiosity as a negative. On the contrary, I can walk down the street and while most of the men will turn away, 90 percent of the women smile at me and that gives me a pleasant feeling. There could be some interest and maybe some pity, but I am not worried about that — it is just nice. That could be the nurturing side of women, but at least I can enjoy it. Why wouldn't people stare? When I see an amputee I think, "He only has one arm" because I do not see myself as being like him. I see myself as a perfectly normal man.

As a young man I used to feel that I had to be independent and take care of myself, but I found out that it can be very nice when people help. You know that you can do it, but maybe not as quickly as someone else can. I began to realize that it is not bad to ask someone to help you, for instance, with things like cutting your meat. People look at me and say, "Oh, let me cut your meat." Initially, I refused help and cut it myself. And I can do it if I have a sharp knife, but I have found that it can be a pleasure to let people do things for me. The only thing I have to be careful of is that they do not try to cut it into small bites like those of a child.

I sometimes get 25 little pieces and it drives me nuts. It spoils my appetite. On the other hand, it feels nice to accept the help. Nothing wrong with that, but you want to be able to do things by yourself if you can.

Of course, it would have been nice to have had my arm all these years. But, after more than 70 years without it, I do not want it back. I get by well without it. Today I rarely wear my prosthesis. It is heavy and can be uncomfortable; getting the perfect fit is difficult. Lately, though, I have been told it is a good idea to wear it because the extra weight balances my shoulders and helps keep my posture more upright. And not having my arm means I can easily get off balance. Right now, doctors can transplant arms, but the recovery process is slow. I would not be surprised if receiving a new arm becomes a routine procedure in the near future. More than likely I will not be here, but I am not sure that I would want it even if the procedure became commonly available during my lifetime. I think I am okay as I am. I do not feel different from other people.

Being an amputee is not the end of the world. You just have to learn to deal with it, and the way you do that is to give thanks for living through the trauma and enjoy the life that you have been given.

When you have been through an experience like this, it is natural to want to share what you have learned. Other amputees are the ones you can help the most. Over the years I have been in contact with other amputees on request by different medical groups or personal friends who knew someone who needed help. I have never tried to make an official counseling service out of it. Doing this kind of helping has been more like mentoring. It is easy to do and I like doing it.

---

In 2007, I had the opportunity to meet with Will Guyman, a young man who had lost his right arm in a boating mishap. His story was extraordinary, and terrifying. When I shared my

Dick with Will Guyman, 2011.

experience of losing my arm, he responded with a thoughtful, gripping description of his accident and its aftermath. It is such an excellent piece of writing that I am including his essay here, with his permission, as an example of what it takes for an amputee to accept his condition, adapt to what is a new reality, and carry on with life in a productive way. Will's essay is the very best example one could read to understand how to successfully deal with the loss of a limb, and it shows the depth of his character and immediate understanding and acceptance of the changes that were to take place in his life.

## THE ULTIMATE OPPORTUNITY

AS TOLD BY WILL GUYMAN

Flying along, smelling the fresh pines in Canada's Desolation Sound Marine Provincial Park, I sat perched in the bow of a motorboat, content and tranquil. I had no idea that a freak accident was about to change my life forever. The water rushed under our 15-foot speed dinghy as my dad piloted our joyful evening cruise. Although I would be painfully tormented during the next four hours, and my life would hang in the balance for the next week, I had no idea that this experience would actually better my life, making me more resilient, grateful, positive, and hardworking. Suddenly, our dinghy lurched as it hit a submerged log and I hurtled headfirst over the bow and under the boat and confronted the dinghy's 60-horsepower propeller head-on. Immediately, I was thrust deep under the surface as the accident happened quickly, but the image would forever play back slowly in my mind. Sharp, electrical sensations gripped my entire body. I felt myself fade from reality as I hovered seemingly neutrally buoyant under the water. Running out of air, I needed to surface, but the strange command of "kick" didn't seem to be working because my body couldn't communicate through the overwhelming, electrical sensations. Somehow, thanks to my life jacket, I managed to break the surface, and my gasp for air was met with another excruciating pain, which emanated from my rib cage. I found out later that one of my seven fractured ribs had punctured my right lung. Furthermore, a crimson cloud surrounded my body, and as I looked at my dad, I spoke in a different voice, a high-pitched, shrill cry.

My dad approached me in the dinghy, his face streaming with tears and stricken with a distinctive look of horror. I followed his gaze to the source of the underwater blood cloud and suddenly realized that the propeller had completely severed my upper right arm. My mind could not compute that my arm was no longer there. My dad grabbed me by my life jacket and heaved me into the boat. My back screamed with pain, the result of a cracked scapula. My dad slammed on the dinghy's throttle to take us back to our anchorage, and within minutes, we roared into the isolated, small harbor.

Kind, caring people rushed out in small boats to help us as my dad and I fashioned a tourniquet around my arm. The next two and a half hours, as we waited for the Canadian Coast Guard, were the longest and most painful hours of my life, but amazingly, I never lost consciousness. Throughout this horrifying accident, I had this overwhelming instinct that I just needed to get through it and survive, and this perception became my mentality throughout the most difficult aspects of my recovery in the weeks and months ahead. As I was transferred to the small Coast Guard super inflatable, an inexperienced crew member accidentally dropped me into the icy water. Using a skill that I later learned to master, I reached up with a burst of energy and pulled my entire body out of the water using only my left arm. Now hypothermic, it took more energy than ever to survive the turbulent journey to the Coast Guard cutter for a helicopter lift rescue. I am told that I was nearly dead when I arrived at the Campbell River Hospital, where I received a blood transfusion and the first of many surgeries. However, the worst was over, and

miraculously, it looked as if I was going to survive. I eventually
learned that this grace was all I ever needed to live happily.

The first two sentences I remember uttering when I woke up
in the hospital were "When can I go back?" and "I'm screwed." I
had been strongly right-handed, and now my right arm was gone.
As soon as I started thinking about the future, I became mentally
chained to the same hospital bed that was physically restraining
me with bandages and tubes. I became overwhelmed with worry
and sadness; however, I began to understand that I just needed to
focus on the next task in order to recover and resume my normal
life. This goal became the paradigm for my recovery: to return
to the same level of competency that I was at before the accident,
in incremental steps that could be checked off one after another.
After two and a half weeks in the hospital, I returned home.
Many friends and family members visited me in the hospital and
provided me with incredible moral support. At home, I was often
able to power through the coming adversity by reasoning that
someone had it worse than I did, so I had no reason to complain.
Although this reasoning alleviated much of my pain, it was still
hard to truly accept myself for who I had become. My doctors
and other strangers were already profiling me as an "amputee,"
and I was labeled as someone with a disability; however, I never
allowed that label to become a limitation. My quest for normalcy
began by beating my doctor's estimates as to when I could return
to my normal life. I did every physical therapy and lung exercise
more frequently than they required — even if it meant more
pain. Despite my back and rib injuries, I tried to walk around as
much as I could. I was also determined to get rid of the pain
medications as soon as possible so that my brain could be sharp
again. I attacked all the one-handed challenges with fervor —
especially writing and typing with my left hand. Most of all,
I wanted to return to school. Three weeks after my accident,
my sophomore year at high school began, and I wanted to prove
that I could start on time. In reality, this task was practically

impossible, considering my complicated schedule of prosthetic, doctor, and physical therapy appointments throughout the week. However, my school administrators gave me the opportunity to return, and I was excited to take it. I started with three classes, which was half my regular load, and went to doctor's appointments in the mornings and classes in the afternoons. Sometimes, I struggled to pay attention in class as the morphine or occasional intense phantom pain in my arm clouded my brain. I soon realized that maybe I had taken on more than I had bargained for, but I couldn't let the school, my family, my friends, or myself down. To combat these challenges, I went in after class to see my teachers about topics that I had not understood. Furthermore, writing and typing were an enormous problem for me. Despite practice, writing and typing one-handed with my non-dominant arm took forever, and my handwriting was almost illegible. So I drew upon a powerful passion that gave me strength: my love of innovative technology.

Although I had always been interested in technology, I could never have foreseen its use during my recovery. I seemed to bond and become energized with technology on a new level. After the accident, with all of my newfound limitations, I searched for technology that would make my life easier. Not only did I find and use important software and hardware (such as the Dvorak-style one-handed keyboard and voice recognition software), but I also discovered how much I loved technology. I immediately joined the school's Artificial Intelligence Club, and the following year, a couple of amazing and generous Microsoft engineers helped me build a one-handed Xbox® gaming controller that resulted in much trash-talking during gameplay against friends. I became passionate about technology, and this passion drove new skills. My accident was already giving me newfound discoveries that worked to my advantage.

By November, two and a half months after my traumatic amputation, school was going well, and my physical recovery was progressing steadily. My rib and scapula injuries, however, still inhibited most of my regular activities, and the coordination of my left hand was not up to par. When I entered school, it was obvious that I would need to find a way to recover my fluid coordination, and I knew just the game. Before my accident, Ping-Pong had been just a recreational pastime, but during my recovery, it became a competitive physical therapy. Playing left-handed, and with only one hand, was one of the most frustrating challenges I encountered. I often broke down in dissatisfaction, but I also understood that repetitive play was the only way to resume normalcy. I also found a table tennis gym, where the best player in the United States, Yiyong Fan, coached. I began training with him and within a month my table tennis skills surpassed those I had possessed before my accident. Not only had I become a better table tennis player, but I had also built better eye-hand coordination that helped me with my writing, typing, daily activities, and sports. Table tennis also palliated my rib and scapula injuries, and I healed much faster than my doctors had expected. Table tennis taught me that with strong persistence I could overcome my frustrations.

Some activities, such as basketball, were harder to resume. My friends stopped inviting me to pick-up games, so I played when it wasn't competitive. Most importantly, though, since my recovery, no activity or sport has been entirely beyond reach because of my accident. I realize that I have more barriers to overcome, whether it's the next repetition of one-handed push-ups or proving my way on the dodgeball court. I have learned, however, that my accident did not give me a disability, just an opportunity to improve.

The most valuable lessons that I have learned from my accident are those of gratitude and appreciation for life. Throughout my recovery, I felt as if I needed to give back in exchange for my saved life. At the start of my junior year, I joined our school's "varsity blood team" that organizes our school blood drives.

In order to attract more donors, I volunteered to speak about how I would not be alive today without blood donors. When I talked in front of the whole school, I was nervous; how could I convey the significance of donating a little time and blood to save multiple lives? It was difficult to talk about my personal experiences, especially to my friends, but I understood that candidness was a small sacrifice to pay to motivate people to donate blood.

Every time I tell my story, I am reminded of how fortunate I was to live, and how there are others continually suffering from adversity far worse than mine. I now know that my accident led me through a set of challenges and opened my eyes to new skills and opportunities that I would have otherwise ignored. I now look forward with optimism to my future, and hope that my experience continues to motivate me and others.

---

There is nothing to add to Will's description of what it is like to lose a limb. Though I have had the privilege and pleasure of meeting and working with many amputees, I have not seen an account and a bravery equal to Will's.

To see Will today, in 2016, almost 10 years after his accident, is incredible. He has filled out physically to six feet one, is lean, and looks as fit as any man of 24 could be. He graduated from Stanford in four years and began searching for a job in technology. Microsoft went after him with an offer of any job he wanted and that opportunity overshadowed two other offers he had from Silicon Valley. He wasted no time and started putting in his 10- to 12-hour days. He has started on his career with all the enthusiasm of any success-bound engineer. It will be fun to watch his progress.

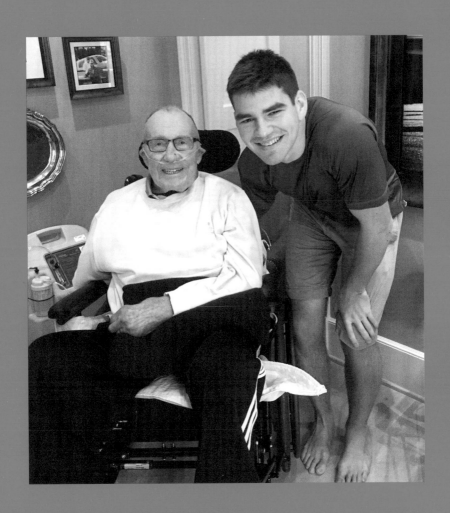

DICK WITH WILL IN 2016.

# Part Two

He said a blessing and I could feel God's presence
surging through me. Although the time spent in the Pope's
company was probably no more than 10 or 15 minutes,
it is something I will never forget. It was so precious,
like God was talking to us. Pope Pius noticed my arm and
asked about it. Then he gave me a special blessing.
It was one of my life's great moments.

Dick could no longer play football, but he still loved to compete, and he golfed, skied, and played squash after recovering from his war injury. In 1953, the Pacific Coast Squash Team won the national championship. They're holding martini shakers, the trophies presented to the team members in recognition of their victory. Shown from left: Ted Clark, Gene Hoover, Dick Cooley, Bob Colwell, and Walter Pettit.

# Peace, Decisions, and a Career

Just as I had studied college brochures during my junior year at Portsmouth, I began to analyze my options for a quick graduation from college. I learned that Yale would give one semester of credit for time spent in the service, so I would need only another semester to complete the requirements for a degree in Industrial Administration and Engineering. For my arm to have the necessary time to heal and the nerves to grow, I was given three months' leave from the army in May of 1945. I applied for an additional month's extension to my army leave, which was granted without a hassle. That gave me four months: time enough to fulfill all course requirements necessary to receive my degree.

My right leg was still weak, but I was ambulatory. I had been off it so long that it was down to skin and bone, but my left leg was strong. During the months at the hospital, I had been confined to a wheelchair, and I spent a great deal of my time traversing backwards through the endless corridors with the help of my one good leg. It was like poling a boat.

Before I was called into active duty, I had completed one month of senior classes and had looked forward to playing on the football team. That dream did not die easily. I had some discussion with one of the coaches about finding a way to rig me up so that I could play, but the idea was complicated and eventually dropped. Besides, I would have been known as the one-armed football player at Yale. Since that option was no longer available, the best thing seemed to be to finish school as soon as possible.

In hindsight, I wish I had not been in such a hurry. In the summer of 1945, I returned for my final semester at Yale. I roomed with a star running back on the football team, Vandy Kirk. We shared rooms in Timothy Dwight College, where I had lived during my sophomore year. Unable to play football like Vandy, I turned my sights to relearning tennis, squash, and golf. These were sports that had always come easily to me, and I hoped I could regain my ability with time. I also bought a bicycle.

During this time I met a young lady who lived in the hills seven miles west of town. Every day after class, I would hop on my bike and make the strenuous trip, eventually ending up at her door. Our meetings were usually just long enough for me to catch my breath and share a Coke. I do not remember how we met or even if we dated, but I do know that by the end of the summer my leg had filled out and was fully functioning.

My classes were organized so that I had one day off a week. On my free Thursdays I would head for New York and enjoy a date in the Big Apple. My date and I would usually go to the theater or to dinner and sometimes dancing. I splurged, spending all of the $1,200 I had saved from my army pay. It was a great summer, and oddly enough, my grades improved. I attribute it to growing up and being thankful for the opportunity.

As I was preparing to finish school and review career options, my father offered to send me to the Harvard Business School. He revered education, making sure that my sisters and I attended the best schools possible, regardless of the fact that he was not wealthy. Every penny he earned was spent on our house, school tuition, and all the rest of the household expenses. I do not know if he ever wanted to do anything else, but I do know that he spent generously on his family and gave us every chance to succeed. Although Harvard Business School was a tremendous offer and would have been a fine choice, I was impatient to start a career where I could earn my own money. What an MBA degree from Harvard could do for one's career was not on my radar screen.

Again, charging ahead somewhat impatiently was my style, which accounted for some missed opportunities.

At the end of October 1945, I graduated from Yale in the class of '44 in Industrial Administration and Engineering. Stepping onto the platform to receive my diploma, I was the only one from my class and the only one in an army uniform. Everyone else wore the ceremonial caps and gowns. It was a mixed-up time. People were coming and going during the war, and most of my classmates were still on active duty. As it worked out, I graduated ahead of my class and missed all the camaraderie after the war. Instead, I focused on what I could, moving ahead and finding a suitable career.

After graduation I returned to the hospital in Indiana, where the doctors checked the growth of the nerves and the status of my leg. They decided that I had gotten what I needed from the "plastic" hospital where all the plastic surgery was done. In November, they sent me to the final stage of the amputee recovery program at Thomas England General Hospital in Atlantic City. During the war Atlantic City had essentially been transformed into a military medical facility with the takeover of a large number of local resort hotels. It was there that they reshaped the stump surgically and prepared me for the prosthesis.

Nothing had been done with my right arm since the initial healing, so the stump needed to be shaped to fit a false arm that would be comfortable and useful. There were some side issues that had to be cleaned up as well. Before I could be legally discharged, I had to undergo significant training with the new arm and pass some proficiency tests.

After healing from the revision operation, I was fitted with a prosthesis. January was an instructional period during which I learned a host of new techniques to maneuver the limb, as well as the proper care and donning and doffing of the prosthesis. After a few weeks of practice I was getting the hang of it, not with the greatest expertise, but enough to pass the tests to prove I could manage on my own. At the end of January '46, with the prosthesis and my overall health cleared, I was able to retire from the Army Air Corps as a first lieutenant and return to civilian life. I celebrated with a short ski trip to Vermont and went to work in mid-February.

———

My father had taken me to the Johnson O'Connor Research Foundation for an aptitude examination. For a few days I went through a battery of tests that we hoped would shed some light on my strengths and weaknesses, and give an indication of what kind of job I would be best suited for. When the Johnson O'Connor advisers reviewed my scores, they found that I would generally be adept at a wide variety of endeavors, not expert, not great, but generally competent in a number of fields. To further illustrate (and confuse) their message, the results of the various skills were put on a bar graph, which showed straight-line profiles. The advisors explained that I was one of those individuals who did not fall into a specific category. Instead they suggested a wide range of career choices, such as lawyer, accountant, or salesperson. Their view seemed to be that whatever I chose to do, I would be a success. Their answer did not give the specific direction that I was looking for, although once again I was thankful for the preparation and broad-based background of the Industrial Administration and Engineering degree at Yale.

As a result, different options surfaced. The founder of Portsmouth Priory believed that I could be a monk at the Priory and offered to help me get a dispensation so I could perform the duties of a priest with one arm. That was an issue because many of the rituals in the church involve two hands. For instance, giving out Communion during Mass requires the priest to hold the chalice with one hand while giving out the Host with the other. You could get by without it, but then you might be leaving out some other specifically important part of the ceremony. However, I did not seriously consider the priesthood. Feelings of guilt or obligation are not enough to support that vocation. I knew I was too materialistic and, I suppose, too selfish to be a priest. I wanted a wife and a family and to create a life like my parents, so I went to work.

My first job was in the commercial printing department at the McCall Corporation in New York City, a publishing company run by Marvin Pierce, who was a golfing friend of my father. He was also the father of former First Lady Barbara Pierce Bush. In looking for that first job, money may not have been my primary incentive, but it was always a welcome moment each Friday when the paymaster came around and paid me $65 in cash. My salary gradually grew until I was making $135 a week.

The company had a large printing plant in Dayton, Ohio, and its own magazines such as *McCall's, Redbook,* and *Bluebook.* They also printed other magazine, including *Reader's Digest, Newsweek,* and my main accounts *Mademoiselle, Glamour,* and *Popular Science.* I made many trips back and forth to Dayton to make sure that each publication was printed on time and with perfect quality. In those days we used the letterpress printing process on enormous web-fed printing machines, which meant that huge rolls of blank magazine paper ("webs") went on one end of the press and came off the other end as perfectly printed magazine-size pages in signatures (sections) of 12, 18, or 24. We had to learn how to diagram each plate on the rollers so that all the pages lined up in the right place when the magazine was assembled. Since then, of course, that process has been replaced by different technology with improved economy and quality.

My first boss at McCall Corporation was Clayton Westland. I had tremendous respect and affection for him because he taught me a great deal about how to work in an office, the mechanics of commercial printing, and many other essentials of the workday world. He ran the business carefully and turned it into a money-maker. The three of us who worked for him had the responsibility of keeping the clients, editors, and production people happy.

The production of each magazine had to be done in a precise, clearly defined way. When changes were made, we had to make sure that every substitution was accommodated precisely. If the color on a Revlon ad did not quite exude the exquisite shade of red that the art director envisioned, we would catch hell. To make amends for a failed situation it often took a three-martini lunch with the magazine's production man, which was typical back then.

Producing magazines was a highly stressful and multi-faceted job. It is a big business, but a quiet one. There is a lot at stake. Each week there was the pressure of deadlines and feet-to-the-fire decisions. We were on our own a lot and responsible for the outcome of many publications. The job was interesting, challenging, and typically took place during the Monday-through-Friday workweek. McCall's Manhattan office was ideally situated directly over Grand Central Station, making it easy to be in the office before nine. I would usually catch an evening train shortly after five that arrived well before seven in Rye, where I was living on my own in an apartment above a family friend's garage. For many New Yorkers, my commute would be considered ideal.

Life began to shape into a general pattern. Rye was a quiet community during the week, with most of the social life concentrated on the weekends. As time went on, my squash game improved enough that I started playing in tournaments during the winter season. With the Yale Club just a block from the McCall's office, I could meet opponents on the squash court during lunch break. My tennis game did not return to form as quickly, but my golf game showed improvement, and I was able to play with my old friends on the weekends. Because I was a former Yale varsity player, tickets to the season games in New Haven were easy to come by. Two-week vacations often resulted in a week of skiing in winter and a golf outing in summertime.

This sounds better than it was. I was 25 years old and I could see the same routine repeating itself when I was 50. I hoped that there was more to life. I began thinking about moving to California, where my family had its roots. Going west sounded exciting, but I had no idea what I could do. I would need a job right away because I had practically no money and the postwar recession was taking hold.

Early in 1948 I began seeing Sheila McDonnell, who was young and spent a lot of her time horseback riding. I met her through her older siblings. Dating turned into courting, which turned into marriage in January of '49. We seemed compatible and both of us were simply ready for that next phase of life — marriage and a home with kids.

The year of dating and engagement taught me how the McDonnells lived with their 14 children and enormous extended family, and it was different from any lifestyle I knew. They were strong Irish Catholics with powerful connections. Mrs. McDonnell's father had been a partner of Thomas Edison. In the winter the McDonnells lived in two spacious apartment floors at 72nd Street and 5th Avenue. The older seven children lived on the main floor with their parents and the younger seven lived a floor below. Sheila was number 10, and dating and marrying me meant she was able to rise in ranking. Normally the younger seven came up to the main floor for a social time before dinner but did not stay for dinner with the older members of the family. Shelia and I were always allowed by her parents to stay for dinner.

In June the McDonnells moved to their summer home on the beach in Southampton, which was a spectacular setting. Everything was organized and beautiful. I was totally impressed with their lifestyle and how great it would be to become part of it all. In a nice way, my father tried to tell me that the wealthy McDonnell family was out of our class, but I did not hear him. In a way, the caution flags he raised only increased my determination to make it work.

The first real lesson on what I was getting into occurred when Sheila and I were thinking about decorating the garage apartment we would rent from our great friend, Mary Harris.

Mr. and Mrs. Basil Harris lived in Rye, and during his working career, Mr. Harris was the chairman of the United States Lines, a transatlantic shipping company. They had a big house overlooking the Apawamis golf course and over their garage was an apartment that Sheila and I moved into for three months after we were married. Mrs. Harris, who was also a very holy Catholic woman, was like a godmother to me, always helping and advising me on what to do. She was a great friend to me and my family.

Before I was married, I had lunch almost every Sunday at the Harris's home. It was always a wonderful meal, with Mrs. Harris's famous peanut butter and bacon appetizers. Life above their garage was comfortable.

The two Harris children whom I knew best were Basil Jr. and Dick. Dick was married to Charlotte McDonnell, who was number four in "the upper seven" of the McDonnell family.

The Harrises, my old friends the Flanigans, and the McDonnells became related to the Cooleys by marriage, but the relationships among them were ages old. Mrs. Flanigan was not a Catholic by birth, but she married Mr. Flanigan and their four children were all raised in the church. When Mrs. Flanigan later decided to join the church, my mother was her godmother for the ceremony. It gave them a special connection that brought our two families closer together.

Sheila's mother offered to decorate the Harris apartment for us as a wedding present, and she sent us to McMillen, a well-known decorating firm that all the McDonnells used and that exists to this day. Sheila was immensely pleased by what they came up with, but it did not look good to me and I said so. At that point in my life I knew nothing about decorating and even less about compromising. It showed, and this dismayed Sheila. After a couple of unsatisfactory visits with the McMillen people, the difficulty of pleasing me got back to Mrs. McDonnell and she informed Sheila that I could please myself, but I would have to pay for it. Unfairly, Sheila had been caught in the middle and must have had some misgivings about the kind of person she was getting involved with.

I wish I had been more tolerant at that time, but the experience convinced me that the best chance for a successful married life lay in getting away from the family and from the New York area. Our honeymoon was planned for the West Coast: Los Angeles, Carmel, and San Francisco, where I intended to do some job hunting.

---

I found two employment opportunities in the Bay Area — one at Standard Oil Company, the biggest company in town, and one at American Trust Company, California's second-oldest financial institution. Standard Oil didn't have a training program, so new employees began pumping gas at a Standard Oil station and earned $250/month. I had never before thought of banking as a career, but American Trust was hiring 50 people to begin a training program that would rebuild its ranks after the war. I was offered the 49th slot, but at a substantial 30 percent cut in pay. At McCall's I was making the great sum of $7,200 a year, while the American Trust training position offered $5,000.

Despite my longing to relocate, I did not accept the job immediately. My plans were met with somewhat mixed reviews. Pop had his doubts. He did not think a bank was the place for a man with gumption and drive. He expected me to do something meaningful, and he was convinced that a bank would do little to foster my ambition. We discussed it back and forth for a few weeks, but he knew that when my mind was made up, I could be bullheaded. Sheila, now pregnant, was feeling uncertain about the move west and the separation from her family and friends. She was young and inexperienced when it came to asserting herself and putting her foot down with me.

It was at this time that a wonderful and unexpected safety net arrived. Horace Flanigan, my best friend's father, was running Manufacturers Hanover Bank in New York at the time. When he heard of my plan to take the trainee position at American Trust, he offered to hire me at Manufacturers Hanover for $50,000 a year. It was a huge sum of money and a tremendously tempting offer. Mr. Flanigan made few conditions with his proposal; in fact he left it open-ended. He told me to take the position at American Trust, but if I did not like it, or living on the West Coast, to call him and he would hire me. With Mr. Flanigan's attractive safety net in my back pocket and a young and pregnant wife by my side, I took the job at American Trust Company in San Francisco.

---

Before moving to San Francisco, we took a six-week summer vacation in Europe. I had convinced myself that if we did not get to Europe before I started work in California and the baby arrived, we probably would never get another chance for a very long time. I had saved $3,000, which was all we had, and planned to spend it on the trip. I purchased a guidebook and underlined everything. In my travel naïveté, I mapped out every minute and calculated every stop so that we never spent more than one or two days at a location. I tried to be sure we saw everything important, but in the end the whole trip was a blur because we raced from place to place.

Our first stop was Rome, where we had the good fortune of meeting Pope Pius XII. Mrs. Harris, the wonderful family friend from Rye, had become acquainted with the Pope when he was a cardinal. Her husband, Basil, had been appointed to escort him around the United States when he visited in 1936. The trip covered a great deal of the country, from the Brooklyn Bridge to the Golden Gate Bridge. When Mr. Harris died in 1948, Mrs. Harris wanted to visit the Vatican and speak to the Pope. That is quite a feat, as the general public usually cannot get that close to the Pontiff, but because Pope Pius remembered his trip to the

DICK AND SHEILA COOLEY MEETING POPE PIUS XII ON THEIR HONEYMOON
IN ROME IN THE SUMMER OF 1949.

United States with Mr. Harris favorably, he graciously granted her an audience. So she flew to Rome and invited us to join her in meeting the Pontiff.

We were taken to the Pope's office, where he was seated behind a little desk—the same desk where I knew he did his work and made a lot of his decisions. Mrs. Harris was crying and the tears were running down her face. She spoke to the Pope about her husband and he listened intently to every word. I too was crying, but with tears of joy. I watched the kindness that Pope Pius extended to Mrs. Harris, and then he turned to me and took my hand. He said a blessing and I could feel God's presence surging through me. Although the time spent in the Pope's company was probably no more than 10 or 15 minutes, it is something that I will never forget. It was so precious, like God was talking to us. Pope Pius noticed my arm and asked about it. Then he gave me a special blessing. It was one of my life's greatest moments.

———————

Sheila had suffered from morning sickness, but we both assumed she was over the worst of it and was fit to travel. We left Italy and were on our way to Vienna and Salzburg, Austria, driving a European Ford that my brother-in-law, Henry, had arranged for us to use. The car did not have a lot of power, and we were trying to get over the Grossglockner Pass. The Austrian countryside was magnificent but rural, and I knew that if we had trouble crossing over the pass, it might be difficult to find help. Sheila was feeling horrible, and eventually I decided to turn around and head back down. Lienz was the next closest town en route to Salzburg, and there was little but picture-perfect farmhouses along the way. At the sight of an inn we pulled to a stop. No one spoke English except for one woman in the area, and we communicated through her. Sheila was getting worse by the minute and at that moment I cursed myself for opting out of my foreign language class. The young woman who was acting as our interpreter called an

Austrian doctor to examine Sheila and through her he told us that she would be fine, although it was imperative that she rest. For a week we stayed at the inn while Sheila regained her strength.

The main thing I remember about that week is that there was very little to do. While Sheila recovered, I walked the Tyrolean countryside, smiling at the locals, which seemed to suffice for those I encountered. Though I could not speak to anyone, I found the people to be incredibly hospitable. As Sheila regained her energy and her appetite returned, the only thing that tasted good to her was chicken soup. This presented a small problem for the owners of the chalet, as every day they had to go out to the coop and kill one of their hens.

Because we did not know where we were or what we would find if a hospital was needed, we were nervous much of the time. After a week's worth of daily doses of soup and much rest, we left the chalet. I don't suppose Sheila felt absolutely on top of things when we drove away, but at least she could manage. We never made it over the mountains to Salzburg and Vienna, but we were able to retrace my steps to the airfield, Benedictine Monastery, and château I had visited during my time in the war. I am not sure whatever became of the count who had taken a liking to me, but I was happy we were able to make a connection with his daughter. She had grown from a 14-year-old girl into an attractive young woman. She and her husband, also a Belgian count, hosted a dinner party for us in Brussels. Just like before, language barriers hindered the special event, though it was a nice way to bring closure to my time there.

---

Shelia and I returned to New York and prepared to move. Given her condition, there was no question of her driving west with me. Instead, I drove alone to St. Louis, where my family had moved from Rye right after World War II. After a brief visit, in the latter part of July, I drove on to San Francisco with my sister, Ann.

I started work on August 1, 1949, and Sheila arrived by plane in mid-August. My nearby family and friends were wonderful and helped in so many ways. We stayed with my Uncle Wake and Aunt Maggie until we could find a place of our own.

Sheila was brave and gutsy. The last thing she remembered before leaving New York was her father saying to her, "Now Sheila, if I write you a letter, do you think you will get it?" For some older New Yorkers, the West begins when you cross the Hudson River.

The Phlegers were also there to welcome Sheila and me when we arrived in San Francisco. The family relationship between the Phlegers and the Cooleys went way back. All through my father's life, Herman Phleger was his best friend. Herman became a great friend to me as well. He was a director of the American Trust Company and gave me good advice as I joined their bank's training program. All through my career he was very supportive. He was still on the board when I became chief executive in 1966, six years after American Trust merged with Wells Fargo.

Herman was the bank's lawyer and a strong man; no one challenged him very often. When he got off the board and his son, Atherton, took his place, Herman told me that Atherton would be a good friend and a big support to me and he was right. Atherton was a member of the Bohemian Group and of the same camp I belonged to at the Bohemian Grove (owned by the Bohemian Club) called Mandalay Camp. As time went on, we saw each other more and more. He asked me to be godfather to his son, Peter, which was an honor. Unfortunately, Atherton became ill with cancer and did not survive it for more than a couple of years. I think about him all the time. He was even-minded, fair, bright, and an outstanding person. He is one of the people I miss. I am sorry that we did not get closer sooner, because my limited years with him were rich in many ways.

As for others who are and have been important in my life, I pray for Atherton every day as well as his family.

Sheila McDonnell married Dick in January 1949.
They were married for 20 years and had five children together.

DICK AND HIS CHILDREN ON A FAMILY VACATION, CIRCA 1960.
FROM LEFT: SHEILA, PIERCE, AND LESLIE.

# Becoming a Parent and a Banker

The training program at the American Trust Company lasted two years. It was largely a retail bank and every two or three weeks, trainees would be sent to different departments or branches, where we would learn the various functions of the banking business. First stop was the collection department, then the bond department, followed by the property division, and so on until we had systematically gone through essentially all the departments and received a general overview of the bank. The theory was that if we were going to be branch managers, we would need to know where everything was located and how it was managed. After moving through the departments, I spent the final year of training in the credit department learning about the larger credits and how they were approved and cleared with the board of directors.

The following year I became a junior loan officer and an assistant to the head loan officer, Ransom Cook. This position would lay the foundation for a long period of mentoring and a friendship that would mean a great deal to me, both personally and professionally. I was Ransom's assistant so I did his flunky work, if he had any, and then he would occasionally let me handle a small commercial loan account. I remember there was one person who came in who had a string of drive-in movie theaters. He would always come in to see "Rans," and after their visit Ransom would turn him over to me and I would get his numbers and find out how he was doing financially and what he wanted to do. It was not big money, but in banking you take care of your customers. It doesn't matter if they are borrowing $25,000 or $500,000, you have to take care of everyone equally. I was called in for the small loans and did the paperwork for the larger loans.

Most of my banking and business know-how came from Ransom Cook, who shared his knowledge and experience generously.

My bank responsibilities were clear, but what was expected of me at home was a different matter. We had a baby girl, Leslie, on January 17, 1950.

The fifties were a much different time when it comes to becoming a parent. Typically, new couples were expected to produce a child after nine months of marriage. It took us 12 months. And men were not expected to have much of a supporting role. I was in the waiting room when Leslie was born, for example, not in the delivery room. That wasn't an option like it is today.

And so, I was not only a new banker but also a new father. When Leslie would cry, I would sometimes kneel outside her door and say the rosary, hoping that she would stop. Obviously, I had a lot to learn about both children and banking.

Two years later, on December 27, 1951, Richard Pierce Cooley Jr. was born. He was a natural athlete, but we were not able to understand his academic challenges until much later in his life, when more became known about dyslexia. He struggled with it. Sometimes is it hard for the son of a successful father to succeed. If I had been around more and traveled less, I might have helped him more. I never cared what career he chose as long as he was happy and was using his abilities as best he could.

Another two years passed and I was well up in the ranks of the bank managers. I traveled more and was home less when Sheila, our third child, was born on November 26, 1953, one day after my birthday. She has become a hard worker, and my father always thought she was a star. She is a star. All of my kids are stars.

---

It was around this time that a senior vice president at the bank asked to speak with me. I went to his office. "Dick," he said, "what do you know about the zoo?" I told him that I knew very little. In fact I was not that big on animals in general, having never had a pet growing up. He said, "We have had the zoo account for a long time, and they are looking for a treasurer. How would you like to be on the zoo board?"

I said, "Sure. Be glad to." Even though I did not have much experience with animals, I wanted to represent the bank and become a part of the community. It turned out that the zoo board was fascinating. It was composed of scientists and businessmen. The scientists worried about the care of the animals, how they developed, and everything to do with the biology of it, and the businessmen were interested in charging the right amount for the hot dogs, keeping the place clean and open, being sure that the admission fees were adequate, but not too much, and other issues of that sort.

The San Francisco Zoo was an interesting organization. Its board met one night a month. I learned a lot about animals and made many friends. One of the more interesting discussions we had was when one of the elephants became ill and the scientists knew he was not going to last very long. They decided they had to put him down because they did not want him to die on a Sunday afternoon with 150 children watching. It was carefully thought out, and while I do not remember all the facts, I do recall that it was a big deal deciding how to euthanize the elephant peacefully and without upsetting anyone. They ended up giving him a sedative and then they put him down on a Monday night. I believe the zoo was closed that night so they were able to move him out without disruption, or an audience. It was a big concern for the board and some of it was over my head. The discussion helped me understand the problems involved with keeping the animals healthy and maintaining a zoo that the city and county could be proud of. The San Francisco Zoo was that kind of place.

————————

The bank decided that I should continue working for Ransom Cook, but split my duties with Senior Vice President Harris Kirk. He was in charge of the bank's business all over the country.

At the time there was a growing feeling that the bank needed someone young to meet the up-and-comers in other banks and clients. I was selected for the position because I came from the East Coast and had connections that the bank hoped would promote strong ties and new business partnerships. That gave me two bosses, one who managed loans and the other who was in charge of business development. My job changed significantly and involved a considerable amount of travel.

All through the 1950s I traveled in the Midwest and Northeast, calling on accounts in New York, Chicago, Detroit, Pittsburgh, or anywhere the bank had customers. The first title I received was assistant cashier, but as I traveled more the bank pushed me up to the rank of assistant vice president. This was not because I deserved it, but because I was representing the bank in different cities and they felt I needed a certain kind of title to be recognized. Eventually the assistant VP position turned into VP for the same reason. The bank had a load of vice presidents who had worked in the bank a lot longer and knew a lot more than I, but the title gave other banks and clients the impression that I was important enough to talk to.

Our national business was growing, so Mr. Kirk brought two more people into his department and divided the country into thirds. I was given the East Coast. Consolidating my focus helped me develop a network, and I made connections with people in other banks with whom we could exchange business and share in large credits.

In the 1950s, banks depended on each other to arrange large loans. No single bank had a sufficient legal lending limit to handle the needs of the big national corporations. Bankers were more cautious then and more interested in spreading large risks. It sometimes would take 50 banks to join in one loan agreement in order to meet the credit needs of a big borrower like the Aluminum Company of America or General Motors. Our relationships with other banks in the country were key to being invited to participate in those large loans. Many of them were initiated and managed by the big eastern banks, which were better compensated than we were. The regional banks like ours tended to get the scraps — the local accounts of those borrowers.

---

During the late 1950s and all through the '60s, money was tight at home. With children, there seemed to be endless expenses, which were beginning to exceed our income. We discussed my leaving the bank and finding employment elsewhere that would meet more of our financial needs. At the time we had three children who were nearing school age. Private school was a strong consideration, but it was not in our budget. I did not have a clear idea of what else I could do, and Mr. Flanigan's safety net seemed a long way away. I had been working hard to build a career in banking and had no desire to start fresh somewhere else when I could see potential for management in the future. Still, something had to be done to supplement my income.

Sheila's older sister, Ann, was married to Henry Ford II. His father had died when he was 21, and he had taken over the Ford Motor Company. It was a tremendous responsibility for such a young man, but he worked hard and did a fine job managing the business. Henry was a humble and generous man. After he married Ann, he continued his kind ways by giving some of the older McDonnell children Ford dealerships. I discussed the topic with some of the fortunate siblings, and then I broached the subject with Henry.

I had only one conversation with him about my strategy and he did not show much enthusiasm. However, he gave me the name of Arthur Hatch, a kind and wonderful man in San Francisco who was the West Coast regional sales manager for Ford. Soon it became apparent that Henry had given us an opportunity to create extra income from owning dealerships with no strings attached. His only desire was that we make money and operate the business with integrity. This chance to become financially solvent would not have been possible without the McDonnell connection with Henry Ford and Sheila's financial support in signing the guarantee, based on her modest family trust, for the necessary loan to own 60% of a brand-new dealership. If these two things had not happened, our lives might have played out in a totally different way.

Our first dealership was in the San Fernando Valley, in a town called Reseda. Mr. Hatch set us up with two experienced auto dealers in Los Angeles who had dealership operations in the area. Once everything was set up, I would go down to check on the dealership once a month to learn as much as I could about the automobile business. During those years auto sales were profitable, so we eventually started a second one in Sacramento. Both of these dealerships were successful and each provided the Cooleys with a new demo car and a salary of $1,000 per month. That meant I was taking home $2,000 monthly from the dealerships and $1,000 from the bank. It seemed like an enormous sum and allowed me to keep up with the day-to-day expenses of running the household.

What a debt of gratitude I owe Henry Ford II. Through his generous support I was able to continue my career working at the bank. Over those years I saw him occasionally and he never mentioned the dealerships, but we did talk about business. I will never forget some great advice he gave me on one of our visits.

"Dick," he said, "everyone I work with is smarter than I am and I know it. That is fine with me, but when they want to do something, I make them tell me in simple terms using five-letter words what it is they want to do and why. I don't approve anything unless I understand it."

In 1960, Wells Fargo President Isaias W. Hellman III negotiated the merger of Wells Fargo Bank with American Trust Company. The new Wells Fargo became the 11th-largest banking institution in America, creating a time of adjustment for many reasons. The merger was dominated by American Trust, which was a $1.7 billion bank, whereas Wells had assets worth $700 million. Harris Kirk became the president and chief executive officer of the merged bank, which assumed the more memorable and historic name of Wells Fargo. At the time of the merger, there were many excellent young employees at American Trust to compensate for the fact that Wells had not invested enough in training programs and lacked young talent, sapped by both the Depression and World War II.

Not long after he took the helm, Harris Kirk died, and Ransom Cook was next in line to become the bank's chief executive.

———————

One Friday morning Ransom sat me down and said, "Dick, you have to learn this business. There are not many people who are eligible for management, and all you have been doing is traveling. We need to put you in a training program." That training program began the following Monday morning, when I was told to report to the Matson branch office as its manager. The Matson office was on Market Street about five blocks from the downtown San Francisco office headquarters for Wells Fargo on California Street. It was called the Matson office because it was in the Matson Shipping Company building.

Ransom felt it was imperative that I learn the day-to-day operations and be aware of how the bank really worked.

At the time, I remember being mad at myself for not accepting my father's offer to attend Harvard's Advanced Management Program, which was a fine course for people who were already in the workforce and were interested in developing skills for higher levels of management. However, Ransom thought I would learn more by staying on the job. In his opinion, I wouldn't need education in a classroom for what I would be doing. Although I didn't know it at the time, I was being groomed to run Wells Fargo Bank and my own management course had already begun.

My training began with my realizing that I did not know how to balance the books or do much of anything like that.

In those days bookkeeping involved a laborious system of hand entries and punch cards. Computers had not yet been significantly employed by banks. Books had to balance to the penny every night, and we couldn't go home until everything added up correctly. I was fortunate to have a skillful assistant manager, James Houser, who knew the ins and outs of the operation, and he steadfastly taught me the ropes. The office was well managed before I arrived. My new job was to learn how it worked and not mess it up. Sometimes there was not a lot to do besides make sure clients felt that they were being cared for and their money was secure and that the staff was happy.

The Matson branch served as my classroom, and it was there that I began to understand management principles such as taking care of the customers, office policies, servicing accounts, and supervising employees. I was at the Matson branch for less than two years. During this time, I did not fully understand that I was being groomed for top management. Still there were times when I sensed that there was some sort of design for my future. One such example came the day that Chase Manhattan's chairman, David Rockefeller, walked in and introduced himself to me. He had been told that I was showing promise and that he should make my acquaintance. Later, we would have more opportunities to meet, including a dinner he gave for me when I was promoted to chief executive officer and president.

––––––––––

On the home front, perhaps it was Sheila's need to fill space left in her life as I spent more time tending to the bank, or maybe it was just God's will, but soon we had a fourth child, Sean, born March 1, 1961. Mark, our last child, was born August 4, 1964.

About the time Mark was born, Ransom Cook decided to reorganize of the bank. He restructured the branch system, separating it into divisions: Metropolitan, Sacramento, and Valley divisions, with a manager for each one. I was made head of the Metropolitan Division, the largest of the three. I moved into the

DICK WITH HIS SONS AT HIS 85TH BIRTHDAY CELEBRATION.
FROM LEFT TO RIGHT, PIERCE, DICK, SEAN, AND MARK.

Wells Fargo headquarters building on Market Street in downtown San Francisco and had a staff that managed business development, loans, operations, and property. It served as a mini-bank within the bank. Part of my job was to visit all the branches and call on customers, but mostly it was to work with our own people to make sure they understood the programs and that we were efficiently taking care of existing customers and growing with new business. I was young to have such a position, and everyone working for me was older and more experienced.

I managed the Metropolitan Division until Ransom Cook moved me back to the main office on California Street, where I was given responsibility for the Property Division. I was in charge of buying new branch sites, building, redecorating, and maintenance. This was considered a large part of the learning process by Ransom, who thought it was the only job in the bank where I would receive practical business experience making the sorts of decisions that clients made with architects and contractors, choosing locations and negotiating prices. This, he reasoned wisely, would help me better relate to customers.

I stayed as head of Properties for nine months before I became head of the bank's personnel department. There were a lot of technicalities that I needed to learn, such as all the aspects of human resources. We did not have unions at the time and we weren't sure when unions might become part of managing our employees, so we did our best to keep people happy and engaged with their jobs. A year or so later, I also became the head of all three branch divisions. Now I had the Metropolitan, Sacramento, and Valley districts reporting to me, while remaining head of personnel. Early in 1965 my title was changed to executive vice president, and in 1966 I was elected to the board of directors. My future as a banker was cast.

Wells Fargo board, 1976. Back row, from left: Regnar Paulsen,
Bob Nahas, Malcolm MacNaughton, Mary Lanigar, Dick Cooley,
Palmer Fuller, Jim Dobey, Jack Mailliard, Ken Bechtel, and
Bob Bridges. Front row, from left: Dick Guggenhime, Ed Littlefield,
Bill Brenner, Jim Dickason, Ernie Arbuckle, Jim Hait, Paul Miller,
Arjay Miller, and Atherton Phleger.

Inspecting an ice sculpture of Wells Fargo's iconic stagecoach
with Ernie Arbuckle.

In the 1950s and onward, the bank had a problem. Its senior managers were nearing retirement, and their juniors were young and mostly inexperienced. During the Great Depression, survival came before succession planning, and the bank had not hired. Then during the war there was nobody to hire. As a result, the bank's management had a decade-sized age gap. As my boss approached age 65, there was no one closer to his age than me to take over Wells Fargo. That is how I got to be on a fast track. By this time, I had run several different departments and entertained clients several evenings each week. Sheila was wonderful with people, and she was great at entertaining. One day the boss told me, "People are defenseless against a young couple like you two . . . you have got to make more friends." And so I did. I began to meet people from all over the East Coast.

When Ransom Cook became chief executive of the Wells Fargo Bank-American Trust Company in 1961, he and the board focused on management succession. He was a fine, intelligent man, who had taught me almost everything I knew about banking, and like my father, he believed in succession planning from your first day on the job. The board tried to hire a New York banker who had roots in San Francisco to line up behind Ransom. He turned them down. Then they tried to hire Tom Killefer, a Stanford graduate and a Rhodes Scholar, who was at the time Chrysler's chief financial officer. Ransom asked me to talk with Killefer, whom I knew socially, but when I did, and Killefer turned down the job, Ransom thought I had said something or in some way expressed an unwillingness to work with Killefer. That was not so, but for a time it put me in the doghouse with him.

If I had to do it all over again, I would still go back into the banking business. It was a good place for someone like me, whose talents are evenly distributed. I was just 41 when I became Wells' executive vice president and a member of its board. Although the board put me in line to succeed CEO Ransom Cook and bank president Steve Chase, they were not totally sure that I was ready. Ransom talked to me about becoming the bank's president and chief executive officer, and I told him that being president was enough. He said, "No, the board wants you to be the chief executive officer. They want to build for the future. I'm over retirement age and Steve Chase has only one year until retirement. I'll stick around for a year and Steve will probably stay for a year, and then you are on your own."

The next conversation we had was about money. At the time I was making $50,000 a year being executive vice president. Ransom told me that I would get a raise and go to $75,000, and that Steve Chase would be making $100,000 a year. He was making pretty close to that anyway, and I did not know what Ransom Cook would be making as chairman of the executive committee.

I told Ransom, "You do not have to make me chief executive officer. I'm happy to be president and I'll work just as hard, but if you make me chief executive officer, I think I should be paid as much as anyone in the bank, which means I should be paid $100,000 if that's what you're going to pay Steve." Either way, it was a lot of money to me, but I just did not think I should be the bank's chief executive in name only, so to speak. The way you keep score is with your salary, and I would not be chief executive officer that way. I stuck to my guns and I think Ransom was a little surprised and miffed, but he talked with the board members (the compensation committee, I suppose), and they decided that I would make the same salary as Steve.

The board named me president and chief executive officer in early November 1966. Steve Chase became chairman. He was already 64, and the board expected him to retire the following year. At 42, I was a young chief executive. When that change took place, Ransom moved off the executive floor and upstairs to the boardroom floor, where he had a beautiful office. But he was by himself up there. He would become chairman of the executive committee for a year and then he would retire from that position. In the beginning, I would be president and chief executive officer, and upon Steve's retirement, if everything went well, I would also become chairman of the bank's board.

It all seemed to happen quickly. I remember that things changed and yet they didn't change. One day Ransom moved upstairs and I moved into his old office on the executive floor, the 12th floor of the Wells Fargo headquarters on California Street (which had formerly been the American Trust Bank headquarters). Imagine that. I didn't know what else to do, so I moved his desk from one side of the office to the other. I was sitting there trying to process the change. Instead of the regular meetings I had always attended, I was now running them. It was difficult, but I got along the best I could and tried not to make too many mistakes. I made some, but nothing disastrous. At the time the bank had assets of about $1.8 billion. In Northern California, Wells Fargo was second only to Bank of America in terms of size, and Wells was the 11th-largest bank in the nation.

I cannot remember what day I was put in charge, but I remember sitting at Ransom's old desk. He and Steve Chase were sitting there in the room, and three or four senior and executive vice presidents were there. We were having a senior management meeting about buying bonds, and I was supposed to be running the meeting. At the time I did not know much about buying bonds, so I was taking the advice of the senior bond officer, Dwight Chapman. He was a good man and had been in the business for 40 years or more. He explained what we should do and people were asking questions. We were discussing a swap, changing some maturities for others, and hoping interest rates would go a certain way so that we would make some money. I said that's fine, but did not have a clue what they were talking about. I had to trust the men and the combined judgment of the group.

I had been working with all those people for years, but that day Ransom took a seat at the back of the room and I took his desk. It was really something. Sweat rolled down my back. In fact, it rolled down my back for almost a full year, sitting in that office trying to be the chief executive with all these older colleagues around me. Everyone was kind, but it was clear that I was not one of them because I was too inexperienced. Nevertheless, they all supported me and I had to fill the role of CEO and do it well. It was the hardest thing I ever had to do as a banker. I never had confidence early on; I just went along day to day. Eventually it worked out and I gained confidence in my abilities, and eventually I understood what needed to be done. Watching a chief executive officer lead and actually doing the job are two very different realities.

In addition to the small monthly senior management meeting that took place in Ransom's former office, we had a larger weekly management committee meeting downstairs in another room for all the department heads, 25 or so. Part of my job as the new chief was to run that forum. It was mainly for communication, so that all the managers would be aware of what was going on in the bank, but it was another big sweat for me. After the first one was over, Ransom took me aside and gave me a few ideas on how to improve. He thought I had let the meeting get away from me and he was correct. He told me that I needed to be more assertive with each person as we went around the table. His net takeaway for me was to keep control of the responses and keep them moving — not to let anyone drag the meeting by provoking questions that could be answered at another more appropriate time. That first meeting we ran 15 or 20 minutes over, but thanks to his constructive criticism it did not happen again.

Banking relationships led to personal friendships, and one example was Bob Miller. He was chairman of one of the Wells Fargo board committees — I think it was the compensation committee. I had to go see him shortly after I became the chief executive. We were talking about some business deal for which I had to get his approval. Then we talked about his health, as he had a weak heart. When I went to see him, he had an operation scheduled at the end of the month. I was giving him a pep talk, telling him that I knew he'd be fine, when he said, "No, I won't. I'm probably not going to survive this operation." He'd had problems before, and I think this was one of those operations the doctors had to try in order to save his life, but they could not guarantee that he would survive it. He was so brave about it. He had a feeling that he wouldn't survive, but he knew he had to do it. It seemed like such a paradox to me that he had to make that kind of decision. In the end, he did not survive. He had the operation and died on the table. He was so dignified and such an outstanding gentleman.

His son, Dick Miller, became one of my best friends in San Francisco. He and his wife, Ann Miller, had 12 children. Dick was godfather to one of my children, and I was godfather to one of his. We lived within a block of each other in San Francisco for many years, and he was always a good friend. Dick and Ann were both Catholics and very religious. Ann Miller was the only child of Donald Russell, who was head of the Southern Pacific Company for years and a well-known person in town. Ann was a live wire in San Francisco and liked to run things. If it moved, she knew about it. If you needed to know someone, she knew them. If you needed help, she could do it. She is the one who introduced me to Father Egon and got me started with Woodside Priory. When Dick was diagnosed with cancer, they prayed and took trips seeking cures, but nothing worked. Somewhere along the way they made a religious promise that after Dick died, Ann would enter a Carmelite convent in Illinois. Three years after Dick's death, with the children mostly grown, Ann entered the order and began to fulfill her promise to become a nun. She had an enormous party just before she went into the convent, and she has been there ever since. People keep in touch with her, and she is able to communicate with her children. Her mother was angry with her because she felt she had all the children to take care of after Ann entered the convent. But the important thing to Ann was to fulfill her promise. I've read about such promises in books, but this is the only time I've known someone personally who fulfilled such a commitment to God. I found it very moving.

---

A year after I became CEO and president of the bank, Ransom Cook and Steve Chase retired on schedule, and the title of chairman was added to my office. It was too much, so I immediately started to search for a person to take over the chairman position. I was uneasy with the directors due to my lack of experience and wanted someone older than I to take the job, and that was when I got Ernie Arbuckle to join the bank's board. He was an incredible person who had been in business in San Francisco for a long time and had many friends on the board. Ernie was finishing 10 years as dean of the Stanford Business School. He had a theory about staying too long in one job. After 10 years in a position, he thought, you might be getting stale and should seek another challenge. His "repotting idea," was why he was leaving the Stanford Business School. He had committed to the position for 10 years and that was it. Initially, he turned down my offer because he had already accepted another position, but that fell apart for some reason, so he came back six months later and asked if the chairman position was still open. I could not have been more pleased.

I hired Ernie Arbuckle at exactly my salary for several reasons. We were going to be partners, and I never wanted monetary issues to become a factor in our partnership. I was the bank's chief executive officer, but it was understood between us that his help to me with the board and the general business community would be important to my success and the success of the bank. Ernie was a great intermediary between my office and the board. He was 11 years my senior and knew the directors, who were also older and more experienced, socially and personally. Ernie also had connections and friendships that I did not have, and he was skilled at handling all kinds of people. Since the directors were clearly watching to see how I was progressing, Ernie was the perfect person to have as chairman.

Ernie became a good friend. He was a fine man and helped me all the way through. I tried to make sure that I never made any big decisions without talking to him first because I wanted him to feel that he was always important. I figured he would go if he felt he was not needed. He was good at dealing with people, which was not always easy for me. He was on many outside boards and was in a great position to advise me on many things that came up and on matters in which I had little or no experience. He attracted people from Stanford, and we had access to the best people that the Business School produced. We put a lot of them to work, sometimes hiring them without even knowing what they would do. We just wanted good people and we had this particular pipeline, which I think made the bank successful at that time. Using the words of Jim Collins who wrote *Good to Great*, we focused on getting "the right people on the bus."

---

It was one thing to acquire a stream of young talent from Stanford, or anyplace else, but it was another thing to utilize, challenge, and keep them. In my experience, commercial banks often behave like a herd of sheep. They all operate in the same bureaucratic manner, and when something new is started, they often copy each other in following a trend. For example, as the money center banks (large banks based in Chicago and New York that work with governments and large corporations) began to do more international business, they looked to the larger regional banks around the country as sources for new customers.

Standard Oil had accounts in California banks, but these banks lacked international connections and the ability to make international transactions. Once the money center banks began to pose a threat to their accounts, the regionals felt pressed to establish offices in places like London, Tokyo, and New York to meet the needs of their corporate customers who did international business. A few years later there were more American banking offices in these key international cities than there was business to support them. At the peak of this trend, there were 144 American banking offices in London.

One thing became clear. The old stuffy ways of banking were beginning to loosen up, particularly as deregulation appeared on the horizon. The Glass-Steagall Act had essentially put a fence around banks to prevent them from investing in other states. A bank was also restricted by how much money it could lend to a customer. In other words, during the days of greater federal bank regulation, banks were not as flexible. So to keep up with the opportunities, and with the competition, a successful organization needed new ideas and new minds. That is how we sought to use the new talent that came our way — to identify better ways to run the bank and newer ways to help our customers. With technology advancing at such a fast pace, fortunately, there were infinite opportunities to offer new products that could help and benefit our clientele.

One concept that attracted me was the mathematical, computerized approach to investing. We were able to attract some of the early researchers in the index fund field and produced significant index-type investment products. I have always been intrigued by good ideas, and I found their research totally convincing. Some of our directors were not as enthusiastic, holding firmly to the idea that superior investment counselors could always outperform a computerized program over time. That did not turn out to be true, and the bank did well on its indexing products.

Like me, Ernie was open to new ideas. Additionally, the young people who came to us felt that Wells was a place where creativity was welcomed and encouraged. These factors may have helped us keep the talent we were able to attract. We also provided a challenging environment, and the people we attracted and hired thrived there. As commercial banks were tightly regulated at that time, there were clear restrictions that limited what could be done. Still, within that framework there were many possibilities for new products.

Earnings were important to banking at this time, but often they did not seem to get the attention that growth did. As a rule, banks watch their published quarterly reports carefully, looking for growth in deposits, loans, and assets. But as the quality of earnings came under analytical scrutiny, some banks began to pay attention. Wells was one of them, empowered by our young MBAs, who thought of banking more as a business, not a profession. This began to have a positive effect on our costs and budgeting. As a result, we were willing to take risks if the idea was good enough (e.g., creating index fund products using the emerging research at the time, and MasterCard). So increasing earnings was another area where good and imaginative ideas were received and welcomed at Wells.

---

With the added pressures of the chief executive's job, I became tense and unhappy, and began to consider a divorce. Shelia did not want that; she didn't believe in divorce. I did not believe in it either, but I felt strongly pressured by Sheila's needs at home, by the responsibilities that came with having five children, and by my job, where I was struggling to be a success. Gradually, the bank and the business became the enemy to her, and when I began to run the place, I turned into the enemy too. We had a difficult time. I had been traveling a great deal, and she seemed to think that I was being urged to work hard by senior management. In fact, I was pressuring myself to do my best. She may have hoped that there would be more time for the family when I ran the bank. That was not going to be the case. On the contrary, I probably worked longer hours and traveled just as much or more.

If I could relive those years, I would not have divorced her. I would have learned to live with the situation and become more accepting. Even though I told myself that family comes first, looking back, it hardly seems true. I was selfish and self-directed, and I would be better about that. I would be more patient and not so gung-ho for my work that I did not take time to experience my children. I made sure they attended good schools and all those things, but I missed out on being a scout leader or a soccer coach. I wanted my own life, and I did what I had to do to manage the business. I did not want it to run me; I didn't want to live that way. It was like holding the tail of a tiger, and I wanted to control it. I could not imagine failure, nor could I have accepted that. In a general sense I had never failed at anything that I tried hard to achieve, and I was not about to start with the bank. In retrospect, I don't believe anyone should take a job like that when you have a young wife and five children at home. That phase of my life was an example of my having too much responsibility too early.

The combination of expectations at work and at home eventually got to be too much for me; that's what I told myself, anyway. Ending our 20 years of marriage seemed to be the only solution. And so, Sheila and I went in different directions. I can't say it was a good decision, but it allowed me to pour more of myself into my work at Wells Fargo.

---

Generally, at Wells, we started the week with a management committee meeting. It was held around the meeting table in my office. There were usually the various division heads plus the chairman and vice chairman — our offices were all on the executive floor. We would talk about the state of each section of the business so that everyone would be aware of what was happening throughout the bank. It was important for communication, but also for dealing with the problems and challenges facing us. Sometimes decisions were easily made and sometimes not. When there were different approaches to be considered, I would speak last and either decide which course of action to take, or put it off until we had more information and could find a better way to attack the problem.

We tried to adjourn that meeting before 10 a.m., after which everybody retired to the coffee room where other staff members would join us. The coffee room provided an informal way of communicating and keeping everyone on the same page. It was also a place where we could introduce new and/or special people to the group. Occasionally, we used this post-meeting time and place to make sure that some of our most important customers could meet other members of the senior management. There was no espresso or fancy coffee carts, as this was the 1970s, before the Starbucks culture took over.

The rest of the morning would be devoted to one-on-one meetings with various division heads concerning things related to their particular business. Typically before lunch, corporate people might bring customers by my office to meet the "boss," or it might be a branch manager from downstate with some people important to him. The chief executive officer's job requires a lot of meeting and greeting all kinds of people who are working for or with the bank. Almost every lunch was an occasion of this sort. Usually we would take visitors to a local luncheon club for businesspeople.

Dinner entertaining was different — more expensive and time consuming — and we went to good restaurants. In the early days of my banking career, there was considerable lunchtime drinking (a one or more martini lunch to mollify an unhappy customer was not unusual), but since I was never a big drinker I am happy to say that was gradually phased out in the '70s and '80s.

Even VIP dinners became more subdued, with far fewer cocktails than in the 50s, and the main meal was usually followed by coffee and going directly home. Occasionally we would go to the theater or a baseball game after an early dinner, which was usually good fun. The West Coast was more laid-back than the New York area, where the evenings were more formal and structured. In the West we did more home entertaining than they did in the East. On the weekends there were golf games and socializing at your club.

Back at the office after lunch, you might be lucky enough to have some personal time to catch up on your phone calls and correspondence. Sitting down with your assistant and going over what was happening that week was important. For the rest of the afternoon, your schedule would be full of various appointments with people who had called and had been given a time slot by the most important person in the office — your skillful assistant. Though it did not necessarily happen on Mondays, there would often be some committee meeting scheduled outside the bank for one of the community "not for profits" like United Way. After that, if you were fortunate, you could take a briefcase full of necessary reading and go home for the evening.

That was a typical day. On other days there were meetings for specific purposes such as going over the company budget or reviewing controversial or larger loans. Almost every week there was a trip away from the office that would take the entire day. Sometimes there were banking association meetings and sometimes I would call on customers with some of our people. On trips east or overseas I might take more time and be gone for a week to 10 days. Many people thought that bank chief executive officers and presidents did too much traveling. It was thought that they should stay home more and tend to their local knitting. I was as guilty as any, and in fact I traveled extensively, trying to expand our international and foreign connections.

Fortunately, we had strong division heads running their business departments successfully, and we had a superb operations head in Jim Dobey, who was the number three person in the bank after Ernie and me. Jim had started out in the bank branches after World War II, and he was a towering success at managing them. He was also an excellent loan officer. Jim was another one of the 50 trainees hired along with me in 1949. His judgment was very good and was based on years of experience. When I was away, I had complete confidence in Jim making the day-to-day decisions for the company. To run any large organization, you need to have good people and then stay out of the way and let them do their jobs.

Banking is a people business. Whether it is a group of employees or an important customer, you spend your day talking to people. That is why successful bankers have to be high-energy people. Each day your calendar is filled up like that of a lawyer or doctor. There is little time to think, as each unallocated time slot will be filled. This is why having an intelligent, detail-oriented assistant is key to your ability to use your time wisely. Your assistant needs to understand your relationships with the various people who want to see you. I have made it a point to get to know the assistants of my peers. These remarkable, talented people are the ones who allocate the majority of a chief executive's time. If you need to get something important done or have to presell a new idea or project, you always run it by the assistant for input on the appropriate way to proceed.

Each month there was the regular board meeting and the committee meetings that accompanied it. We would prepare carefully for those meetings, as they often represented a complete review of the business for the directors. We would practice our presentations and take great care making the various agendas. The directors were our bosses and we treated them accordingly. One of our most important and senior directors was Ed Littlefield. He was chairman of the compensation committee, a job he seemed to like and one I found hard to rotate him out of, which made him a very important director.

In general, Ernie and I liked to rotate the board members through all of the committees so they would each have a good general grasp of our business. Also, we did not want anyone to have an overly strong hold on any one part of the bank's management. I believe all directors should be equal. Ed was bright and highly respected in the business community, and having sold his company to General Electric, he had become the largest individual shareholder of that company. Occasionally there was a conflict with the dates of those board meetings, and Ed told me that if I wanted him to come to the bank's meeting, it had better be more interesting and thought-provoking than GE's.

Board meetings can indeed be dull and uninteresting, particularly when they don't make use of the experience and intelligence of the directors. Ed's ultimatum was a good wake-up call, and we tried hard to have each meeting be informative and clearly describe what was going on in the bank's world so the directors would go away having learned something useful and interesting that they might apply to their businesses. We also tried to find ways to tap into their expertise to solve problems that were not clear or easy for the bank to fix. They had to feel that they were needed and that they were contributing.

I always tried to have a one-on-one breakfast or lunch with each director a minimum of once a year. It was a time to find out what they were thinking about, which perhaps would not have come up in the meetings. Certain directors are uneasy bringing up controversial points of view in a setting with their peers, but they will level with you when it is just the two of you. You work for the directors, so it is important to get to know them. Any chief executive officer forgets that at his or her peril.

The board meetings used to be on Tuesday mornings. After the meeting the directors and senior staff would lunch together in the board dining room. When the lunch was over and things had gone as planned, I would go back to my office and breathe a big sigh of relief. It was like I had passed an examination and could feel secure in my job for another month.

When you are in the midst of making daily decisions as chief executive, you sometimes cannot see how it will play out, but you intuitively know that it is the best decision for the company now and in the future. Years after I left Wells, I read *Good to Great*, a book written by Jim Collins. It was first published in 2001, and it has stayed on the business best-seller list for a long time. Collins mentions the companies that possess Level 5 Leadership. According to Mr. Collins, a Level 5 leader is a person who is very humble, but has the indomitable urge to succeed and who is perseverance personified. When you put those attributes together, according to the book, it leads to greatness in leadership. In Collins's and his research team's view, a great leader is "self-effacing, quiet, reserved, even shy." Additionally, Collins noted that the good-to-great leaders "never wanted to become larger-than-life heroes" and "never aspired to be put on a pedestal or become unreachable icons."

Out of thousands, Collins picked 11 core companies that over a 15-year period maintained a good-to-great standard. Wells Fargo was one of them, but Collins picked a period after I retired, so I did not get or deserve credit for it. Carl Reichardt was responsible for that. The Collins team took those companies that were selected and compared them to another competitive company. The companies they chose to highlight were Abbott, Circuit City, Fannie Mae, Gillette, Kimberly-Clark, Kroger, Nucor, Philip Morris, Pitney Bowes, Walgreens, and Wells Fargo. Wells was compared to Bank of America for the study.

Collins found that "Wells Fargo began its fifteen-year stint of spectacular performance in 1983, but the foundation for the shift dates back to the early 1970s, when then-CEO Dick Cooley began building one of the most talented management teams in the industry (*the* best team according to investor Warren Buffett).

Cooley foresaw that the banking industry would eventually undergo wrenching change, but he did not pretend to know what form that change would take. So instead of mapping out a strategy for change, he and chairman Ernie Arbuckle focused on 'injecting an endless stream of talent' directly into the veins of the company. They hired outstanding people whenever and wherever they found them, often without any specific job in mind. 'That's how you build a future,' he [Dick] said. 'If I'm not smart enough to see the changes that are coming, these people will. And they'll be flexible enough to deal with them.'"

Collins further noted, "Cooley's approach proved prescient. No one could predict all the changes that would be wrought by banking deregulation. Yet when these changes came, no bank handled those challenges better than Wells Fargo. At a time when its sector of the banking industry fell 59 percent behind the general stock market, Wells Fargo outperformed the market by over three times."

Collins interviewed a former president of Ford Motor Company and a longtime director of Wells, Arjay Miller, who found the Wells Fargo management team to be similar to Ford's "Whiz Kids" who had been recruited right after World War II.

"Wells Fargo's approach was simple," said Miller. "You get the best people, you build them into the best managers in the industry, and you accept the fact that some of them will be recruited to become chief executive officers of other companies." Bank of America recruited so many Wells Fargo executives during its turnaround in the late 1980s that people inside began to refer to themselves as "Wells of America."

According to Collins, Carl Reichardt, who became Wells Fargo's chief executive officer in 1983, "attributed the bank's success largely to the people around him, most of whom he inherited from Cooley. As he listed members of the Wells Fargo executive team that had joined the company during the Cooley-Reichardt era, we were stunned. Nearly every person had gone on to become CEO of a major company: Bill Aldinger became the CEO of Household Finance, Jack Grundhofer became CEO of U.S. Bancorp, Frank Newman became CEO of Bankers Trust, Richard Rosenberg became CEO of Bank of America, Bob Joss became CEO of Westpac Banking (one of the largest banks in Australia) and later became dean of the Graduate School of Business at Stanford University—not exactly your garden-variety executive team," concluded Collins.

*Good to Great* also mentions a quotation by Warren Buffet regarding his $290 million investment in Wells Fargo despite his serious reservations about the banking industry: "They stick with what they understand and let their abilities, not their egos, determine what they attempt."

The lessons that Jim Collins and his team analyzed and wrote about were good ones. They make sense and are well worth studying and using.

When you sit in the chief executive chair, you make decisions and you make the best ones you can. Rarely is it easy or black and white. There is a lot of gray. A chief executive makes those decisions and lives by them. If your judgments are half right, you are probably pretty successful. I used to agonize over my choices, but now I realize you have to make a lot of decisions if you are running an organization and you can't or won't always be right.

You cannot worry about what others think, or the consequences of crossing someone. It is human nature to want others to respect and approve your judgment in management, but being in charge means setting the tone and making decisions for the good of the company. You make big choices about buying millions of dollars' worth of bonds and hope that the interest rates will be favorable to you. That is a big decision, but there are also plenty of small decisions others pass your way that can be distractions you need to manage — like being asked to choose the color of the new decoration in the coffee room. Silly things like that.

Sometimes you have contemporaries in the bank who offer good advice on how to handle a certain situation. There are others who would rather have you make any questionable decision so they will not have to. Making those choices can rattle nerves when you are only 42 years old. That is how I started out as president and chief executive of Wells Fargo Bank.

———————

My first major decision after becoming chief executive officer was to expand the bank to Southern California. It seemed to me and to my confreres, the younger part of bank management, that we had to expand our territory south in order to compete statewide. Besides, there was a lot more money and economic activity in the Southland. We had always been one of the top banks in Northern California and our principal competition was Bank of America, which was the largest bank in both ends of the state. Security Pacific was ranked number two in the South, and Wells Fargo was ranked number two in the North. At one point we started merger talks with Security Pacific in an effort to provide statewide competition for Bank of America. When we got to a discussion of feasibility with lawyers, they told us that the Antitrust Division of the Department of Justice would not allow it. It was also likely that Bank of America would see that such a merger did not happen. We dropped the idea and continued on alone, planning to build slowly and methodically, one branch at a time. But we knew that such *de novo* banking (state-chartered banking) would be expensive.

———————

Early in 1967, we made the decision to open a branch on Pershing Square in the heart of downtown Los Angeles. Wells Fargo has long had its stagecoach trademark, so we took the coach we had on hand for marketing events to the square and rode around in it wearing top hats. The little bank branch opened in a modest locale, not classy at all and with little business to speak of, but it

CLOCKWISE FROM UPPER RIGHT: TV ACTOR JAMES DRURY OF *The Virginian*;
JACK BREEDEN; DICK COOLEY; WELLS FARGO MANAGER BRAD DAVIS;
AND TV ACTOR DALE ROBERTSON..

gradually grew into something. I remember one of the directors said to me, "Dick, this is going to take you 15 years before this becomes anything at all. Hope you do not lose your shirt in the process." We knew it would take a long time to get off the ground, but we had to start. We did not think it would be a profitable thing, but we thought for the growth and future of the bank in the decades ahead, we simply had to be in both ends of the state.

We were acting on our expensive *de novo* plan for developing a system of 50 branches in Southern California when we had an opportunity to purchase Los Angeles-based First Western Bank & Trust. It had 54 branches in Southern California and assets of about $1.1 billion. It was owned by World Airways, and bank regulators had ruled that banks could no longer be owned by nonbanks. At the time we had assets of not quite $8 billion and most of our 285 branches were in Northern California. It could have been a great marriage for Wells, but the Department of Justice again denied our efforts, claiming the merger would reduce competition in both lending and customer service. Had it been completed, it would have been one of the largest mergers in U.S. banking history.

Although our plan for setting up branches in Southern California had been expensive, it turned out to be a good plan 40 years later. Moving south was probably the biggest decision that I made. Ransom and Steve Chase were not enthusiastic, given where they were in their careers, but the idea was well supported by the younger bank managers. They and I thought that such development needed to happen. So although it was challenging and difficult to launch, it was a strategically positive move. Today the bank is well established in both markets, and it offers strong competition to all the other banks.

During my early years as president and chief executive officer, we continued to look around for new merger candidates that might pass the antitrust tests, as well as new branch locations. Some people in San Francisco did not think much of Los Angeles in those days, but on the other hand, it was an economic powerhouse. LA was where it was happening. People in San Francisco were more conservative and not quite as open as they have since become.

Basically, California's growth during that early part of my career far exceeded the vision we had when we started. The overall growth of the bank was a combination of mergers and *de novo* branching that is too lengthy to detail here. We needed more capital, more people, and a tremendous amount of energy to keep up with the opportunities in Southern California. It was exciting and stimulating and demanded much hard effort from all involved.

As we built the branch system, we had another major problem — installing senior management and representing the bank to the Southern California community. In our corporate business we already had many important customers in the area that we serviced out of San Francisco. We needed to build on that base and be able to service business in the south. Jack Breeden, who ran our corporate business from San Francisco, volunteered to go to Los Angeles as our executive vice president in charge of Southern California operations. Jack took early retirement when he turned 60, moved to Hawaii, and for a time worked there as a consultant. Years later his place was taken by Bill Barkan, who took early retirement after a medical scare.

At this time, Carl Reichardt, having joined Wells Fargo & Company to start our Real Estate Investment Trust business (REIT) in 1979, was made president of the bank. He was from Southern California and had worked for Union Bank in that area so he knew that part of the state. As a potential successor to me, we wanted to move him north to San Francisco so he could become familiar with that part of California as well. To accomplish this and to convince people in the south that Wells Fargo was serious about becoming part of the community, I moved to Wells's Southern California headquarters in Los Angeles, though the bank's headquarters remained in San Francisco. By 1980 we had 383 branches statewide, and 125 of them were in Southern California. Carl moved to the San Francisco office as president. He was ranked fourth in executive management, behind me, Ernie, and Jim Dobey, who was vice chairman.

While I was officially in Los Angeles, I usually spent two days a week in my San Francisco office, which meant constant travel back and forth. I bought a home on the beach in Orange County, and the bank provided me with an apartment in San Francisco. Getting to know people in LA was a challenge compared to San Francisco, where I felt I knew everyone.

Bank of America's chairman lived in Los Angeles. Security Pacific was second in size to Bank of America in the Southern California market, and always a possible merger consideration for Wells, but we were starting from scratch. Our competitors were already entrenched. The Southern California market was a tremendous source of deposits, and there were many opportunities to loan money. To get to know people, I went on the boards of nonprofits in San Francisco and Los Angeles. Civic dinners in Los Angeles were as important as in San Francisco, if not more so, leaving me plenty to do.

Looking back on it over four decades, I know that moving Wells Fargo into southern California was the right choice and one that ensured the future of the company. I will forever be grateful and glad that we moved to Southern California when we did. As I mentioned earlier, chief executive officers make a lot of decisions, some good and some bad. If some of your right decisions are among the important ones, the mistakes will not kill you.

Through it all, putting the customer first always seemed the best way to go for me. Putting the customer first sounds like an oxymoron for a large retail bank, but it is not. When one truly makes the total thrust of an organization to always put customers first, many choices are made, some of which may not seem to benefit the shareholder or the staff. However, in my experience, if a bank sticks to this policy and doesn't dilute it with strategies that seem to benefit the customer but actually benefit the bank, everyone wins — customers, shareholders, and staff.

Dick with Ransom Cook (middle)
and Stephen Chase (far right).

# International Interest and Investments

New York City banks like Citibank and Chase traditionally handled international transactions, but as businesses grew in the West, Wells Fargo accounts more often needed services that required international banking relationships. In the beginning we would fulfill these needs through Citibank or Chase, but as the volume of this business increased, we looked to establish our own international banking connections. Wells was not alone in expanding banking beyond U.S. borders. Bank of America and others were also shunning the costly services of New York banks, choosing instead to establish their own relationships.

Carlos Rodriguez-Pastor Sr. was our man at Wells Fargo in the International Division. He had been the chief executive officer of Peru's central bank, but then his politics got caught up in Latin American volatility and a nonviolent military coup, so he was forced to leave the country permanently. I was told that he had to swim across a river to make his escape and avoid arrest. Once in California and reunited with his family, he began to explore the possibility of working in the U.S. financial sector. It happened to be good timing for Wells, and because we were focused on building our business internationally, we hired him. Carlos was experienced, and because of his numerous connections all over the world, he could open doors anyplace in Europe or Latin America. He also could play the piano beautifully, and everyone enjoyed his company.

Through Carlos we got to know Miguel de la Madrid. He was a senior credit manager at the Banco de Mexico, the Mexican central bank. We visited him regularly and watched as he advanced politically in the PRI (Partido Revolucionario Institucional, or Institutional Revolutionary Party), the dominant political party in Mexico at that time. Soon after we connected with him, he became his party's leading candidate and ultimately president of the country. Carlos felt that Miguel de la Madrid would be the candidate who would clean up the corruption in Mexico.

How much he accomplished in his six-year term I am not sure, but I liked him a great deal. He was personable, well-educated, and the only president of a foreign country I have had the pleasure of meeting. One evening we were invited to his house for dinner, and we ate around the table with his family. Everyone was speaking Spanish except me. Miguel spoke English well, as he had gone to graduate school at Harvard. I found him a gracious, intelligent, and sincere man.

When Miguel de la Madrid became president, Carlos took me down for the inauguration. We liked the fact that Miguel would be the president, because we thought he was a competent technocrat more than an old-style PRI politician. We were eager to support his efforts. As we went through the reception line, he was speaking in Spanish to his hundreds of guests. When it came my turn to shake his hand, he shifted over to English and said warmly, "Hello, Dick. I'm so glad you came down." Out of that mass of people, he recognized me and made the adjustment to speak English. It was something that I will never forget.

There was a time when Carlos thought doing business in Spain would be a good connection for our Latin American business. He hired a young, personable, well-connected man in Madrid to represent us. Our new young man was a cousin of King Juan Carlos. In 1976, Carlos and I went to Madrid to make ourselves known to the bankers and the business community.

It was the only time I have ever been there, and it was memorable because of our new representative. Amidst the regular calling, he arranged a personal visit with the king for the three of us.

The king and queen were popular there and were considered to be doing a good job. We were invited to go to the palace in the late morning for coffee and a personal visit. When we arrived we were taken upstairs to a large room that had the appearance of a comfortable family room here in the United States. There was a large chaise against the wall in front of which was a wooden coffee table. Two easy chairs were at each end of the coffee table.

After we were ushered in, the king arrived from the opposite side of the room, informally attired in short sleeves, with a smile and a welcome in English. He sat in one of the easy chairs, was relaxed, and appeared to enjoy seeing us. Having his cousin there seemed to give the visit a pleasant family tone. He wanted to know about the bank and what we were hoping to do there. No problems of state came up, and the time passed easily as we had our coffee. He was cordial and friendly, and you could not help but like him.

I have always found that smaller, more intimate groups suit my personality better. I was never good at going through a cocktail party and shaking hands with everyone in the room, and I never found small talk particularly captivating. I know it is a technique that you can learn, but it has never been my style. I was always better at standing in one place and visiting with whomever was around me. Having a good conversation was easier and more pleasing to me than moving about the room.

You meet a lot of people in the course of a career. One of the basic things in life is the wonderful people you encounter along the way. Some may be around for a while and then they tend to fade out of your circles. And I have found it to be true that even the richest man in the world may be grumpy in the morning. You cannot be a star every day. If you are in a position in life where you meet many people, you will notice that unless you find each

other agreeable and you are able to do things together as friends,
meeting another person does not change anything, especially
who you are. As I learned when I was much younger, the mere
fact that someone is famous does not make that person more of a
human being or more special than you.

One memorable occasion took place in the 1960s when David
Rockefeller offered to host a business dinner for me in New York
City. I was both flattered and pleased. The impetus behind the
dinner was that I was a young bank CEO and he wanted his bank,
Chase, to be our principal New York bank. He informed me that
there would be several important executives there, but I told him
that I would rather have a smaller dinner with some people he
found interesting. That might have surprised him because I am
sure he probably had to organize this type of dinner every night
of the week. David invited his wife and daughter, the president of
Rockefeller University, a few professors, and the U.S. Secretary
of Health, Education and Welfare, John Gardner. They were all
fascinating people in their own right.

The dinner was held at one of his old New York clubs, which
was the kind of place that would not make the society pages in
the newspapers. New York has many such clubs people do not
know about, where families who have lived in the city a long time
can have a private place to entertain. It is not that it was so fancy,
although it was a fine place and the food was very good, but the
protocol is the same. If your manners have been taught to you by
your mother, then you can enjoy these events in fine places with
well-known people and be at ease. David Rockefeller was always
at the upper level of things, so for him to have a dinner for me
was quite an honor. I hope he enjoyed himself, because it was not
just another bank dinner. Maybe he was glad to find someone
who wanted to do something different. David was a kind man and
for me, this evening was most enjoyable.

David Rockefeller of Chase and Walter Wriston of Citibank
ran the two largest banks in New York, and they were known to

compete. Everyone liked David Rockefeller, although some did not think he was the same caliber of businessman as Walter Wriston. Regardless, David Rockefeller was an impressive man who was known by kings and queens, and all the Saudis. On the international scene he was without peer and enormously well regarded as a person. David spent much of his time as chief executive officer of Chase making connections for the bank. Wells Fargo had a long-standing relationship with Chase by then, and David's interest in our West Coast bank was gratifying for us.

Walter Wriston wanted his bank to be successful, and he was more aggressive about it than Chase. When he decided Citibank had made a mistake when they started in the credit card business with the Everything Card, he made a classic Wriston move. He did not stick with something simply because he had created it, and he realized that the Everything Card was not a good name. It did not work for Citibank, so he made a 180-degree turn. He decided to dump it and asked to join our MasterCard Association. That was fine with us, and we were glad to have him.

Our bank had started MasterCard with three other California bank partners to compete with the BankAmericard, Bank of America's early Visa card. Jack Elmer of Wells was the organizer of the original MasterCard, and he ran the project with the three partner banks, Security Pacific, Bank of California, and Crocker. By the time the research, planning, and organization were done, we had 70 banks in the MasterCard Association. Adding the biggest bank in New York to the association would give us critical mass, and we welcomed Mr. Wriston's interest — and Citibank.

---

In 1965, when the board decided to make me the head of the bank, they put me in a special training program. It was during this time that Ransom Cook took me and our wives to Europe so introductions could be made to the proper bankers in London, Paris, and elsewhere. He also took me to Japan to visit the bankers there, introducing me as the man who would succeed him.

That was the old-fashioned way, and it was important for building relationships and keeping the bank's connections intact.

As part of my training under Ransom, I regularly went to Tokyo and Osaka. The bank had a small office in Tokyo that was staffed by only four people, one American and three Japanese. One of the men in the office was an old Japanese fighter pilot named Sidney Shimizu. He had been shot down five times in World War II. His English was excellent, as was his knowledge of Japanese banks. He arranged everything for my visits and accompanied me wherever I went.

The Japanese trips were always business related. There was an interpreter on each call, and as it turned out, there was more calling on banks than corporate calling because the banks served as advisors to the corporations. Additionally, the bank would entertain clients they had an important relationship with. If you had 10 major banks that you were dealing with, most would entertain you, particularly as a new young bank president and CEO. Not only were you entertained graciously, but there were also welcoming gifts. In time much of the custom was done away with, but during my early years in Japan it was still very much a part of the protocol.

Ransom told me that I should always bring bottles of Johnnie Walker Black Label. Recently, a Japanese friend confirmed that this preference was still alive and well in his country. Since that is what these bank executives liked, I brought some with me on each trip as a courtesy. I learned that although Japanese bankers did not make a lot of money, they had huge expense allowances because they ate most of their dinners while doing bank-related business. All the entertaining was a large part of their job. They got home late, but that was viewed as normal by their wives, who usually ran the households.

The dinners were always formal and lengthy. We would go into a private room in a restaurant and sit across the table from the man who was hosting the dinner. He would have a geisha on each side of him, and I would be flanked by two geishas. They would fill your sake cup or your glass if you were drinking Scotch. I was always terrified to drink the sake because I did not want to over imbibe with these bankers. Usually it did not bother the Japanese men, who drank the Scotch copiously.

Sidney told me that they had geisha parties nightly. Since he was the one who arranged the dinners, I knew this was probably true. We played childish little games, and sometimes the geishas would dance for us and sing in Japanese. The music did not hit my American ear as pleasantly as it did the Japanese. Dinners usually consisted of 10 or 12 courses. I always tried to do my best with the portions, but the dessert course was always a welcome sight because I knew that I could leave soon and get into bed. It was not my kind of food, but there were never difficult things to swallow. The Japanese presentation is very important, so the food looked appetizing; it just wasn't always warm and excitingly edible for my tastes.

There were formal calls at the banks, but never drop-ins. The dinners were always separate and not a place to discuss business. Geisha dinners involved party talk. Nothing was ever solved. It was a time to form a relationship and a friendship. In time I became acquainted with one of the bank chairmen, but I was never invited to his home. It was always a dinner party out at a restaurant.

On one trip I brought my wife. At the time, I was married to Judy Chase Ludwig and the Japanese bank executives included her in the dinner invitation. She was seated at the main table and was given her own two geishas. My friend, the chairman, who was hosting the dinner, broke precedent and brought his wife. She sat in the row behind us and was not allowed to sit at the table. His wife had never been invited before, and she was happy to be included, even if it was in the second row. That is how they did things back then, but I am sure that as time went on, the entertainment became more modernized.

One time a Japanese banker took me golfing. Being part of a golf club is important to the Japanese, and the banks pay enormous sums for those memberships. Afterward, we had a steam bath where people scrubbed our backs. It was an all-day affair. The caddies were women and what I found impressive was that they never lost a ball no matter how bad you were or where it landed. We played nine holes and then stopped for a wonderful lunch, followed by another nine holes.

The Japanese were big at forming societies when they wanted to deal with a problem and I belonged to a few of them. Bank of America also participated. I am not sure how much good they did to enhance trade between customers or countries, but we certainly learned about Japanese culture and how to do things in Japan. It was also a chance to be close to some of the American businessmen with whom I wanted to establish relationships.

Wells was a member of the Japan-California society, which would meet one year in the United States and the next in Japan. All the heads of the largest businesses in California — some 20 or 30 important executives — joined the society. It was a way to try to be friends and do business with Japan. The meetings were conducted in a very gentlemanly way, but not much came from the discussions. Topics mostly fluctuated between imports, tariffs, and exchange rates. The thing that was bothersome to the Americans was the Japanese yen. It was a controlled currency, and it was very low at that time. This made it especially difficult for California businesses to make products that were competitive with Japanese products.

For 20 years I made business trips to Japan. As a West Coast bank, we had customers who did business in Japan and we wanted to serve them there. Bank of America was everywhere, so we were also trying to hold on to our customers and compete. It did not work out well, and the Tokyo office was eventually sold to a Swedish bank.

Despite all my travel to Japan, I have yet to take a vacation there. Once in a while there would be the odd day off when I could go exploring or possibly have a weekend free, for which the office would arrange a room at an inn on the side of Mount Fuji. It was a nice way to see the beauty of the area as well as walk and take the steams. If it was the right time of year, the bank might arrange a golf game.

On the occasions when I could get away for a few hours, I was able to see some of the temples and beautiful meditative gardens. These exquisite sites offer time to think and reflect about what is going on in the great cosmos. My Japanese friend told me they are places for prayer. In addition to Tokyo and Osaka, I visited Nagoya and Kyoto to see the temples and a performance of the traditional tea service.

Only once or twice did I stay in one of the Japanese inns where you pull the mattress out of the wall and sleep on the floor. My rooms usually had a hot tub, which added to the ambience and made it totally different and fun.

---

In 1976, at Ernie's recommendation, we initiated the Wells Fargo Bank International Advisory Council (IAC). Many American banks had established special boards or advisory groups to aid them in becoming more international in scope. Through Ernie's connections we got Lord Roger Sherfield to take on the chairmanship and help us gather an extraordinary group of talented people.

Lord Sherfield was an active member of the House of Lords and had been the United Kingdom's ambassador to the United States. His wife of more than 30 years, Alice, was American. His experience, not only in the United States but also in Europe, made him an ideal person to help us build our IAC. The council had two major purposes. First, its members were to keep Wells Fargo's senior management apprised of their views on the world economy, particularly in their own countries and regions. Second, the individuals served as experienced senior advisers in discussions of the company's plans and strategies for domestic and international markets.

The first two IAC meetings were held in London in 1976. The meetings were to be held every eight months, alternating between California and a foreign location. When the first regular meeting took place in San Francisco in 1977, there were 12 members from nine different countries.

In addition to Lord Sherfield, Ernie, and myself, the initial members included Göran Ennerfelt. Ennerfelt was from Sweden and was president and chief executive of the investment company Axel Johnson AB, one of the three major companies in that country. Early in his career he had spent a year with Wells in a specialized bank training program learning about American business. He was smart, friendly, and he fit in easily with this group.

Another member, Eugenio Garza Lagüera managed his family's industrial conglomerate, Valores Industriales, in Monterrey, Mexico. He also became chairman of the Monterrey Institute of Technology and Higher Education. He was one of the important businesspeople behind the PRI government's modernization of the Mexican economy, and he provided valuable insights into Latin American business and finance.

North American IAC members included Belton K. Johnson, who was a part of the King Ranch family from Texas. He owned several ranches and was a beef industry expert. He was also a noted philanthropist. Educated at Cornell and Stanford, he sat on a variety of boards including AT&T, Signal Companies, Campbell Soup, and the National Cowboy Hall of Fame. Like me, he had served United Way as a trustee, and we were both members of the Bohemian Club in San Francisco.

Ahmed Juffali was a Saudi living in Jeddah. While he was not a member of the royal family, he was part of the business elite. He and his brothers owned the Juffali Group, which was a

joint-venture partner with international stalwarts such as
Daimler-Benz, Dow Chemical, Fluor Corporation, Ericsson, IBM,
and others. His background and knowledge provided IAC remarkable insight into both the politics and business of the Middle East.

Lord Lawrence Kadoorie was one of the richest men in
Hong Kong, one of the original *tai-pans* ("big shots"), and a key
English investor. He and his family owned, among many other
entities, a famous old hotel—The Peninsula. He advised the IAC
regarding China's and Hong Kong's sphere of influence in Asia.

Adolf Kracht was Wells Fargo's German banking friend. He
migrated from banking to one of the large old German family
insurance firms during the 1970s and ended up running Gerling-
Konzern, one of the country's largest insurance companies.

Roger Lapham Jr. was a Wells Fargo director whose interests
were primarily in insurance and finance. His father had been
mayor of San Francisco. Roger was chairman of the Rama
Corporation Ltd. in Paris. He also represented the Wells Fargo
bank and holding company boards on the council.

Monroe Spaght was a retired senior executive from Shell Oil
Company and a close friend of Lord Sherfield. He contributed his
observations from the United Kingdom and his knowledge of the
petroleum business.

Jacques Terray was the chairman of the Credit Chimique, our
French investment partner, and adviser to the IAC regarding
European business and finance. I worked with Jacques on a
regular basis as a board member of Credit Chimique.

William Turner represented the Canadian business sector
on the IAC board. He was chairman and chief executive officer
of Exsultate Inc., a holding company for Newmont Gold
Company. He was vice chairman of the Carnegie Institution of
Washington and a director of Proudfoot, a Canadian management
consulting firm.

Sir James Vernon was IAC's only member from the Southern Hemisphere. He ran a major sugar business in Australia and was an expert on the Australian postal system, among other interests.

We were looking for meaningful international financial know-how to make available to our customers as the business world became ever more global and our overseas business expanded. Much of the West Coast business went to European, Latin American, and Asian companies, and that business was reciprocal.

Initially we decided to try for one meeting a year in some part of the world that was important economically and interesting in a business sense. It was a large and continuous task. We were lucky to find Jackson Schultz, a retired U.S. Navy captain working in the bank, to take on the job of planning and caring for this group. All of these people were highly placed in their own countries and required intelligent and thoughtful handling. Jackson's wife, Rhoda, was a perfect complement to him in this effort, as one of the conditions of each meeting was the inclusion of the members' wives. This was important to the bank, because we felt the wives helped us better understand the various cultures we would encounter when making international investments. Plus it was attractive to the busy executives we wanted to attend our meetings. We wanted everything to be first class, and the Schultzes helped us accomplish that goal.

After the London and San Francisco meetings, we ventured to Mexico City and a year later to Brazil. In between, we continued to have our California events once a year but moved them up and down the state. The business part of the meetings usually ran over two days and was like a regular board meeting, except that there was no need for resolutions, votes, and so on. We wanted their help and advice, so we had to make the members aware of how the bank was doing and what we were working on. Often a department head would come and talk about a part of the business that had little or nothing directly to do with our international efforts, so it was essential that these sessions not only be interesting, but also in sync with the members' thoughts and experiences. The variety and depth of experience represented on the council was awesome and we took advantage of that, used our time with them as wisely as we could, and as a result these meetings were a great help to Wells Fargo.

My last trip with the council was to Saudi Arabia in 1982. In most places we traveled to, one of the council members acted as an unofficial host, which made it possible to see and visit places that would have been out of reach otherwise. These hosts facilitated meetings with key persons in government so that we better understood the economic life of the part of the world we were in. At times, these fascinating key government people were willing to participate in our meetings.

Over the years the membership in the IAC varied, as some stayed only for their initial term of six years or occasionally less. As new members were added, we more than maintained the high quality of the initial group. Of the original nine, five were still with the council when it was disbanded in 1995 when our priorities shifted.

Jim Collins noted in his book *Good to Great* that Wells Fargo studied its results and made adjustments. "Wells Fargo had tried to be a global bank, operating like a mini-Citicorp, and a mediocre one at that," wrote Collins. "Then, at first under Dick Cooley and then under Carl Reichardt, Wells Fargo executives began to ask themselves a piercing set of questions: What can we potentially do better than any other company, and, equally important, what can we not do better than any other company? And if we can't be the best at it, then why are we doing it at all?"

In a table that illustrates the attitudes of companies that successfully transitioned from good to great, Collins wrote: "Wells came to two essential insights. First, most banks thought of themselves as banks, acted like banks, and protected the banker culture. Wells saw itself as a business that happened to be in banking.

'Run it like a business' and 'Run it like you own it' became mantras. Second, Wells recognized that it could not be the best in the world as a global bank, but that it could be the best in the western United States."

In another table that features the qualities of good to great companies, Collins presents this statement: "It wasn't a single switch that was thrown at one time. Little by little, the themes became more apparent and stronger. When Carl became chief executive officer, there wasn't any great wrenching. Dick led one stage of evolution and Carl the next, and it just proceeded smoothly, rather than an abrupt shift."

In 1966, when I became chief executive officer at Wells, I was clearly the youngest man on the management team. Ernie Arbuckle came on board in 1967. I stayed as president and chief executive, and Jim Dobey became executive vice president. We were the three senior executives of the company. Ernie did not have banking know-how, but he had tremendous business experience. He focused on bank policies and helped us get things done at the upper level. Jim was the operations person. When I was not there, he was in charge of the day-to-day business.

Ten years later, in 1977, Ernie retired. There were a lot of changes in between, but gradually we built a management team of younger people. At the time of Ernie's retirement, I became chairman as well as chief executive officer, and Jim Dobey became vice chairman along with Ralph Crawford. We were the oldest of the bank's senior officers. We brought Carl Reichardt up to San Francisco from Wells's Southern California unit as president, but according to the bylaws he was number four in executive rank, after Dobey, Crawford, and me.

Ernie Arbuckle believed that I should never have stayed as long as I did as CEO. He once said, "You are over your limit and that is when you lose your zing and zang. It is hard to be a CEO longer than 10 years in this day and age." I lasted 16, but I knew what he was saying. He retired when he was 65.

Since moving to Los Angeles, I had been going back and forth to San Francisco every week. It seemed to me that lots of problems came up, and the best way to handle them was with face-to-face meetings. The team around me was good; they were younger, and clearly they had their own ideas of what they would like to do. From my perspective and perhaps because I was older, I thought they were somewhat impatient to have a new plan, one of their own creation. They were a group of outstanding young people, and I knew they could take the bank in whatever direction it had to go. This should have been comforting for me, but it was not. Although it was unintentional, this group made me feel uncomfortable. They were like young lions nipping at my heels.

Dᴉᴄᴋ ᴀᴅᴅʀᴇssɪɴɢ ᴛʜᴇ Wᴇʟʟs Fᴀʀɢᴏ ᴀɴɴᴜᴀʟ sᴛᴏᴄᴋʜᴏʟᴅᴇʀs
ᴍᴇᴇᴛɪɴɢ ɪɴ 1981.

# Wells Fargo and Board Work

When I started moving up the ladder, the bank made me sell the car dealerships and remove myself from all for-profit boards with the exception of the Pacific Gas and Electricity (PG&E) board, which I will talk about later in this chapter. At the time, I was also on the board of United Way, a nonprofit. It took a lot of my time, but I was nearing the completion of my five-year commitment to the campaign, so my bosses did not consider it to be a problem.

From the bank's standpoint, it was felt that my overall attention should be concentrated solely on the job and not distracted by outside obligations. Although there were invitations, I turned them down. It was made clear to me that if I wished to join another for-profit board, I would have to seek approval from the executive committee of the bank. I found I had plenty to keep me occupied as president and chief executive officer of Wells.

The first invitation to join a board that I felt compelled to discuss with the board arrived about three years after I became the bank's chief executive. It was from United Airlines (UAL, Inc.), the holding company and the airline. One of our directors, Paul Bissinger, had been a member of that board for years and had unexpectedly died of a heart attack. The United people came and asked if I would like to take Paul's place. I was intrigued and talked about it with Ernie Arbuckle, who by then was chairman of our board.

United Airlines was a major carrier to and from San Francisco International, and its ties to the Bay Area were historic. To develop and prepare hot meals for flights, it opened the nation's first flight kitchen in Oakland in 1936. And in the 1960s, United had become the largest airline in the world, with many flights initiating in San Francisco International Airport, which also was the site of United's maintenance facilities.

The prospect of joining the UAL, Inc. board appealed to me because I was interested in flying and airlines, and I also thought I would learn a lot that could be beneficial to the bank. Customers get to know airlines through flight attendants. The men and women who run those cabins have a tremendous effect on how a customer regards and uses the services provided by the company. This is also true of a bank. Other than a few upper-level corporate accounts, most customers meet the bank through its tellers. When people cash their checks and make deposits, they use a teller's window. We have money in the bank and an airline has airplanes, but we have similar kinds of opportunities and problems with customer relationships.

Ernie and I talked about it quite a bit. He agreed that my reasoning was probably sound, but he was not overly enthusiastic about my choice. Still, he went to the board and explained to the members that I had this opportunity and he thought I should take it. After all, the place had not blown up so far under my leadership, and we seemed to be doing relatively well by most standards. He convinced the executive committee that it would be acceptable, so the decision was approved.

It was early in the 1970s when I joined the United board, and I stayed on it for 25 years. Meetings were held monthly in Chicago, and the board members would fly in from all over the country in time for dinner on the night before the Thursday meeting. At least a couple of members of the United management would be present on those evenings, and this became an opportune time to discuss relevant topics or some current project that otherwise would not receive adequate time during the meeting. The directors of United were a diverse group, each of whom usually ran a major business in one of the key sites that the airline served. We sometimes had more than one representative from a hub city, but we always had someone from Seattle, San Francisco, Los Angeles, Denver, Chicago, and New York, as well as someone from the Midwest and Washington, D.C.

In the course of these Wednesday night dinners we had some incredible and informative conversations. I would say that most of the board members were Republican, but not all. One of our important directors was Andy Brimmer, who was a governor of the Federal Reserve Bank in Washington, D.C. and the first African American to hold that position. He was appointed to that position by President Lyndon B. Johnson and he was a strong Democrat. The political discussions were engaging because we had some heavyweight Republican executives on the board, and then we had Andy, who was well respected by the group. His presence and outspokenness made those discussions lively. I learned about what other companies were doing, and besides that I made some good friends from all sectors of the business community.

The following morning there would be the regular board meeting and then everyone would go home after lunch. I would return from most meetings with notes in my pocket about ideas that could improve our customer service or make the company run more smoothly. These were ideas sparked from hearing about other companies' pension plans, HR decisions, and other corporate know-how. It was different from our board in some ways, but the issues were often similar. There was usually something that United was doing that we could implement at the bank to help improve performance.

At the time I joined the UAL board, the company was in the process of reorganizing management. The situation came to a head when the airline's chief executive officer made the mistake of coming to the board with a loss budget for the year. The board members would not stand for that and wanted someone else to run the company. To his great displeasure, the board replaced the CEO with board member Eddie Carlson, who was chairman and chief executive of Western International Hotels and was living in Seattle. United's holding company, UAL, had decided to buy a hotel company, and later an auto rental company, Hertz, to try to get their arms around the whole travel experience. When UAL bought Western Hotels, Inc., Eddie Carlson and Lynn Himmelman joined United's board. Without conducting an expensive search, they moved Eddie Carlson from running the hotel to running the whole company. Lynn Himmelman, who was number two at the hotel, took over for Carlson and ran the hotel business.

Eddie did not know much about airlines, but he understood the travel business. He also did not know about pilots or maintenance or buying airplanes, but he did know about building hotels and taking care of customers. In its February 1971 issue *Fortune* magazine wrote, "The in-joke among the airline's employees these days is that Carlson will ground all 747s and make them into hotels."

Given his lack of experience with the airline industry, Eddie did an interesting thing as he took the helm. Using business acumen and his skills at working with employees and customers alike, Eddie quickly recognized that morale at United was bad. For the next two years, he traveled to the major United employee bases to talk with all the employees he could. The pilots and flight attendants were based in Chicago, Denver, Los Angeles, Seattle, New York, and some other locations. The mechanics were concentrated in large operations centers. Eddie met employees in each location, answering all their questions and listening to what they had to say. He would tell them what he hoped to do with the airline and how he intended to work on issues such as raising company morale and providing good customer service. His efforts paid off. He was well received. The employees liked him, and ultimately he was able to breathe new life into the troubled airline, helping it turn a profit less than two years after he took over.

I took Eddie's example and applied his tactic to our own management challenges. A shift in attitudes at the bank was causing us to experience a troublesome period. So we started having meetings with our employees. I would stand in front of the tellers for three hours on a Saturday morning and answer all their questions — whatever they wanted to ask. I did a lot of that — and a lot of listening — and I think it really helped. Because I got the idea from Eddie and United, I felt that alone had justified the time I spent on the board. I believe you should never join a board if you cannot learn something and offer your ideas in return.

The United board did some other things that helped alter my views on management style. The board would go on trips to new locations. If they were opening a new plant, say a big maintenance base in Denver, the board would have its meeting there that month and probably stay an extra night. To help the company entertain big clients, a director from the board sat at each table to meet local business owners. It was public relations, but it was appreciated. It gave the directors a means of selling the company, and it also helped them understand what people were thinking about in that part of the country. When you are dealing with an entity that goes from coast to coast and almost north to south (United didn't fly to Florida or Toronto at that time), there are a lot of different things to consider. It is important to understand that the culture varies in each area and you have to be able to adjust to it.

Wells Fargo was an in-state bank for a long time, and we would take the board on trips to see different parts of the state we served. We also used the board to sell ourselves to the customers in that part of the state. It was another idea that I took from United and implemented at Wells. I saw how effective it was, and I thought we could adapt it to our purposes.

Getting the board together outside the boardroom became basic — something that almost every board chairman understands and does. I learned more about that from my experience at United. Whenever there was a chance to do something with the board, like an annual dinner or a meeting, it was good to get the group together in addition to just coming for an 8 a.m. meeting and finishing by noon. The meeting itself is formal, and you do not have much of a chance to interact. A luncheon in conjunction with the meeting was useful. The board needs to be a team, and if that is accomplished, you have a good chance of running a really strong business because everyone is moving in the same direction.

Shortly after I became the Wells Fargo CEO, I was asked to join the board of PG&E, the major Northern California utility. It was an old relationship — the bank signed on their bonds — and the Wells chief executives have been on the PG&E board forever, so I was expected to join. The experience was completely different from the one at United Airlines. PG&E meetings were run strictly by the rules, and there was little chance to connect with the members in a more neutral, casual setting.

Running an electric utility in a state like California requires a lot of lawyers, who were important in dealing with the state public utilities commission and the state legislature. It was almost equally important to have engineers, although lawyers typically dominated the scene. The main objective of the utility was generating electricity and gas and making it consistently available throughout its segment of the state. The company had an enormous need for capital expenditures to build plants and equipment to keep providing electricity and gas to local residents and businesses.

PG&E was one of those boards where there was not a lot of discussion and what discussion did transpire was highly technical. I am not a lawyer or an electrical engineer, so I did not always understand the details of the legal or technical issues. However, I did gain an understanding of how that board operated.

The executive committee was composed of the older people on the board. They would often meet just before the regular board meeting and go over the agenda, seemingly deciding which way things would go. The board, which was maybe twice the size of the executive committee, would then go over the same agenda. It seemed to me that we were voting on subjects that had already been approved by the executive committee. We just ratified their approval and there was not a lot we could do about it, even if we wanted to. There were two classes of directors: those four or five who were on the executive committee and 12 others who were on the regular board. The board was set up so that people were there to represent a group or a community. I was there because of the bank's connection with the utility's bonds. And because I was young and coming in, I was part of the regular board, not the executive committee. The directors were not circulated annually among the various committees like they were at United or at the bank.

At that time the head of the company was Sherm Sibley. He was a little older than I, an engineer, but not an attorney, and we had gotten acquainted through community and social activities. Sherm was well liked, and going on the board with him running it was one of the big pluses as far as I was concerned. Then a terrible thing happened. While fishing in Oregon he got caught in fast water, which flooded his waders and carried him out to sea. No one ever saw him again. It was a tragedy for me because I knew his wife and family and for the community because every-one liked him.

The effect on PG&E was tumultuous, and the way the company handled it was disappointing. The executive committee met immediately to discuss the situation and select Sherm's successor without talking to the rest of the board. When the subject came up at the special board meeting, the successor's name was already in the resolution. One of the senior directors denied that it was true and told us that they were just thinking about having this new person take over. But they had already decided who they wanted to promote, and they did so without the approval of the whole board. It was maybe a good choice or maybe a bad choice, but it was a clear demonstration that there were two classes of directors. In a business sense, you never want unequal directors on a board. Everyone bears the same liability, and if all the decisions are being made by just a third of the directors, it puts the other two-thirds in an untenable position. It was the first time I had ever witnessed such a division. It was not good business, and it made me feel reluctant to continue being on that board.

The PG&E board has probably gotten away from such practices now, but that was the way it worked 20 and 30 years ago. I clearly remember that day and how incensed I was at the outcome. There was nothing I could do except grin and bear it. I could not get up and resign because of the bank's business relationship, although there was nothing I would have liked more. It was apparent that the executive committee did not feel a need for the whole board's decision-making abilities. That was my first experience with two classes of directors, and I have talked about it a lot since. Where such a situation exists, one should take steps to get rid of it.

------------

I'd like to say a few words about nonprofit organizations in general, and the United Way in particular. Most banks are heavily oriented toward nonprofit community activities. I do not mean the money-center banks in New York or Chicago, but the strong regional banks, which encourage their managers to become involved in all kinds of local activities. These regional banks are represented on many boards for organizations like the United Way, the Red Cross, Boy Scouts of America, and various hospitals, schools, and colleges. The theory is that if a bank is situated in a healthy community, that is good for the business of the bank. I found that people expect bankers to jump in and help.

My first nonprofit board work was as a trustee for the San Francisco Zoo, and as I said before, I'd never had pets and really didn't know much about animals. I quickly found out that I wasn't asked to be on the board because I was an animal expert. I was invited to join because the bank had relationships with the zoo. It was a gratifying experience and I learned a great deal about nonprofit organizations, which always need money, and animals, which always need caring for.

My association with the San Francisco United Way began when I was a senior vice president. One of our major clients at the bank was the Southern Pacific Company, parent company of Southern Pacific Railroad, where my friend Benjamin Biaggini was the number-two man and heir apparent. He had moved to San Francisco from New Orleans to take over the operations of the railroad, which he did from 1964 to 1976. He then served as chairman of the Southern Pacific Company's board of directors from 1976 to 1983.

Ben had been selected to run the Bay Area United Way Campaign. He took me to lunch and said, "Cooley, I want you to head the corporate section of the campaign." I thought he was joking. In my mind I was far too young and inexperienced and did not know enough key people in the area to handle that responsibility. Ben told me, "You are on the threshold. You can do it, and more importantly, I need your help." Because Ben was a man I liked very much and greatly respected, with his promise to keep me on course, I sought permission from my bosses and took the job.

The corporate section of the campaign was the biggest. The campaign was divided into divisions for individuals, homes, geographical areas, lines of business, and major corporations. There were 50 large companies in the Bay Area that provided the lion's share of United Way funds. To take that on seemed like a lot to me, but there was no way that I could say no to Ben. He insisted that I could do it. That was the first of five years working for the United Way. We did the campaign, and though we did not make our goal, we were close.

Being involved with the United Way was like going through the chairs of a fraternal organization. You ran a segment of it, then every year there was a new leader in each division and you moved to a new position. From starting out as a chairman of the corporate campaign you went to vice president of United Way and then to campaign chairman. Then you made the move to president, and the following year chairman of the board. In your last year, you became chairman of the executive committee. In the last two years, the time commitment was not nearly as heavy as in the previous two. For continuity, one tried to get people lined up to take these positions far in advance so there was a planned leadership team from the community to support this organization each year for two or three years ahead.

The United Way in San Francisco was a big operation that represented five counties. There was a large paid staff who did all the detail work, but the organization also required a huge number of volunteers. Businesses liked working with the United Way because it provided a connection with numerous charities. At that time, about 148 agencies in the five-county area were represented by the United Way in San Francisco. That meant that businesses did not have to pick one person to represent the Red Cross, another person for the Boy Scouts, and someone else for all the rest of the agencies that asked for help. By working with the United Way, banks got all their charity work accomplished at one time. Only one campaign per year was allowed to take place within each corporate organization.

A company would appoint someone to run their internal United Way campaign, which was organized so that during a certain week in the fall, all employees would be asked to contribute. The chairman or the president of that company would have a meeting with the senior people and would ask them to consider making a certain level of gift. Forcing them to give was frowned upon, but there was supposed to be a slight push (sometimes more than slight) to stress what a good idea this was for themselves and the company.

The donation money was deducted from an employee's paycheck. The payroll system was set up with only one charity box to write in this donation. What made it attractive was that instead of 20 different boxes on the payroll system for different charities, there was only one to cover the gamut of community needs. Then there was the corporate gift. Each company would decide on its corporate gift and add that to the combined offerings of the staff. As a result, a donation could get pretty large. In a sense, the United Way had a monopoly on asking for money from corporate employees. Many years later it broke down, but that was the basic idea in the beginning.

The year I became chairman of the campaign (two or three years before I became CEO of Wells Fargo) there was an enormous goal, something like $50 million. It was similar to being in politics: you had to have your version of a United Way stump speech. I always felt that if you pushed the right spot on my chest, the United Way speech would start coming out. The staff would make appointments all over the area and I traveled around continuously. That year I must have given 60 speeches at breakfasts and lunches, or in-between times. I gave my speech about the United Way — all the benefits to the community, how necessary it was to contribute, what the needs were in the community, and how important it was to have a healthy community — to many different groups.

Giving all the speeches was good because I had never done much public speaking and I was nervous. I could do it, but I did not enjoy doing it. I was timid and not at ease talking to an unfamiliar crowd. When I was discussing the United Way, I knew what I was talking about, and I gave the speech so often that I became an effective and knowledgeable advocate for the organization. It developed my ability to speak in front of people and to think on my feet. I learned a lot from the experience. It was good for the United Way, and the United Way did a lot of good for me. And because the United Way was established across America, you could learn from what was happening at United Way branches in other parts of the country.

From the bank's point of view, Wells contributed my time and my efforts to doing this program, so the bank was "off the hook" from handling other charitable requests. I carried the bank's load for that five-year period. United Way was considered part of my job. There was another benefit besides learning how to think clearly and finding out how to present yourself in front of a lot of people you did not know. You also met lots of new people throughout the five counties. Even if you were not doing business with them, they got to know you and you got to know them. If they liked you, there was always the chance that you might do business with them someday. It was fun and there were good people involved. And because the whole business community supported the program, it was an opportunity to spread my wings and become better known in the business world.

---

Jumping ahead maybe 15 or 20 years, when I moved to Seattle from San Francisco, oddly enough, within six months of my arrival three distinguished elder citizens of the community came and asked me to run United Way in Seattle. I told them that I could not do that because I'd already done it in San Francisco. They said to me, "That's just why we are asking you. We want you to do it here. We need you." Again, it is one of those things that happen to bankers. I was new in Seattle and it was a great way to meet people. In the end, I did say "yes" and ran the United Way in Seattle. But it was so much work—the speeches, the moving around, the time it took—all while I was constantly worrying about running the bank and making enough money to keep it afloat.

There was one aspect of the Seattle experience that was different from San Francisco. In San Francisco, we had something called Corporate Circles. It was a special name for people who gave $10,000 or more per year. That is a large sum, and it was definitely a large sum in those days. To be successful you had to have major donors, and they were not all going to be rich people. A lot of them had to be corporations where employees made large salaries and could afford larger paycheck deductions. In San Francisco more than 100 people were giving $10,000 or more. When I came to Seattle I found out, to my horror, that only three people had given $10,000 or more in the last campaign. That was shocking to me.

As it was getting closer to my turn to lead the campaign, I went to see one of the senior citizens who had asked me to take the job. I asked him for his contribution and told him that I wanted to start a Circle Club where whoever belonged would give $10,000 per year. He looked horrified. He said, "Dick, you don't understand. In Seattle we do not do things like that. If you gave more than $1,000, people would think you were showing off. People just don't do that." I was shocked again. Here was a very wealthy man who was feeling that he could not show his wealth by giving generously to the United Way. That was an idea that we had to break down, and eventually we did. Now, many years later, we have over 700 people in the Alexis de Tocqueville Society who give $10,000 or more each year. In fact, we have a $100,000 Annual Giving Club, which is amazing. People are generous in Seattle, but they do not want to do the wrong thing; they need to feel comfortable about sharing their money.

That first United Way experience in San Francisco was wonderful for many reasons. You find out what is going on in the community that you didn't know about before. You discover causes and people who really need your assistance. And you have the opportunity to help make things better.

If you are going to build a hospital, or a gym for a school, or a law school, that is a capital project and a different kind of fund-raising program. The United Way campaign goes on every year, and it takes care of the annual needs of organizations that are helping disadvantaged people.

I know the United Way has had its ups and downs across the country. There have been some abuses, but by and large, it has done a good job and I am glad to have been associated with it.

———————

Bill Hewlett and Dave Packard, founders of Hewlett-Packard, were great friends of Ernie Arbuckle. One day, sometime around 1970, Bill Hewlett came in to see Ernie. He told Ernie that he was completing his tenure on the RAND board and he thought it would be a great organization for me to join. In his opinion I was young, and this would be a way for me to learn what was happening in the world. To be honest, I did not think I was intelligent enough to join the board. The members were scientists, physicists, and economists, and I was just a young, inexperienced businessman trying to get along.

RAND is a highly regarded policy research institute that's been around since the late 1940s. Its mission is to help improve policy and decision-making through research and analysis. It does not manufacture anything, but uses brainpower to solve problems and develop solutions. Other people construct and run the programs it devises, but RAND provides the blueprint for how to get things done. RAND is doing so many worthwhile things in the world, and it was incredible for me to know I could participate in shaping a better future.

For one reason or another, and with Bill's help, I was accepted on the board in November 1970. It was a 10-year term for a trustee. If you started early enough, you could take two or three terms, but board members had to complete their terms by their 70th birthday. I learned that most trustees served one term, but

Bill got me in early enough that I was able to complete two terms as a trustee, with the standard one year off between terms.

When Bill first spoke to me about RAND, he gave me a report that had been written sometime during the late 1940s. It described a design for an experimental world-circling spaceship. It also expressed hope that the spaceship could accommodate a person and return him to earth safely. At the time the report was written, the idea of sending a satellite into outer space was the stuff of science fiction — as was the idea of putting a man on the moon. In the summer of 1969, like millions of others, I watched the launch and touchdown on the moon, and I watched our astronauts take the first steps on the moon's surface and plant the American flag. But it wasn't until I read the report Bill gave me that I realized that this tremendous accomplishment was actually RAND's vision put into motion. It was RAND's detailed engineering feasibility study, combined with its call for a major national space initiative, that had made this possible. Eventually I met all three of those astronauts: Neil Armstrong, Michael Collins, and Buzz Aldrin. Neil Armstrong was on the board of United Airlines, Michael Collins was on the RAND board, and Buzz Aldrin I met socially after he retired.

RAND is a fine group of approximately 1,900 staff (roughly 950 researchers) from more than 50 countries around the world. It has three principal U.S. locations: Santa Monica, California; Arlington, Virginia; and Pittsburgh, Pennsylvania. Other staff operate from the RAND Gulf States Policy Institute in New Orleans, Louisiana; RAND Europe in Cambridge, United Kingdom, and Brussels, Belgium; and RAND Australia in Canberra. Located alongside RAND's Santa Monica headquarters is the Frederick S. Pardee RAND Graduate School, founded in 1970. It offers the nation's largest public policy Ph.D. program, serving about 100 students from more than 20 different countries. After I turned 70, I became an emeritus trustee and also served on the graduate school's Board of Governors for several years. It has been a rare honor and a privilege to be a part of such an illustrious group.

When I was on the RAND Board of Trustees, a typical business meeting consisted of 15 or 16 people, mostly scientists and a few businessmen. I was asked to offer insights about the business world as it related to their projects. At these meetings members would describe their latest assignment, such as helping the Air Force be more efficient in getting supplies to the front. Usually they would give us a presentation or a report, but we did not vote on it. Instead, we would ask questions designed to help strengthen the project. Then the briefing team would convey suggestions to the project's researchers, and sometimes these suggestions would be incorporated into the report before it was delivered to the client or grantor supporting the work. Sometimes the board was able to identify something that the researchers might have missed or was able to anticipate controversy and help address it in the report.

RAND held two board meetings each year, one in the spring and another in the fall, and they were two-day meetings. Often they were held in the Santa Monica headquarters and other times in Washington, D.C., but the location moved to different sites such as New York or anywhere around the world if there was a reason. When I joined the board, it seemed hard to justify the time away because there was always pressure to be visible in the bank, but now two days does not sound like much at all. Although the time away seemed difficult to schedule, everyone on the board agreed that once we were there, it was an incredible experience and well worth every moment.

During my first term Donald Rumsfeld was chairman of the board. He is very bright, very quick. He liked to be involved and get things done. If he decided that he wanted to do something, he did it. At different times Alan Greenspan, Condoleezza Rice, and Brent Scowcroft were on the board.

Early on at RAND, researchers focused largely on work useful to military decision makers, although they also contributed to America's space program, digital computing, and even artificial intelligence.

In addition to studying issues of interest to the Air Force, Army, Department of Defense, and other national security organizations, RAND looks at health care, education, poverty, and municipal services, to name just a few of its research areas. I was always drawn more to this nonmilitary work. Even now, I still receive regular newsletters from RAND about its current slate of projects and about the scope of its research and analysis in the Middle East and other parts of the world.

Most members of the RAND board were well versed in what was going on in the government, although they had to be nonpartisan in their work for the board. We were rooting for the country, not a political party. You had to have a top-secret clearance to be on the board, which I had for many years but do not have anymore.

When New York City went through its bankruptcy period in the 1970s, the New York City–RAND Institute was established to look for ways to run the city more economically. Among the institute's many projects were two that stand out to me as noteworthy and helpful. First, researchers worked on improving the efficiency of the police department. They analyzed crime reports to find out when the crimes were being committed, finding a clear time frame when crime activity heightened. So, they proposed reorganizing the police force into shifts and increasing the number of policemen during the peak times when crimes took place. The police started to get a handle on it, and effectiveness improved tremendously. Second, researchers took a look at the city's fire department and came up with several ingenious solutions to improve its response. RAND scientists invented something called "slippery water." They found that adding a polymer to water allowed it to go through hoses faster than regular water, making it possible to get more water flow to a fire quicker. Slippery water cut costs and minimized fire damage.

In addition to conducting research and analysis for external clients, RAND has a program through which it supports projects of its researchers' own devising. Much of this work is funded using money from donors. Being associated with RAND for over 30 years has been a broadening and fascinating experience. I have enjoyed my affiliation greatly and my friendship with many on the board, including Jim Thompson, who was the head of RAND from 1989 to 2011. He is currently a President Emeritus and a professor in the RAND graduate school. The new president and CEO of RAND is Michael D. Rich.

For those who wish to gain a greater understanding of what RAND tries to accomplish in our times, I encourage you to visit their website: www.rand.org. Here is a list of some RAND achievements since 2000:

After Hurricane Katrina, RAND helped create Louisiana's long-range master plan for a sustainable coast. To guide investments and to help people plan for the future, RAND developed a new hurricane flood risk model that planners can use to assess the effects of different projects designed to reduce damage from flooding.

During the wars in Afghanistan and Iraq, RAND published a study of the prevalence of psychological injuries in veterans of these wars, finding that nearly one in five had symptoms of PTSD or depression but only half were seeking treatment. This work spurred the creation of treatment programs that are helping veterans and their families all across America.

For the Department of Defense and NATO, RAND looked at Russia's resurgent threat in the Baltics, examining what types of strategy, operations, and forces would be required to counteract Russian aggression in the region. Researchers did this work in part through gaming, which is an area RAND was active in even before I joined the board.

In the U.K., RAND researchers analyzed the consequences of a future in which viruses and bacterial infections have become resistant to antibiotics. They calculated that this resistance could reduce the world's population by 11 million working-age adults by 2050 and also compress the world economy by at least $53 billion each year.

In 2015, RAND published the results of an analysis of the economic costs of the Palestinian-Israeli conflict. Using different scenarios, they found that 10 years of peace, with a Palestinian state built alongside but apart from Israel, would boost the Palestinian economy by $50 billion and the Israeli economy by $123 billion. Yet 10 years of violence would cost the Palestinians $50 billion and the Israelis $250 billion.

RAND is researching the operations, structure, and finances of the terrorist group called the Islamic State, and it is helping various organizations develop a strategy to neutralize it. RAND is also studying terrorist recruiting and the threat posed by Western recruits returning home after fighting for the Islamic State in Iraq and Syria. Very early on during my time on the RAND board, researchers there established the nation's first database of terrorist incidents, and this work has continued for decades.

RAND researchers studying dementia in the United States estimated that the yearly costs of treating dementia in this country are between $159 billion and $215 billion. They found that middle-class Americans in particular struggle with these costs because many can't afford long-term care insurance policies and often don't qualify for government help under Medicaid. RAND developed a national blueprint designed to provide relief to those with dementia and to their caregivers.

RAND researchers are exploring how self-driving cars and other autonomous systems are changing the world. They published one of the first papers on the liability implications of self-driving cars and are helping to answer questions about data privacy, infrastructure upgrades, insurance claims, and regulation.

During the national debate over the Affordable Care Act, RAND continued to focus on the facts, providing objective, nonpartisan information on a host of issues, such as the employer mandate, enrollment in individual exchanges, and government subsidies. RAND has been studying the complex interplay between cost, quality, and access to care since before I was on the board — I was a trustee when it launched the groundbreaking RAND Health Insurance Experiment.

———

Among the most interesting nonprofit organizations that I had the privilege to serve as a trustee was the California Institute of Technology, best known as Caltech. It is a private school, although it receives substantial grant money from the federal government. I was on that nonprofit board for more than 30 years. It is another incredible Southern California institution, different from RAND but equally fascinating. Caltech is in the same category as MIT, but it's about one-fifth the size of the Massachusetts institution.

Caltech students and staff work on all kinds of scientific endeavors. At any given time, they have a number of Nobel Laureates (in 2016, it was five) on the faculty doing research.

The school was founded as Throop College in 1891. Over time it developed numerous courses of study, including geology, humanities and social sciences, and biology. Under the direction of the renowned aeronautical engineer Theodore von Karman — one of the founders of the Jet Propulsion Laboratory, which is managed by the school — Caltech began to establish itself as the world's center for rocket science.

Being on the board at Caltech, you are not quite as involved creatively as you are at RAND; you're more involved in raising money. In the recent decade, Caltech completed a $1.5 billion campaign to build new buildings and fund new telescopes, new labs, and research, as well as increase the scholarships available for students to further research and discovery.

———

I joined the Kaiser Family Foundation board in 1987 and served as a director through 1994. This came about through Eddie Carlson, who was a friend of the Kaiser family. The term was seven years, and when Eddie went off he suggested that I take his place.

The Kaiser Family Foundation had problems when I first joined the board. I soon became part of a group that was trying to keep the factions together and make some changes at the top, which we did. As part of their interest in all things medical, the foundation wanted to stay on top of the country's medical policies, influence decisions that were being made, and determine where their research focus should be and how it should be organized in order to provide the best health care to all our citizens.

Regarding health care policy, the Kaiser Foundation has been very influential. They have a strong media division and good relationships with the broadcasting companies. I do not know what their concerns are now, but when I was on the board, they had a focus on and big reach into Africa. They spent money and time in South Africa to figure out how the change in government and policy under the leadership of Nelson Mandela would affect health care and the local citizenry. The foundation opened an office and put someone there to follow how the change would play out. About 20 percent of the budget went for improving public health in South Africa. The Kaiser Foundation board is selected carefully, and there is one member of the Kaiser family on the board at all times. The family has passed it around to various members over the years, and I think the system has worked pretty well.

---

My work on boards was satisfying, but I felt a growing need for a change. It was the early 80s. I had been working at Wells Fargo in one job for 15 years, and I needed a fresh start.

WELLS FARGO'S EXECUTIVE OFFICERS IN LATE 1980, ABOUT TWO YEARS
BEFORE DICK RETIRED AND MOVED TO SEATTLE. SEATED ON THE LEFT IS
CARL E. REICHART, PRESIDENT, AND DICK IS IN THE RIGHT CHAIR. STANDING,
FROM LEFT, ARE PAUL HAZEN, EXECUTIVE VICE PRESIDENT, ROBERT L. KEMPER,
VICE CHAIRMAN, AND RICHARD M. ROSENBERG, VICE CHAIRMAN.

# Transition to Seattle

In 1966 at 42 years of age, I was by far the youngest man on the Wells management team. That was no longer the case in 1980 after 14 years of being the bank's chief executive. The early retirements of Crawford and Dobey, who by then had become vice chairmen of the bank, meant that at 57, I was now the oldest person on the senior management team.

Things were not as flexible in the banking world then, and I did not know what else to do. We had a strong succession plan built in, and Carl Reichardt and his team were coming along fine. He was younger than I by the right amount of years and was fully capable of running the bank. I don't think he was aware that he might take it over as early as 1983, but he was ready. And I was finally ready to leave if only I could find some satisfactory way to support myself.

I was 58 when I started to think about what I was going to do at 60. Was I going to make Carl president and chief executive then wait around as chairman until I was 65? That did not sound like much fun. And yet, I did not know what kind of job I could get outside Wells Fargo Bank. I did not know what I could do or where I could go and was very uncertain. I talked to a headhunter, an old friend, and he told me what I might be able to expect. I had a conversation with one of the significant board members, Ed Littlefield; he assumed that any job I took at that point in my career would be a tough one. In other words, I would be working for a company that was in trouble and wanted me to come in and fix it. "You could not just expect to move into a comfortable job and add whatever you could add to an already successful company," he counseled. "Instead, you would have to straighten out somebody else's mess and put it back on track."

My whole career had been in banking except for those early years at McCall's, and that appeared to be a problem because I did not have the confidence to move into Boeing or Pepsi-Cola or any other business that I did not understand. I was a banker. That was Littlefield's view, and I agreed. I did not think I could strike out in a completely new direction, even though I had become a little burned out in my job. I had led the bank by then for about 15 years and did not feel that I was in tune with the younger staff as much as I could or should have been. With all these concerns looming, my headhunter friend said he would look around. In one of our conversations he told me about an opportunity in Hawaii. One of the big five companies in Hawaii was looking for a chief executive officer, and he asked if I would be interested. It was a food company, which I knew nothing about, but it was something to consider.

---

Then, Seafirst bank in Seattle got into trouble. It had made sizeable, largely unsecured or poorly collateralized loans to the petroleum business, and when that blew up in the early 1980s Seafirst's chairman, Bill Jenkins, quickly fell out of favor with the board. The bank's board decided that he had to go and initiated a search for a replacement. The chairman of the search committee was Harry Mullikin, who had been a friend of mine for a long time. We had been on the United board together and knew each other well. In the summer of 1982, Harry came down to see me and said, "You've been in this business a long time. What should we be looking for in a candidate to replace Bill?"

I had a good talk with Harry about various people I knew and he suggested business skills that might be important for someone to be successful in Seattle. Afterward I started thinking about that conversation and, more specifically, the job. Harry came back later and talked to me about whom he had in mind and what was going on in the search. By October of 1982, the Seafirst board had whittled its list down to four candidates. That was when I started to seriously consider the job for myself. Seafirst was about two-thirds the size of Wells Fargo at the time, but it was not as important. It was a good bank, the biggest and oldest bank in the state of Washington. Its assets were a little over $10 billion, but it had problems.

I arranged to see Harry in Vancouver, B.C. I said, "Harry, what would happen if you put my name in the hat for this search you are running?" I do not know if he was surprised or not, but he said, "Oh, well, that's interesting. I'd be glad to talk to the other members of the committee about it if you are truly interested." Harry asked why I would consider the job, and I told him that I thought I had gone stale at Wells and it was time for me to make a change. I had that opportunity with the large food company in Hawaii that needed a CEO, but I felt more comfortable going into a business that I already understood. I did not know Seattle but I did know the banking business, and I felt comfortable that I could do something with Seafirst if it was necessary. Looking back, I will never know if it was my idea or if Harry had subtly put the idea in my head to consider working for Seafirst.

One thing led to another. Harry talked to his people and told me that it was good news as far as he was concerned, because the committee wanted to meet with me. I went to Seattle and met with the selection committee and did some due diligence with the bank's senior staff. It seemed to go well, although one can never know for sure. Toward the end of November, without going through all the details of meetings and such, I was trying to get to the heart of Seafirst's problems. Essentially it came down to bad loans. Seafirst had made energy loans in excess of a billion dollars, and the portfolio was poorly secured. The bank's energy loan department was small, and it had little or no experience with the technical side of contracting perfected collateral — which meant they did not have sufficient collateral to support the bad loans. A significant part of the total exposure related to Seafirst's practice of participating with Oklahoma-based Penn Square Bank.

When Penn Square Bank failed in July 1982, Seafirst was left holding an empty bag.

Bill Jenkins thought things were not as serious as they seemed and that the industry would correct itself in time, but the board did not agree. It was a tense time because Jenkins did not think they should be getting rid of him, but the board persisted. Things got tougher and the bank had to write off more and more of the loans that went sour. There was an incredible loss coming up, and no one saw it coming. No one knew how bad it was going to be, including me.

The search went ahead, and Harry told me that my name had been added to the four finalists. I had been put in front of the executive committee, and eventually the whole board decided that I was their man. I was told that they would be delighted to have me come up and take over the bank. It happened quickly, and that presented some problems. I had to talk to everyone on the Wells board about what I had decided to do and why I was doing it. I suggested that Carl Reichardt take my place. I knew the bank would do well because the key managers were all pros. They were good and aggressive, and the bank would be fine. The board agreed.

I had to talk to every member of the Wells board by early December. The final board meeting of the year was nearing, and that seemed to be the best time to formally announce my retirement. The meeting was on a Tuesday morning, but the Seafirst board meeting in which I would be named as that bank's chief executive was not to take place until the following morning. The timing of the meetings was awkward because I did retire from Wells on Tuesday and the change was announced. I was able to leave the bank that day to fly up to Seattle. The next day, the Seafirst board made the announcement of my hiring at their meeting in Seattle. By Wednesday evening there were only a few noses out of joint over the way it was handled, but by then it was a *fait accompli*.

The transition was to be effective on January 1, 1983. Having had dinner with the board of Seafirst, I took a week off and went skiing in Aspen with my friend Mary Alice Clark and some of our respective children. After that I moved to Seattle and was there to take over on the first of January. Those days were a rush of meeting people and interviews. I was excited about the new challenge and establishing myself in a new city.

When Bill Jenkins found out I was the one the board had selected to take his place, he never batted an eyelash. He was always friendly, considerate, and helpful in every way. We had known one another for years and had done things socially together in the past. We had also served on the United Airlines board together. He could not have been more of a complete gentleman and good friend in helping me get started in Seattle. I will never forget how he treated me with the utmost respect and graciousness. Bill's problem was with the bank, not with me. His removal was the board's decision, and I was the one who was elected to take his place. That was the way it was and the way he seemed to look at it publicly. I do not know how he felt inside, but he certainly handled himself well and in a constructive way as far as I was concerned. He did things he didn't have to do, like introducing me to his friends and the town.

There were others who went out of their way to introduce me to the community. Certainly Harry Mullikin and his predecessors, Eddie Carlson and Lynn Himmelman, were great supporters and good friends. They sponsored me many times and were helpful with the local knowledge that is so essential to getting started in a new city. We had been together on the United Airlines board for years and knew each other well. Another old friend, Chuck Pigott, was also warm and welcoming. Shortly after I arrived, Chuck offered to give a lunch for me at the Rainier Club to introduce me to some of his friends in the business world. The people I met that day became friends for as long as I have been in Seattle. It was a generous and thoughtful event that

I enjoyed and appreciated greatly. It was as if he were mentoring me and letting his friends know that I would be able to bring something to the community.

In the end it all happened quickly, although the move came about after considerable thought and angst over a year or two while I was still at Wells. Ernie's advice came back to me: I may have overstayed my welcome at Wells and no longer felt comfortable. Additionally, my personal life was not great, and I just did not want to be in San Francisco anymore.

---

Seafirst's management team was good, but the system was flawed. The bank's structure had been changed in response to a consultant's report in the early 1980s. It became top-heavy and expensive, and many of the bank's problems were justifiably well publicized. Still, we hoped that the high level of professionalism at Seafirst and the personal strengths of its management team and other employees, combined with the continued support of the bank's customers and shareholders, would save the day.

We revised the corporate mission statement to clearly define our new strategy, which helped return the bank to profitability: "Seafirst's primary mission is to be the major provider of quality financial services to profitable segments within the personal, business, and corporate markets in the Northwest. Seafirst will also compete within selected areas of the Western United States and Western Canada whenever a significant presence is sustainable. Nationally and internationally, the company will be active in those areas and countries where providing service to major corporations and foreign operations will directly support and enhance Seafirst's primary mission as the leading Northwest regional financial institution."

During my first three months in Seattle, it became clear that Seafirst was in much worse shape than I or anyone else had imagined, and each month it got worse. Its book value was fast becoming a negative number. Seafirst's nonperforming loans represented nearly eight percent of its assets, and they exceeded the bank's shareholders' equity and loss reserves by more than seven percent. It became clear that the bank had to be sold or it would be taken over by the FDIC. In the latter case, all the shareholders would have been wiped out. Initially, to keep the bank in business I had to secure a $3 billion line of credit from the nation's largest banks. The line could be collateralized by good loan assets pledged at the Federal Reserve Bank. This credit was not long lasting, and it only gave us time to see what we could do about getting a large capital infusion or selling the bank. The credit line provided Seafirst some assurance that it could withstand a possible run on the bank.

The board and I had launched Westnet, an effort to form a consortium of major western U.S. banks that would provide common services and products to customers throughout the West to compete with Bank of America. We were making good strides toward this and other objectives — exceeding our own expectations — when we began to offer Market Rate Savings accounts, which were popular with our customers and allowed them to enjoy interest rates that were in keeping with the market.

During this time, and after many trips east and overseas, it became clear that a sale of Seafirst was the only opportunity short of an FDIC takeover, and Bank of America became the chosen buyer. A special vote by the Federal Reserve was needed for Bank of America to acquire Seafirst, or any other bank within the state for that matter. The acquisition was hotly contested by our competitors. They feared the strength of what they understood to be a financial behemoth, but the relevant law was amended to allow "failing" banks to be acquired by out-of-state banks. In June 1983, the transaction was complete and by the end of the year Seafirst had written off almost $1 billion in failed loans.

The deal preserved about 50 percent of Seafirst stock's peak value, and that was better than many had expected. If the FDIC had taken over the bank, the shareholders would have received nothing for their investments and the government would have owned and operated the institution until it could be liquidated or sold. In theory, the FDIC would have kept the bank's management, including me, until the bank's business was straightened out and resold to the public. From my point of view that would have been a good outcome, but that was not what I had been hired to do. I was there to try to save the bank and protect the existing shareholders as much as possible. Either way, the customers of the bank were going to be protected and the operations would continue to serve the community.

Seafirst went through some difficult and perilous times. The board stuck together and was supportive of management's efforts. When Bank of America acquired Seafirst, they maintained the board, kept me on as its chief executive, and put one of its executives on the board. Subject to little restraint, I was allowed to run the business, plumb the depth of its losses, and continue the effort to return it to profitability. As usually happens in a case like this, the effort to stabilize took longer than I expected. There were lots of changes in organization and policy to be established, and after the first year a large turnover in the top management had occurred. I brought only one key person with me from Wells: Glenhall Taylor. He became our senior loan officer. He took over the immense job of sorting out the loan portfolio while I tried to straighten out the organization that had created the mess in the first place. Those were our two key responsibilities. The personnel for the other management roles came from among the existing staff.

I did not remove anyone for the first year, but then I began to make changes that I hoped would help meet our goals and create a new operating environment. It was a nervous time but also stimulating. As we went through the difficult times, it seemed to me that all I had learned at Wells in those 16 years as its chief executive was being put to good use. I became more confident and comfortable with what to do and how to do it.

Bank of America let Seafirst's board and management plan and run the operations as if we were an independent entity. We kept our name and operating procedures and the immense financial strength of our parent allowed us to move ahead. By 1986 our assets totaled $10.3 billion. We were still the state's largest bank, but we faced increased competition. Washington State banking law facilitated the merger of prosperous banks, and in 1987 I found myself again competing with Los Angeles-based Security Pacific when it acquired Washington's second-largest bank, Rainier Bancorp. By then, Seafirst had once again become profitable.

At the time I came up to Seattle I had just been divorced from Judy, my second wife. We had been doing the best we could to iron things out, but I asked for a divorce and saw it finalized in the fall of 1982.

My relationship with Judy had begun during a period of great loneliness for us both. I was in the process of divorcing Sheila when I first found out about Judy Ludwig, who was going through a set of problems similar to mine. Since neither of us had formally left our homes, communication was limited to the phone. Still, through those conversations we became closer. When the divorces were finalized, we got engaged and then married before taking enough time to understand all the implications of what our different families and backgrounds would entail. Judy knew what was expected of me by the bank, its board, management, and clients. She had grown up around banking. Her father, H. Stephen Chase, had been my boss at Wells Fargo, and I succeeded him as the bank's chairman. She tried hard and was a good person and a good wife, but the marriage did not last.

About the time that Judy and I married, Sheila, my first wife, married Dick Collins. He was an equestrian and ran the equestrian center at Pebble Beach. He also was busy in the real estate business and over time taught Sheila all she needed to know to be successful in that field. She became the top salesperson in the Monterey area and held that position for 10 years.

Dick Collins was older than Sheila and died several years after they were married, but not before making a tremendous impression on Sean and Mark. He was the father for them that I was not. They loved and respected him, so I pray for him as a way to thank him for all he did for the boys and for Sheila. By then Sheila was in declining health, and she sold her home in Pebble Beach and moved back to San Francisco. She died in the fall of 2008, surrounded by our children. It is never easy to see your mother die, but the children all told me she had a peaceful death surrounded by family.

---

Before retiring from Wells Fargo and moving to Seattle I had grown quite fond of Mary Alice Clark. Her husband had recently died, and in fact, she had been widowed three times. Her third husband had succumbed to cancer about a year before Mary Alice and I became friends. She was dating other people and so was I, but the move to Seattle precipitated a change in our relationship. I asked her if she would consider moving to Seattle if I relocated. She thought she might be open to the idea, but it was a lot to consider and she was not sure. We firmed things up in January after I had moved and she had come to Seattle for a visit.

Boeing President Mal Stamper became a good friend. He and his wife, Mari, gave a dinner party for us shortly after I arrived in Seattle. He wanted to introduce me to some people they thought I would enjoy meeting. I asked if it was all right to bring Mary Alice, being concerned about appearances in a city I had been led to believe was somewhat conservative. As I was new to a very visible job at a well-known Seattle company, I asked Harry Mullikin his opinion regarding any exposure of my personal life. He told me that it would be just fine for me to bring a lovely lady to Seattle. "No one would care, and people would be happy about that," he said. There was no pressure either way and I was happy to share the evening with Mary Alice.

I was able to say to Mary Alice that if we did get married and she moved to Seattle, she could pursue anything she wanted. I told her that she did not have to join a lot of boards or work for the bank. That was my job. Mary Alice was an artist and wanted to pursue her education and art degree, which she was able to do. In January we decided to marry. The ceremony took place in the Westin Hotel on February 20, 1983. It was a wonderful day and just happened to fall on the same day as my parents' wedding some 67 years before. That is how I began my life in Seattle with Mary Alice. Ten of our combined 11 children attended, making it a great occasion. My time in Seattle has been a significant period of my life, lasting more than 25 years and counting. More importantly, it has been the happiest time in my life.

---

The decision to move to Seafirst Bank and get married in Seattle happened so quickly that I'd had no time to search for a place to live. The bank gave me three months to get settled and during that time put me up at the Westin Hotel. Initially, I was not too concerned about my accommodations, but even the best hotel room makes me feel like a transient. That changed when Mary Alice and I decided to get married. She had a large classic home in Beverly Hills where she lived with three of her children. There was much to be done, as she had decided to rent rather than sell her home. And where and how did the children want to live? We traded weekends off and on at both locations in those first three months, and spent considerable time looking around Seattle for a rentable condo or apartment. We found a nice penthouse apartment overlooking Elliott Bay — less than a mile from the bank headquarters — and took possession in April.

We furnished our new place from scratch. Mary Alice's youngest child, Bruce, was the only one of her children who made the trip north to live with us. His brother, Jim, got an apartment in Los Angeles. His sister Anne-Marie went to UC Berkeley as a freshman. She went straight through in four years, earned a degree in history, and then took a job at a San Francisco brokerage firm. Being a broker did not turn out to be a good fit for her, so a year later she went back to school to get her teaching credential. During this period she married and moved to Hillsborough, California, where she began her teaching career at the Crocker School.

Mary Alice, widowed three times, had four of her six children — Karin, Susan, Michael, and Jim — during her first marriage. Anne-Marie and Bruce were from her second marriage, to Bruce Cordingly. Karin, Susan and Michael were out of the house and gone before I came onto the scene.

---

I gradually settled into my job and my adopted city, but there were still many trips back and forth to Beverly Hills. In our first year together, Mary Alice discovered a lump in her breast, which was diagnosed as malignant. It had to be removed. After the first operation in Beverly Hills, her care was transferred to Seattle. Through our internist, she was fortunate to be put in the hands of Dr. Kaplan, an oncologist at Swedish Hospital. When we met him for the first time and talked about the prognosis of the disease, I asked him if we could hope to see our 25th wedding anniversary. He smiled and said he could not promise that, but he was sure that 15 years was within reach. Though not the news we were hoping for, it could have been a lot worse. It would be hard to imagine a more thoughtful and competent person to help her through this ordeal. During that time we did go to the Mayo Clinic, and to be on the safe side, Mary Alice elected to have a double mastectomy. After those first two years of treatments and the successful results, she was allowed to take a rest from the chemo and, with the exception of regular checkups, began to live a normal life again. The initial course of treatment seemed to be successful and she remained in remission for five years.

Our apartment was downtown and within walking distance of most places we wanted to visit daily, so we found that we walked much more often. If we had a destination that was farther away, the bank arranged for a car and driver for me, making transportation to and from the airport and places like that convenient. It also became an enormous help when we attended various social events, as we were able to enjoy the entire evening without having to worry about who was going to drive home. People were kind to us and we both made many good friends. My business travel continued, but at a much less intense rate. I took Mary Alice with me whenever I could, and she was willing to go.

We worked hard at combining our 11 children into one group. The ages were staggered a year or two apart, and they all seemed to get along well. In those first four years we took everyone, grandchildren included, to Vail for the Christmas holiday and they became good friends. In smaller groupings there were summer trips to places like Sun Valley or bike trips to France and Germany.

---

I found the work at Seafirst interesting and satisfying. The bank continued to recover, and it became a good investment for Bank of America. At Wells, being chief executive officer of the third-largest bank in California was challenging and rewarding, but when you are the biggest and oldest bank in your state, as was Seafirst, it is a slightly different situation. There is a greater opportunity to set the tone and be an influence in the community. There is a chance to lead rather than just react to the competition. Being the biggest entity in any market gives one a chance to take a constructive leadership role that can have a positive effect on providing new services or ideas that may help many people. There is an opening for greater creativity in the work one does for the whole area.

Although not as large as San Francisco, Seattle was no backwater Pacific port. It received a fair amount of attention, especially around the time of national elections. President George H. W. Bush was one of those people who had a Phi Beta Kappa key from Yale. George and I played tennis together in our teens. He was highly intelligent, an excellent athlete. While still in college, he married Barbara Pierce, who, you may remember, was the daughter of Marvin Pierce, my father's close friend and my first boss at McCall's. I was a year ahead of George at Yale, but we knew each other because of the family connections and growing up in the Greenwich-Rye area. During World War II and afterward we went in different directions. On the rare times we ran into each other, Barbara and George were always cordial and friendly. George Bush and Miguel de la Madrid were the only two presidents of state I have really known — and both were kind enough to remember me out of long lines of presidential greeters.

When George was running for his second term as President, the campaign brought him to Seattle. As a modest donor, I was invited to meet him at the Westin Hotel, along with a multitude of others. In the back of the hotel, down the spine of the building, was a floor of meeting rooms that were connected by a service hallway. We were divided into appropriate groups, probably by size of contributions, which put me in the third or fourth room. The President went from room to room using the back hallway as he passed. In each room he gave a short version of his stump speech and answered a few questions. When he came to our room, I was in the back of the group and not able to make eye contact with him. He was probably with us for 10 minutes or so before sliding out the door and on to the next room.

After he left, the group filtered out gradually, and I was left standing in the middle of the room across from the door to the back hallway. Soon there were some cheers and hubbub and people moving back down the hallway in the opposite direction, signaling that the President's party was leaving. I looked up and there he was, glancing into the room, and our eyes met. He stopped cold, smiled, and came quickly through the door right to me. He stuck out his hand and said, "How are you, Dick? Great to see you here! How are your parents?" It was short but friendly. It had been more than six years since he had seen me. It was impressive that he picked me out so quickly in that short glance as he was rushing to his next appointment. Later that evening, Mary Alice and I went to a larger reception to hear the full speech and had our picture taken with George and Barbara. He never forgot his friends.

From time to time in Seattle I would run across someone connected to my past, such as Peggy Vance. I found out that her father was Sheila's older brother, Murray McDonnell. Murray had married Peter Flanigan's only sister, Peggy, and they had nine children together. One of them was Peggy Vance. She married Cyrus Vance Jr. and moved to Seattle sometime in the late 1980s. Mary Alice and I got to know them quite well, and while we were not in the same social group, we saw them fairly often. They had two children here, and Cy did an outstanding job with his Seattle law firm. He was a Democrat and interested in politics, which he might have inherited from his father, who was secretary of state under President Carter.

---

As the bank recovered, the board began to think in terms of management succession. They did not want to have my five-year contract mature and not know who was going to manage the bank. So I began to think about a successor. Dick Rosenberg, an old associate from Wells Fargo, had gone to Crocker Bank as its number-two person when Carl Reichardt took over at Wells. After a time it was clear that Dick would not move up to become Crocker's chief executive. I knew that being head of a major bank was his goal. He had been a talented marketing guru for Wells and was very bright and ambitious. I thought he would be a good fit at Seafirst, so I cleared it with the Seafirst board and the Bank of America management then went down to San Francisco to sound him out. He was thinking of moving and was considering an interesting offer from a bank back east. I told him that if he came to Seattle, I would retire in a year and he could run the bank on his own. He was concerned about Bank of America's ownership, but the fact that Seafirst had kept its name and board of directors was a plus. When Dick decided to move to Seattle, it made a lot of people happy.

Not long after Dick and his wife, Barbara, arrived in Seattle, Bank of America's loan problems were exposed and its management changed. Tom Clausen was brought back from retirement to head the bank. Bank of America had been going through some hard times with its international investments and loans. Its management bench needed strengthening, and some competent Wells bankers had moved across the street. Glenhall Taylor, who had done such an outstanding job pulling together Seafirst's portfolio, was taken down to San Francisco to do the same for Bank of America. It was a big challenge for him, as Bank of America was so large and so diversified globally. Turning around a bank that size was not going to be easy or happen too quickly, but he was ultimately successful.

I had been elected to the Bank of America board while Sam Armacost was running the bank. As the head of an important subsidiary, I was an inside director and not involved with the executive committee and all the actions that were going on. Still, I was able to see and understand the progress of the changes. With increasing problems, the deposit line of the bank began to waiver. Its large California branch network was its biggest asset. The board elected Tom Clausen to succeed Sam Armacost as the bank's chief executive, and Tom decided he needed a strong marketing head to turn it around. There was no one better than Dick Rosenberg for that job, and Tom came after him. Dick was happy in Seattle and doing well operating the Seafirst organization, and he was not too excited about going back to San Francisco in the marketing slot. He turned down the first two offers, and Tom was getting frustrated.

One night after a long and discouraging Bank of America board meeting in Los Angeles, Tom took me aside and asked me what he had to do to get Dick to come to San Francisco and take that job. Among other things, I told him that he should think about coming up to Seattle, taking Barbara and Dick out to dinner, and making them an offer they could not refuse. That offer was a much bigger salary increase than Tom had been thinking about and a clear opportunity to succeed him when he stepped down as chief executive. Having come back from retirement, Tom was not going to be around too long. I did not think Dick would go for any less than that. They finally worked it out on the third try, and I was back in the succession business looking for my replacement. Dick went down to San Francisco as vice chairman. He came up with a new deposit and loan plan that was sold successfully through the branches. The deposit line of the bank stabilized, and the loan product turned the losses into profits. Dick saved the Bank of America, though he never received the proper credit for it. However, he did get more important recognition a few years later when the Bank of America board voted him chairman and chief executive officer and he succeeded Tom Clausen.

When Seafirst's board initially asked me about a successor, I told them that I did not think anyone in the current senior management was ready, but there would be candidates in the future. Almost two years later, as we began our second search, I concentrated on people inside the bank. Of all the top managers, I thought Luke Helms was the best person for the job. He was smart, experienced, and well liked in town. Dick Rosenberg agreed and so did the Seafirst board. Luke succeeded me when I retired at the end of 1990. The board kept me on as a nonexecutive chairman of the executive committee while Luke ran the bank on his own and did well with it. I was given a small suite of offices on a lower floor in the building and continued providing administrative help. I rarely went up to the executive floor, and then just for scheduled meetings. After 42 years as a banker, I learned that you acquire connections and relationships that do not die the day you retire. And you continue to provide help to people and customers who need it. It is the nature of the business. But in Ernie Arbuckle's words, it was time for me to be repotted.

# Banking Before the Repeal of the Glass-Steagall Act

I have been retired from Seafirst for almost 26 years. People who have known me as a banker often ask me if I'm happy that I am not in the business today. I used to smile and duck that question, but of late it is becoming easier to answer because conditions in the financial world have become so flexible and open to greed.

From 1933 to 1999 there was a clear distinction between commercial and investment bankers. Commercial bankers were regulated carefully, primarily through the Glass-Steagall Act and by the Federal Reserve Bank, the Comptroller of the Currency, and the Federal Deposit Insurance Corporation, while investment bankers were governed by the marketplace. Governmental regulation put strong controls on risk. Commercial bankers took in deposits from people and corporations and used those deposits to make loans and clearly defined investments. These loans and investments were subject to management review and also to rigid examination by governmental regulators. Investment bankers had no such restraints and were able to borrow funds from banks, insurance companies, and the general marketplace. Because they were controlled by regulators, commercial banks were not allowed to leverage themselves so freely.

An example of how this worked is the housing market. In the 1980s our bank would be able to lend 80 percent of the appraised value of a $500,000 home, while our savings-and-loan competitors could lend 100 percent, plus a separate loan for furniture. As market conditions changed in the 1990s, sub-prime loan packages could reach 130 percent of value. With the economy booming, housing prices went up, which made the loan seem less risky than it was. The success of these loan packages depended on rising home prices and full employment with consistently rising payrolls. If the economy slowed and wages decreased, there was no way to keep the mortgage payments on track. In addition, some lenders applied fewer restraints and made numerous loans at less-than-appropriate credit standards. And when the bubble burst there was no way to service these debts.

That is a simplified description of how homes came to be financed in the new century. Imagine bundling thousands and thousands of this kind of paper into collateral for a bond issue that would be sold all over the world as a "safe" investment. The risks involved in the sub-prime bond market were exceedingly high. And this is a simple example that does not even take into account surrounding financial vehicles such as derivatives, counter-party risks, default insurance, and all the other financial contracts that accompany investments in general. Putting all these instruments together in an accelerating stream of activity produced enormous profits, which led to cutting corners and fraudulent activities pushed hard by greed.

After the repeal of two key provisions of the Glass-Steagall Act in 1999, it became hard to distinguish between commercial bankers and investment bankers. As that happened, the business of the old commercial bankers changed. Much has been written about the new financial vehicles that have come to the market in the last few years. Until 2008 the vast increase in risk was not talked about as much as the tremendous profits that were being generated. When the bubble burst, that changed dramatically and the word greed was on everybody's lips. The assumption that things could never get so tight that even a firm like Lehman Brothers could not borrow a dollar proved erroneous. People forgot the rules, pushed on by greed and the assumption that everything would keep going up. It is hard to buck a trend like that. Basically, it was not the kind of banking I was trained for and grew up in. So even though I missed the big paychecks, albeit they were small by comparison to those paid to investment bank management, I am glad that this frenzy was not part of my career.

# Part Three

*As the years stockpile, I have learned to accept help
from others and be grateful for it.*

Dick's Seattle-based community commitments included three years
as president of the Seattle Symphony board. Here he is shown
with Chairman Emeritus Sam Stroum.

Chapter 13

# Retired Productively

Walter Wriston, a business friend of mine, ran Citibank for many years. When asked what retirement was like he responded, "Retirement? It's like walking down a pier and falling off the end into the water."

The day you give up the office and the responsibility of leadership in a large, publicly traded company, you're faced with a new challenge. Even though you may be receiving a generous settlement, as some definitely are, it is hard to prepare yourself for the change in lifestyle. There is the table at 21 in New York, or the box seats, or the jet and the personal car and driver. All of a sudden all that stops and it is hard to slam on the brakes. Everything you have worked for has been passed to the incumbent. The workforce feels like it has moved on with a new momentum and tide. Fresh policies are implemented. People are hired and fired. The media quotes the new guy instead of you. Retirement is a hard thing to do gracefully, but I have seen it done well.

One particularly good example of a graceful exit was Chuck Pigott's retirement from PACCAR, Inc. After 33 years as that company's chief, he retired and people were no longer following his orders. It is a hard thing to get a handle on, but I think he managed to step down with dignity and let his son Mark run the company with tremendous success. Though he never admitted it to me, he saw that experts had trained Mark carefully for the job. Transitioning his lifestyle, Chuck supervised the building of an impressive yacht and traveled the oceans with many of his friends. When he is not traveling, he shares himself with several community activities of importance. In my book that is an A grade in retirement.

Unfortunately, many people who retire discover that they have lost their tailwind. What motivated them before, whether it was the salary or the pressure from others, is gone, unless they put considerable thought in beforehand to find a new reason to get out of bed in the morning. You wonder: Should I reinvent myself or simply drop into a lower gear?

The transition was not as difficult for me as it might have been for someone who had no idea what to do. Many chief executives who retire have not planned for anything besides more time to play golf and gin rummy. They are too old to go out and raise hell, and they may not want to do that at 65 anyway. One has the old connections to the business world, but those relationships fall away, and one is left with a lot of unscheduled time.

For me it was different. When I retired from Wells Fargo after 33 years, I was not really retiring but moving on to a new challenge that excited me. After eight years at Seafirst, my retirement at 68 was more conventional. I was alive, energetic, and looking for something to do. I had some ideas but not a clear plan.

When I retired from Seafirst at the end of 1990, Mary Alice suggested that it would be good to get out of town for a while. She thought I needed the rest, and she also believed that Luke Helms and his team would have a better chance of getting their own programs underway if I were not around to look over his shoulder. She was right on both counts. A change of scenery was the perfect solution. We settled on London and the U.K. In most of our European visits we had traveled through Heathrow, never spending more than a day or two before going to a new destination. We decided to dedicate the entire sabbatical to the British Isles.

Renting a flat for three or four months in London seemed like the best way to go about our plan. In mid-December of 1990, we stayed a week in London at the Berkeley Hotel while looking around for a place to stay. There were many flats/apartments for lease, but they were hardly exciting. Finally, through a friend at United, we found a lovely flat in Chelsea, which we took even though it was a six-month lease.

We arrived at Tedworth Square in Chelsea in the middle of February. There was snow on the ground and a chill in the air, and we were lucky to have a new two-level flat that was warm and cozy. Within the first week, on February 18 to be exact, an IRA bomb blew up in Victoria Station about a mile away from us. In spite of the closeness of that bomb going off, we managed to get settled in, although it took a couple of weeks. It was not like living in a hotel with all the conveniences already in place. Instead we had to find everything from scratch, and that took some know-how because the culture was different. For example, there were two TVs, but they would not work until I found the Chelsea Old Town Hall and purchased a TV permit. I had to buy a parking permit so we could park in front of our flat. There were all the usual necessities of daily life: the markets, the cleaners, the newspaper stands, the florist, the Church and Mass times, etc. The Thames was about four blocks from the square, and we shared many fun and interesting walks.

Our idea had been to experience all we could see and learn about England. With that in mind, I purchased two British Rail passes and we made plans to see much of the countryside on the weekends. We also had a desire to experience the London theater scene. I would look through the *Times* and pick out several plays that were recommended and appealed to us. Getting tickets was not a problem. If I arrived at the theater in the morning and stood in line before noon, I was usually able to pick up reasonable seats for the most popular plays without difficulty or a big surcharge.

Since we expected to stay three or four months, we each wanted to have something of interest to do during the day. For Mary Alice this meant finding an art school where she could continue her painting education that she had been working on at

Cornish College of the Arts in Seattle. As luck would have it, there was an arts college only 30 minutes from our flat. I was also fortunate to find the London School of Flying about 17 miles west. Mary Alice rode a big red double-decker bus to within a block of her school, and I drove through the countryside and roundabouts out to the airfield three times a week. These were great experiences for both of us.

Through friends of friends, we met people who were kind enough to offer assistance so we could learn the system and get things done. Someone suggested we check out a tennis club called the Vanderbilt, and we learned that they offered a temporary membership. That was a great boon, and we tried to use their indoor courts regularly. The club's claim to fame was that Princess Diana played there occasionally, though we never saw her. It was not the weather for golf, but the wet and cold days lent themselves to brisk walks exploring the city and visiting marvelous museums and historical sites.

We stayed with our original plan to see as much as we could of England by whatever means. When Mary Alice's daughter Anne-Marie and her friend, Stephanie, were with us, we spent a night in Oxford and had a chance to visit the wonderful University of Oxford. Later we went out to see Cambridge, which seemed a little friendlier to me. One of our English friends strongly recommended a visit to Bath, and that turned out to be quite wonderful. Since we were driving there, we routed our way back via Downside Abbey, a 400-year-old Benedictine school from which many of the Portsmouth monks had come. Mary Alice and I used British Rail for both shorter and longer trips. We traveled to Cambridge and Salisbury and took longer trips to the Lake Country, northern Wales, and of course, Glasgow and Edinburgh. It seemed like the most civilized form of travel, as we did not have to think about driving ourselves or mapping out our destinations. Six to eight hours on the train gave us the freedom to relax and enjoy the countryside.

All in all, the time passed quickly and it was hard to leave. But we had some things to look forward to as we began our lives together in Seattle. In the early 1990s, Mary Alice and I started looking around Sun Valley for a vacation home and in 1992 found one that suited us and the kids. We did not have enough beds for everyone in our combined family at once, but we were able to fit all those who wanted to ski sometime during the winter. Mary Alice loved to ski, and we would often spend a week or two on our own, taking advantage of all the great runs Mount Baldy presented. It was the right time for most of our young grandchildren, and we found that summer visits were just as desirable as those during the ski season, if not more.

In addition to our family activities in those first post-Seafirst retirement years, there were other interests that took up considerable time. One was our airplane and flying. There was a lot to learn and a lot to practice. Mary Alice and I both earned our private licenses, taught by Phyllis Baer, a fine instructor with more than 10,000 hours under her belt. I was trying to learn enough to get my instrument rating. Mary Alice and I flew together often. There was the occasional longer trip to Sun Valley or San Francisco, but more often it was the $100 hamburger trip to Tacoma or Port Townsend on a weekend. Once we flew down to Tucson to see our friends, the Mullikins, and from there across the country to Augusta, Georgia, to play golf. On our way, we encountered inclement weather and had to spend an extra day in Waco, Texas, before getting out late in the afternoon and making it to Little Rock, Arkansas, where there was another weather delay before we could leave. I remember just barely being able to see the Mississippi River as we flew across it at twilight. From there on we were in the dark until we landed at Augusta around 10 p.m. We took turns flying and navigating and it was fun.

Another interest was the Washington State Health Commission. Democratic Governor Booth Gardner had initiated a strong legislative effort to improve the health care system in the state, and this was well before he was diagnosed with Parkinson's disease. Paul Redmond from Spokane was appointed the first chairman. At the time, he was busy as Washington Water Power's (now Avista Utilities) chief executive officer, and after a year of getting the commission started he wanted to be relieved of the responsibility. I was offered the opportunity to replace him and I accepted. I had never taken a job like that for a state, and thought I had the time and should do it. Randy Revelle was in charge of coordinating the program and getting the report done on time. There were many meetings in Olympia and other parts of the state, as well as a series of public hearings where the commissioners would listen to ideas and recommendations from all parts of the health care delivery system.

After getting as much information from the various parties as we could accommodate, we were to prepare a report and recommendations for the legislature and the governor that was to be the basis for legislative action. It was hard to accommodate all the specific interests of the many groups who made up the system. We came up with a compromise report that would have helped a lot of people, though all were far from satisfied. In the second year of the project, there was an election in which control of the legislature went from Republican to Democratic shortly before the report was submitted. With the normal controversy surrounding the subject and the change in legislative control, the report languished and failed to generate strong political interest on either side of the aisle. It was clear that this was a subject in which it was very hard to please everyone. Still, it was a good experience and I learned an incredible amount about health care and how the state government worked.

While these two items took up a lot of time at the beginning of my retirement in Seattle, teaching at the University of Washington Business School was constantly on my mind.

When I was still at Seafirst, the then-acting dean of the University of Washington School of Business asked me to teach the Executive Master of Business Administration (EMBA) classes that took place "off campus" and in the mornings during the first week of the program. Since I had come to Seattle to take over Seafirst, the dean wanted me to take students through the trauma and the actions it took to keep the oldest and biggest bank in the state alive and functioning. Several of the students worked for managers who worked for me. Because the story was topical and related to me personally, I was able to make it interesting and got through the week in good shape. The real-life experience and the students' ability to ask questions about it went over very well. However, the story of the Seafirst demise was not sufficient as a base for an entire class and neither were the six slides (which later became seven) I came up with (see "Teaching About Being a CEO" on page 209), but they provided me with an idea of how to proceed. However, it did not come easily.

I had not been successful in working out an understanding with the school before we left for London. The department heads thought they could use me for spot appearances in various finance classes and as a "brown bag" lunch lecturer on an irregular basis. I wanted a regular class where I was officially part of the school. The program managers were friendly, but not receptive to the idea of making me a part of the faculty. I had taught relatively successfully in the special week's training program for the EMBA students during the spring quarter, which was the group that appealed to me the most. Students in this program still had their regular jobs and their experience level was that of managers who worked for senior management people, the group of people I was most recently familiar with in the business world. I thought the EMBA students were more mature and interesting to be with. However, the professors and the chief staff member who ran the program were close-knit and wary of the private sector. They let me know that there was no room for me in the group.

I had hoped the university would welcome someone of my experience in the "real world," but that was not the case. The same story came out of the regular MBA finance department when I offered to teach bank management. My persistent visits were a problem for them, and they did not know what to do with me. Finally, Bud Saxberg, one of the department heads, asked me what I really wanted to do. They questioned what I thought I could teach. My answer was that I was going away on a sabbatical, and when I returned I would have a plan and talk to them. In the bank my experience interviewing MBA graduates had been disappointing, and I thought the University's School of Business needed to expose students to the practical business world. But that was not high on the academic agenda. And the fact that I was not an MBA, not to mention missing a graduate degree, made me an outsider in this academic environment.

While in London I spent considerable time thinking about teaching. I questioned my ability to teach something new and different from the standard curriculum. After all, what did I really know enough about to share with business students who were interested in successful careers? For the past 24 years I had been chairman and chief executive of two major NYSE-listed banks, so I thought that I could teach about the chief executive position with some authority. Along with that came my experience with boards, how they worked, and how a CEO or director works with them. There was no one in the business school with that kind of experience — and no courses on these subjects at the UW. As I thought more about it, I decided teaching a course on being a CEO and working with a board of directors would solve both the university's problem of what to do with me and my problem of figuring out how I could add value to the student experience. I began working out the details.

The job of handling me seemed to fall to Professor Bob Woodworth, who was kind, smart, and became a true mentor to me. We talked through my ideas for a class, and he went over them with Bud Saxberg, the head of the management and organization department. They discussed it and decided to give me a try. Bud offered me a job as an adjunct lecturer teaching a course called The Chief Executive Officer and the Board of Directors. The class was to meet once a week for three hours in the spring quarter. The pay was $3,000 and it was to be an elective in the regular MBA program. It was not what I had hoped for but it was a start, and I was grateful to Bud for the opportunity.

I ended up teaching The Chief Executive Officer and the Board of Directors at the School of Business for 10 years and then took a year's sabbatical because I thought I was becoming out of touch. The students were young and fresh out of college, and unlike my older students, they didn't understand why I valued and wanted to teach them what I called the "ABCs" (i.e., the importance of working hard, listening to people, and putting the customer first, to name a few). However, about the time I took a break, the dot-com bust happened. After that both the students and I realized that the "ABCs" were important in the business world. You can't take shortcuts; the ABCs — the "golden rules"— are always keys to success.

After my year-long break in 2003, Louise Kapustka, the new director of the EMBA program, invited me to come back and teach. Over the years, Louise has been a wonderful supporter of my teaching and relationship with the UW Foster School of Business as well as a dear friend. My new EMBA students ended up being older and having real-world experience, exactly the kind of people I had wanted to have in my classroom from the start.

I always thought I would be best suited to teach the people who were higher up in their careers. The typical business student runs from 25 to 35 years of age and has much less experience in the business world. The EMBAs are usually individuals in middle management. In the past, their companies would pay for their participation in the program, but as companies began to cut costs, these people had to pay out of pocket. In 2009 at the University of Washington it cost about $30,000 a year to be in the EMBA program. When you combine lost pay, living expenses, books and field trips, it's closer to $75,000 to $80,000 a year. Although some students are still paid by their companies to attend the program, many have to borrow money to participate.

The chance to be involved with these more experienced young businesspeople was rewarding beyond all measure. In addition to the classwork and presentations and in place of an exam, students had to write a four-page paper on an appropriate subject they had studied during the quarter. "Why I want to be a chief executive officer" was a popular topic, which produced many interesting papers. Occasionally the students would write about their experiences in their own company, which often was fascinating and sometimes a little scary.

While I was teaching at the University of Washington, Steve Sundborg, president of Seattle University, invited me to one of the breakfasts he was having for community leaders about what was happening at his school. He was looking for ideas and responses on how to make Seattle University better and more relevant locally. After that breakfast, which included three or four people outside his staff, I offered to try my course at Seattle University's Albers School of Business and Economics. They did not have a program like the one I was teaching at the UW, and I thought it might be helpful for them. Gradually, I was turned over to the dean of the Business School, Joe Phillips, who then turned me over to one of his department heads who decided to give me a try, although there was not much excitement or interest. As it turned out, the Seattle U. students were slightly older than the UW students and it was a night-school class, running from six to nine, with the same format. We had the teams, visiting speakers, and all the rest. It took a while to get off the ground, but when it did it went like gangbusters. It was well regarded and the reviews were excellent.

All through my 15 years of teaching, I made adjustments to improve the class so that by the time I got through my last quarter in 2006, I was comfortable with the format and enjoyed the class reviews. Of course, reviews went up and down, and some classes were easier to deal with than others. However, I found it was always a pleasure to teach, and my second career was thoroughly satisfying and engaging.

In my last quarter at Seattle University, the faculty decided to continue the program. My replacement, Annette Jacobs, has kept the same general curriculum and question-and-answer sessions with business leaders. The University of Washington Foster School of Business continued the program with Bill Ayer, the retired CEO of Alaska Airlines Group. As of 2016, the classes are going forward, although I am sure the format has probably changed considerably.

When I was teaching, I learned that getting good speakers comes from who you know and what you've done with them. As I have gotten older, my friends are at least in their seventies and not as active in business anymore, and I know only a few current chief executives. Mark Pigott is a wonderful example of someone the class could relate to. He is in his mid-fifties and highly successful. I just didn't know enough people like him and you cannot keep going on the same old stories. Besides, a big story to me doesn't mean as much to one of these younger students. Additionally, my hearing was fading and it was hard to keep on top of a "discussion" class. That is why it was important that I retired from teaching when I did. However, Bill Ayer still brings me into the first class each year to help set a tone. I emphasize the importance of the basics: listening, having good common sense (which I learned from my father), and striving to do the right thing. It is always enjoyable to be in the classroom again.

Dick Cooley with Hannah Su, one of his students in the
University of Washington Foster School of Business EMBA
Program, from the EMBA 20th Anniversary event, May 2005.

# TEACHING ABOUT BEING A CEO

Filling the void after retirement is not an easy task. After my initial transition period that included living in London, I taught graduate-level business school classes for 15 years with the MBA and EMBA programs at the University of Washington and the MBA program at Seattle University. It was a new challenge, as I had never felt particularly comfortable behind a podium, but it was exhilarating. Teaching gave me something to focus on and it moved me into a different world of academia and campus life.

While in London I had spent some time thinking about my career and what had been important to the success of the jobs that I'd had. What I came up with were generalizations on business and ethical behavior. There was nothing outstandingly different or precedent setting in these statements, but they represented an update of several of the old golden rules I learned from my father. Initially there were about 30 or so statements about ideas that had worked for me. I thought about how to make these ideas into the basis for a class. They turned out to be what I called a "low tech" leadership presentation, which I felt would be useful to students in their careers — whether they aspired to be a chief executive or not. I combined the statements into seven slides, as follows:

I. WHAT IS A CEO LIKE?
Bullet points: CEOs work hard (12 to 14 hours a day); CEOs have a mission, corporate goals, and a plan; CEOs work to make a team; and CEOs let associates do big jobs and make decisions.

When I talk about this slide, I emphasize that CEOs really have to be on top of things and understand what they are trying to do.

When you have a mission, you have goals. The goals are used to create a plan. Since no one does anything by him/herself, it is important to have a team and to get the right people on the team. This is especially true for effectively managing technology in the workplace. Once the person in charge picks the right people, he or she can let them make decisions. Then it's important to have a time frame for getting things done. On all of these counts, Ransom Cook was a good mentor to me in getting me ready to be CEO of Wells.

## II. Useful Skills For A Ceo To Have

Bullet points: Listen more than you talk (because you cannot learn while talking); Cut down (and eliminate if you can) office politics (one way to do this is to pick the right team of people to work together); Speak well and clearly (you cannot sell your ideas when you mumble); Be fair, be firm, and be sure there are no misfits in key jobs (each person under you should be the right person for the job so that you have no need of favoritism; no one likes favoritism — it hurts everyone); Ask lots of questions (this is the only way to learn what other people know).

I use this slide to state that to get the best people in key jobs, the CEO has to be good at picking talent. It is important to always ask lots of good questions so that you know what other people know. Listen. You hear more and are less likely to miss key details.

## III. Get Along With Others

Bullet points: The best CEOs form strong teams to do a superior job; Trust your people (give your employees responsibility and hold them accountable); Offer regular feedback to those who work for you (everyone likes and needs to know where they stand); Lead by good example all the time — in all things (when the boss gets to work early, so does everyone else; when the boss dresses well and appropriately, so does everyone else; when the boss is excited about the firm and its future, everyone else is too).

I use this slide to point out that the people you work with need to want you to succeed. Don't fuss about trying to hold people accountable. People have to know that they are expected to do a good job. In today's world, it is more acceptable to be casual at work. Nevertheless, it is still important for the person in charge to set a good example, particularly in being excited about the company and what it is doing.

IV. Personal Behavior
Bullet points: CEOs are paid to make decisions; Use common sense and good judgment (trust yourself, get as much help as possible, and think decisions through carefully, then decide what seems best to you); Make decisions and have good reasons to believe you are right (don't waste time second-guessing yourself; when you make a choice, stick with it and do not worry over it); Have no fear of failure (if you are right half the time, you will be successful; nobody is always right); It is okay to make an honest mistake (everyone does, but it is dumb to try to cover it up); Take no actions on assumptions (yours or anyone else's; so many people accept the general herd mentality without finding out the facts to prove or disprove it); Be physically and mentally strong and disciplined (there will be long days in the office and hours of important negotiations in which you will need to be sharp; your mind and your body have to be in good shape to stay on top); Have personal goals (corporations have plans and goals and so should you; when you write down and speak about your plans and goals, you are more apt to accomplish them).

Using this slide I tell my students, if you are going to be a CEO, you have to make decisions. Be confident. And some parts of this slide are from what I learned in the military. For example, being physically and mentally strong, being disciplined, and being sharp — these qualities are very important in the military and they have served me throughout my career.

## V. Personal Communication

Bullet points: Communicate clearly, frequently, and in all directions (so many careers and good projects have foundered on a lack of communications); If people understand what you are doing and what you want them to do, the chance of success is high (think about this point with regard to your personal life and it becomes even clearer); Control your ego (try to be humble; fatheads rarely win and people enjoy bringing an egotist down to earth — don't let it be you); Be honest (have good ethics and don't take shortcuts; your reputation will be the most valuable thing you have; make it good; keep it good); Always have a successor able take over your job (having a successor means there is nothing to prevent you from moving up the ladder).

## VI. How To Be Successful

Bullet points: Take intelligent risks (without risk-taking, you will die on the ground; every successful CEO has to take lots of risks; there is no way to play it safe); Decide to take chances that have good odds of succeeding; Do not be afraid of new ideas (no business can stand still and repeat itself year after year; new products and new ways of doing things are the name of the game in this competitive world); Be imaginative (stimulate creativity and add value); Create a climate where new thoughts flourish and where people are rewarded for great ideas; Keep learning (any CEO can be taught new subjects, techniques, and knowledge; smart CEOs are always studying something by going to seminars and adding to their experience); Think ahead (don't get complacent, even with success; always think about what you can do next; look at today as the beginning of a better tomorrow); Be lucky (or have the mind-set that you are lucky); Be confident; Be a winner.

## VII. THE BOARD–CEO RELATIONSHIP

Bullet point 1: How a board manages the CEO relationship (directors should expect, and get, an overview of the firm's total business at each meeting and in between meetings if necessary; directors must approve of the vision, goals, and plan that the CEO has for the company; directors must know if the CEO has the right people on his/her team to execute the vision, the goals, and the plan).

Bullet point 2: How a CEO manages the board relationship (the CEO needs to share his/her ideas with the board at all times; the CEO should meet with each director alone at least annually and try to know each director personally; CEOs should create occasions where the directors can be together on a retreat or a trip to see a market or plant and get to know each other better; most importantly, the CEO needs to understand clearly that he/she works for the board and act accordingly).

I tell my students that the board is responsible for seeing that the vision, goals, and plan are well executed. If the directors do not see performance, they must change management. The CEO must have a succession plan constantly reviewed and approved by the board. In turn, the board must give timely and frequent feedback to the CEO.

———————

My class at the University of Washington began in the spring quarter of 1992. Over the next 10 years it gradually evolved into a format that worked well for the students and satisfied me. During that time the academic requirements at the school changed, and two classes per week rather than one became the minimum.

It was clear to me that I could not entertain, much less teach, for three hours straight, and even two was not productive or easy.

I looked for a curriculum that would involve the students either as individuals or in teams throughout the time period. I decided that having outside speakers from the business community would be interesting and useful to the class. The curriculum had to be a series of subjects having to do with chief executives and their boards. While it varied a bit over the years, the following is a list of the basic subjects.

1. Audit Committee
2. Board Mechanics
3. Chief Executive Officer and Retail Operation — Customer First
4. Chief Executive Officer and the Community
5. The Chief Executive Officer Job: Getting It, Keeping It, Being the Boss
6. How the Chief Executive Officer Relates to the Board
7. Corporate Ethics (covered by a team of students)
8. Corporate Governance and the Sarbanes-Oxley (SOX) Act of 2002 (designed to protect investors from fraudulent accounting by businesses they invest in; covered by a team of students)
9. Corporate Leadership
10. Corporate Strategy
11. Diversity: Women/Minorities on Boards (covered by a team of students)
12. Evaluations of the Chief Executive Officer and Board
13. Executive Pay (covered by a team of students)
14. Family Holding Companies

15. Mock Board Meeting (teams of students participate over a two-day period)
16. Risk: Managing it in Business (covered by a team of students)
17. Small Business Boards — Entrepreneurs (covered by a team of students)
18. Succession Management (covered by a team of students)
19. Turnarounds (a management process that helps a company get back on track; covered by a team of students)
20. What an Outside Director Expects from the Chief Executive Officer

Once I began to bring other people to talk to the class, the format evolved and soon developed into a class of participation. The students had to be involved. They had to ask questions. I started splitting the classroom into teams then taking different business subjects and having each team prepare a presentation for the class on that subject. That was combined with bringing currently active chief executives and businesspeople into the classroom to talk to the students about their experience and what they were interested in. Each year I tinkered with the format a little, making a conscious effort not to repeat anything and bring something new to the students.

I decided I did not need a textbook. Instead I made my textbook from the media. It was going to be a class about business practice, because after all, that was why I was there. I wanted the students to be prepared to understand the "real world." That meant I would read books and select text from the ample business literature available, then read magazines, newspapers, periodicals, and essays. I tried to make sure the articles were timely and practical. Clearly, students would have to understand how the corporation worked and the mechanics of running a company, from the board of directors down to the operating levels.

I learned to ask questions as well as leave a lot of questions for the students to ask. And there had to be homework. When one is teaching a subject based on personal experience, it is not easy to find existing materials to cover the topics most pertinent to class discussions. The media articles provided the necessary background reading and exposed these potential MBAs to the way businesses truly functioned instead of relying on textbook analogies. I would clip media articles, for instance, from the *New York Times*, the *Wall Street Journal*, *Fortune*, and *BusinessWeek*, among others. Typical subjects included:

1. What kinds of people are there in the company for future management?
2. How should a company handle a takeover?
3. How does a chief executive officer deal with his board?
4. What does an independent director expect from his board?
5. How do you develop a future strategy for the corporation?
6. How do you plan for management succession?
7. Where do you go for product?

Each class was divided into teams of four or five, who were asked to research a topic, prepare a presentation, and present it to the class on a certain date. Some of the presentations were fabulous, the question periods afterward were intense, and everyone learned a great deal about the subject. Some were average, but rarely did a team bomb. Usually the guest speaker went first, with the day's team following after the break. The class structure was flexible enough so that the students and I had time to comment and I could raise my own thoughts about the subjects in between the presentations.

The exciting thing about this format was that I could get someone such as Jim Sinegal or Mark Pigott to come in and talk about his company. Jim would always talk about Costco, and Mark, of course, would talk about PACCAR. Speakers usually had slides, and afterward students could ask questions to help them form a good overall understanding of what was going on in the company. Depending on who it was and how quickly questions were answered, we might get in 25 to 30 questions. The point for the class was that they had a chance to ask someone who was currently doing a good job in a chief executive position to explain what it was like to work there and hold that position. The questions covered topics such as: What do you have to do to get there? What kind of promotion can you expect? What kind of career trajectory can you anticipate? What do people in charge look for in a new employee? What is important in climbing the hierarchy ladder? There were personal questions as well: How do you manage all the travel with a family? What do you do with your children? Many were questions students would have never had a chance to ask a high-level executive in any other forum.

I also asked chief executives of privately owned companies to speak to the class. Mike Garvey explained the chief executive's role from the perspective of a serial entrepreneur. He was a founding partner of what became Chateau Ste. Michelle. He was also the principal owner of Saltchuk Resources, a holding company for maritime interests including TOTE and Foss Maritime.

So the class was split into the visiting speaker part and a student presentation part. Gradually I got better at it. Sometimes I reviewed what I had heard, and I asked a lot of questions to emphasize what the students should have learned. We would discuss the meat of what the visitor had to say about his company, as well as his presentation and some of his answers to student questions. That was very popular. There also would be a chance to discuss the subject that the team presented. When the class was over, hopefully they had covered two different important business subjects thoroughly.

The class itself was a discussion of key business ideas. There were certain subjects that did not lend themselves to speakers, so I covered such subjects as corporate governance and the community. And always I gave a quiz. I liked quizzes because I wanted to know if students had done the reading. In the early days, I would have them write out answers in class, but I found that their writing was rarely legible. That was something I wanted to improve on, but there wasn't much I could do about their handwriting skills at this level. Eventually, I gave them a question to take home so they could type the answer on their computers and bring it back to the next class. The students were also required to write a paper on one of the subjects presented in class. I would give them five or so topics, and they could pick one to write about. In some cases the mark they received was a pass/fail, and for other courses I had to give them an absolute mark. The overall grade consisted of 25 percent for the quizzes, 25 percent for the team performance, 25 percent for the four-page paper, and then a subjective mark on their class participation. This last was the hardest thing to do because it was difficult to keep track of, but I was able to get a sense of how often certain people participated and whether they had something intelligent to contribute to the discussion or just sat on their hands and took it all in as entertainment. I had to speak to several of them on that latter subject more than once. I was not a hard grader. I would say I was fair, but I did expect them to do the work and contribute to the overall discussion. It was important that they collaborate with the other students and present ideas in a constructive way, the whole point being that it was an interactive class where they could learn from one another. They certainly learned from the speakers who so openly shared their knowledge and expertise.

As I transitioned into the EMBA schedule, the same class format worked well. Over the entire 15 years, the speakers came and went as their schedules varied. Some came in only one year, while others came in year after year to help these students. A sampling of the quality of their different backgrounds is indicated by this partial list, which includes the position each speaker held at the time they came to speak: Bill Ayer, chief executive of Alaska Air Group; Renée Behnke, chief executive of Sur La Table; Jeff Brotman, chairman of Costco; Phyllis Campbell, president and chief executive of the Seattle Foundation; Joan Enticknap, president of the HomeStreet Bank; Dan Evans, governor and senator from the state of Washington; Anne Farrell, founding chief executive of the Seattle Foundation; Mimi Gates, director of the Seattle Art Museum; Gerald Grinstein, chief executive officer of Delta Air Lines; Joanne Harrell, president of United Way of King County; Kerry Killinger, former chairman and chief executive officer of Washington Mutual; Harry Mullikin, retired chief executive of Westin Hotels; John Nordstrom, retired co-chairman of Nordstrom; Mark Pigott, chairman and chief executive of PACCAR, Inc.; Judy Runstad, attorney and former chairman of the Federal Reserve Bank of San Francisco; Mal Stamper, retired president of Boeing; and Kathy Wilcox, chief executive officer of the Washington Software Alliance. To these and all the other wonderful people who shared their experiences with the EMBA/MBA students, I say thank you for your time and generosity in giving students the exposure they had never had before and which they treasured.

MARY ALICE PLAYING TENNIS ON HER COURT IN BEVERLY HILLS BEFORE
MOVING TO SEATTLE IN 1983.

*Chapter 14*

# Lost, Found, and Remembered

Toward the end of our stay in London, Mary Alice developed pains in her side. She had passed her five-year stretch of remission from her tumor problems, so I was hoping it was nothing big. Though it was disturbing, she felt well enough to continue our trip. We traveled to Stuttgart, Budapest, Vienna, and Berlin then dropped off her new Mercedes-Benz to be shipped home and flew back to Seattle on May 19, 1991. Our stay overseas was a time that I will long cherish. When we arrived, snow had covered Tedworth Square, and as we left it was a garden of green and a profusion of flowering plants and trees. What a privilege those months in England and the short trip on the Continent had been.

After we returned home, the first and most important necessity for Mary Alice and me was to visit Dr. Kaplan about the pain in her side. The news was unexpectedly bad. Scans showed tumors in her ribs. After six years of remission, her cancer was back. Mary Alice began another program of chemo and regular visits to Hank Kaplan's office. As time went on, the effects of this insidious disease became apparent. She gave up flying and lost her stamina to play tennis. She was more often tired now and had to pace herself. She may have had more pain than she let on, but Mary Alice went on with her life almost normally, although her exercise was limited to easy walking. If one were not aware of her condition, I doubt that anyone would have noticed the change. She was warm and affectionate, reaching out to everyone she encountered. During our time in Seattle, Mary Alice made many good friends and came to cherish the people here.

The treatments and various kinds of chemo continued. In the latter part of the 1990s, the treatments became stronger and more difficult to sustain. It took a lot of courage to face those trips to the hospital for visits that were painful and all-around not easy. By 1999 the cancer was out of control and was affecting Mary Alice's daily life to the point where a normal life was no longer possible. We knew there was not much time left, but we did not talk about it. It was too hard to discuss the end of a wonderful life and what to do about it. There were obvious things that we did discuss, but mostly we just addressed what we were doing to help her physically day by day. She became very close to Hank Kaplan and his assistant, Jeanie. They were both tremendously supportive, and Mary Alice felt truly blessed by their care.

On October 4, 1999, Mary Alice died at home in bed. Her daughters Karin and Susan were holding her hands when she took her last breath. Hank had come to see her that Saturday afternoon and told us it would probably happen within the next day or two, so we were trying to make her as comfortable as possible. Mary Alice carried a lot of pain at the end. When she passed away, it was hard to believe that it had finally happened because even when it is expected, one is never prepared.

I did not cope well. I was surprised by my reaction because I knew she was going to die, yet I could not grasp the fact that she was going away and I was losing her. Rationality flew out the window with her passing. I loved her deeply and found that in the weeks and months after her death, I dwelt increasingly on the ache and hollowness and absence. I have learned about myself that if something awful happens, I try to absorb it. When my parents died, I knew they were going to die and I was prepared for that. I miss them more today than the day they died, but they were older and had lived long and productive lives. I marvel at what they taught me and how they loved me.

Mary Alice was my wife from 1983 until her death. While we did not live together before 1983, we saw a lot of each other, and it was an experience not to be equaled. When I pray for Mary Alice, I pray that she will be full of love and close to God in heaven. She was an extraordinary mom and a wonderful wife. She contributed to everyone she ever met in her life, and she will always have a prominent place on my prayer list.

My prayer list is a special part of who I am. I haven't discussed it much in this memoir so far, but all of the people you have been introduced to in these pages are on it. I explain what I mean by my prayer list after the last chapter.

I tried to cope with my sorrow at losing Mary Alice, but it got worse. For the first time I was unable to find a place to tuck my grief. Absorbing this one did not happen. After Mary Alice died, my thoughts and dreams became extremely upsetting. I had to take sleeping pills for a couple of months just to get through the fretful nights. I was living in a space that we had shared, and memories overtook me. She had been such a wonderful friend and partner to me.

Her death did not come as a shock. We had been preparing for it. The momentum had been building and building until the last second. I did not know the exact date and time it would happen, but it was a reality that we both accepted. At one point in the final stages of life, those left behind are faced with the physical demands of those who are dying. We are asked to facilitate the body's demise and the soul's departure. At that time, one becomes so involved in the present that there is no time to think about the future. Then in an instant, I had to cope with her passing and that was enormously difficult.

I never expected to get married again and had no interest in trying to find someone to duplicate the kind of relationship I shared with Mary Alice. We had built something unique to us, and I wanted to savor and preserve it. For a while I was almost "anti-casserole." It was a time when I didn't want anyone to come by the house with food or be nice to me. I wanted to be alone in my pain, even though below the surface I understood that all attempts to help were offered by people with huge hearts, who only wished to do whatever they could to honor Mary Alice and lessen my sorrow. I may have seemed ungracious and selfish, for which I am sorry, but I desperately needed to grieve.

When Mary Alice decided to move to the Northwest, it solidified our life together. We came to Seattle unmarried, with many questions as to whether it would suit us well. As it turned out, we soon realized that Seattle was a city where each of us could pursue interests and thrive. It became apparent that the move would create a marriage of love, friendships, new beginnings, and experiences. Many people helped in our transition to Washington. We enjoyed our newly formed life together among many great friends who genuinely wanted us to embrace the city and its citizens. I loved sharing the experience with her and making those friendships. Rightly or wrongly, when Mary Alice died, a part of me left those connections behind. There are people who draw comfort from familiar settings, but for whatever reasons, I drifted away. I had built a life with Mary Alice that I treasured. It seemed that any effort to diminish that memory would take away from my love for her. In case anyone may have felt slighted by my disappearance after her death, I wish to assure you that it was no reflection on your kindness or friendship. It was strictly my absence of coping skills.

Sometime after Mary Alice's death, a friend told me that it takes three years to recover from the loss of a loved one. Although I am sure there is validity in his statement, I had no desire to find a replacement for my loss. It is not that I felt my life was over, but I did not think I would find anyone to share it with. And I was not looking for anything but peace.

---

I suppose this is the perfect time to admit that along the way I found many opportunities to make mistakes, or as my tolerant family may attest, blunders that set me back in their eyes. I was confused, unsettled, and had little idea of where I was going. Time passed.

I paid slight attention when an attractive woman came up to me in the middle of what had become my daily workout at the Seattle Tennis Club. She was fascinated with flight, and a friend of hers had told her that I had flown a P-38 during World War II. As I was reading a book and working through my 30 minutes on an exercise bike, she walked over and introduced herself. I was immersed in the words on the page when I heard someone say, "Hi. You don't know me. I'm Bridget McIntyre. Someone told me you flew a P-38 in the war." I did not know how to react, or how to reply. It was a true statement, of course, but it rattled me a bit and I did not say anything for a moment. It didn't matter because she continued to question me: "What is a P-38? Do you fly now?"

It turned out that Bridget was a pilot and was working on getting her instrument rating. I told her that I was flying now, but not in a P-38. Then I gave her a brief description of the plane and what it did in World War II. Bridget seemed curious about all things flying. As she turned to leave, she told me that she wanted to hear more stories about the P-38. I let it go and went back to my book and my 30 minutes on the bike. Still, I began to wonder about this woman who had interrupted my exercise program and wanted to hear war stories about my favorite airplane.

Seven months went by, and at times we would pass each other in the hallway heading to or from a workout. Other than smiles, nothing was exchanged. Then one day I saw her coming toward me. She had a hat pulled low over her eyes, and her face was red as a beet. I was expecting another smile when she blurted out something about wanting to hear my stories about the P-38. Again I didn't know how to respond, so I said, "Your face is red." She explained that she had just come out of the sauna. I invited her to lunch, but she turned me down. She said, "I don't take lunch breaks." So I asked her to dinner, only to be turned down again.

As my personal mending continued, I thought more frequently about Bridget. She started it with her quizzing me about the P-38, and there were her smiles. But she turned me down when I asked her to lunch, and again when I asked her out to dinner. Bridget became a puzzle and a bit of a challenge. After several weeks, and with my damaged ego under control, I called her. She must have given me her number. She was out and I was only able to leave a brief voicemail message. Finally, after several efforts, we made dinner plans for a Saturday night in May. A Saturday night dinner seemed more like a date than I had intended, but I was determined to get beyond my fear of any involvement following Mary Alice's passing.

I stood at her door with no expectation, and knocked. The door opened and there stood a young woman I had never seen before. Her hair was short and very blond and she had on a dark leather coat. The smile was the only thing I recognized. The other times I had seen her at the club, she had been wearing a baseball hat and sweats. For a moment I thought I had made a mistake because the reality was so different from what my mind's eye was expecting. I was able to charge ahead and hope that she would not catch my incredible hesitation. We went to a nearby restaurant on Capitol Hill that I liked. Bridget ordered water. I went straight for a martini and entered a conversation that went on from there as we began to find out about each other. Small talk included family and kids. She had been single for about six years and lived alone in the Edgewater Apartments, about a mile from my house. She had worked for Piper Jaffray for 18 years and was a broker's assistant. In time, I learned that she rowed competitively at the national level, swam beautifully and competitively (and she was a joy to watch in the pool doing 100 or 200 laps), ran marathons, and skied fast and furiously on the double-black trails at Sun Valley. She was a natural athlete honed by an addiction to speed and competition. Her principal interest was to develop her flying skills. At one point I asked what her goals were for the next five years, to which she answered, "My goal is to get my instrument rating, my commercial rating, my certified flight instructor rating, do volunteer work, and then get married, in that order."

She did get around to my family, starting with my late wife. Mary Alice and I were listed in the Tennis Club roster and she had looked us up. When she asked about Mary Alice, I wondered what she was thinking, as I assumed she had heard that Mary Alice had died the previous October. That was a bad assumption, as she knew nothing about me except the listing in the Tennis Club roster and the fact that I had flown a P-38. I was not as strong as I thought I was, and unannounced, the tears quietly started rolling down my cheeks. Bridget was somewhat startled. It was my first date-like dinner since Mary Alice had died. So we talked about her and what our life had been like in Seattle. She found out about my job and my 11 children. I drove her home after dinner, said my good nights, and went home confused and stimulated by a pleasant evening that had turned out to be so different than I expected.

By the next afternoon I was more curious and excited, and I was ready to try it all over again. I called her and invited myself to her apartment for a drink. Since Bridget did not imbibe, I brought the vodka, the cheese, and the crackers. She had some glasses and a nice sitting room where we could spread out and begin the exciting business of learning about each other. We discovered that we were both Catholic, and for us both this was important. It was the start of an adventure that went on for three years, until we were married in July 2003. We've now been married for 13 years, and the adventure is still going on.

In 2002, as our relationship deepened, we planned a trip to Europe. It would be a tour of major cities, with heavier emphasis on Italy and the foundations of our Church. Over three weeks we traveled to London, Rome, Florence, and Paris. Bridget had not been in Europe for more than a decade and she found traveling there stressful. She was not crazy about Rome, but fell in love with Florence. That trip did not lead to the succession of travels abroad that I had hoped for. In fact, the next big trip we took was entirely within the borders of the United States.

I inquired about the airplane I had purchased with Mary Alice and had sold. It seemed that the woman who bought it had little time to use it and was willing to let me buy it back. It was a fast, four-seat, single engine Beechcraft Bonanza. I began flying again, and it was once again fun. Bridget and I flew across the middle of the country through Nebraska, Iowa, Illinois, and as far east as Providence, Rhode Island. We returned by a more northerly route. At the time only Bridget had her instrument rating, but not for the plane we were flying, so we were ducking July thunderstorms all the way. Bridget completed her complex high-performance training after we returned to our home base. She went on to receive her commercial license, multi-engine rating, and has since earned her certified flight instructor rating.

The best way to summarize our adventures is to say that through it all, our relationship has kept growing and maturing in an incredible way that I had never hoped for in my wildest dreams.

Dick with Bridget on their wedding day in July 2003.

Helen Cernik (left) and Bridget next to The Princess.

# ATLANTIC ADVENTURE

## AS TOLD BY BRIDGET COOLEY

As I approached an altitude of 11,000 ft. to cross over the
Greenland Ice Cap, miles of glaciers flowed by as far as I could see,
with mountain peaks the shade of steel blue poking up as though
trying to get a breath of air. Blue skies were wrapped around all
of it, including Helen and me in our silver bullet, or as we call her,
"The Princess," the single-engine Beechcraft Bonanza carrying
two women pilots on a journey over the Atlantic to London.

Dick Cooley, my dear husband since 2003, has given me the
world in many ways, but he gave me the moon when I had the
opportunity to make this trip. Originally, the trip was more
elaborate and we had planned to fly on to Florennes, Belgium,
after our London stop; it was from Florennes that Dick had
departed right before his crash. But due to unforeseen circumstances, we were a few days behind schedule by the time Helen
and I departed from the White Plains airport, and we got
further behind along the way. As you will see, it is important to
"expect the unexpected" when you fly. This adventure reminded
me of the phrase again and again. Nevertheless, I loved every
minute of it. The opportunity to do it is something for which I
am forever grateful.

---

I was taxiing out of Boeing Field Airport in Seattle when I noticed
a woman at the last hangar putting an airplane away. She waved
and gave me the signal that the tip tanks on my wings that hold
extra fuel would clear her truck. Then she threw me a big smile.
I remember thinking, who is that? She had a commanding way
about her and a look of fun along with it. I had been looking for
someone to help me understand my new Garmin 430 GPS, a piece
of equipment that was especially useful for flying in the clouds,

so I decided to track her down. One month later I met Helen Cernik for the first time. Helen and I started working together and right away she was able to take a lot of the mystery out of instrument flying, including with the Garmin 430.

In conversation one day she asked if my husband and I did a lot of traveling, to which I replied that my husband had been all over the world and loved to travel and that I was not as well traveled as he. I mentioned that Dick would love to live in London for three or four months, but I preferred to stay in Seattle so as to fly in and out of Boeing Field. It didn't take her but 10 seconds to say, "Why don't you just fly your airplane to London?" My heart raced as I exclaimed, "Fly our airplane over the Atlantic?!"

Helen said, "Yes, fly the polar route." As soon as I heard her say that, I knew I was going. My fears of traveling to new places disappeared in that moment, but they were replaced with new thoughts such as "what if our engine quits?"

Nevertheless, I could hardly wait to approach Dick with the idea. But I had one stop to make before seeing Dick. I had to run the idea by my mom, the woman who took more risks than anyone else I know and loved to be out on the edge, living life to its fullest. I entered her house, looked at her now trapped in a chair with an oxygen mask, and started to tell my story. Before I finished she leapt up, sending her nasal cannula flying, and said, "Go!"

But she did have one question after I told her about all the risk involved: "Do you have your Mother Cabrini medal?" "Yes, it's in the plane." "Then go. She'll protect you."

After my encouraging visit with Mom, I went home and approached Dick with the idea and his response was, "Can I come?"

---

Helen is a flight instructor and she is also a ferry pilot. At the time I met her, she had done five solo Atlantic crossings to deliver aircraft to Europe. This was all the qualification I needed to start planning with her. Helen explained that there were two important tests that we had to accomplish before beginning the trip. The first was to see how the airplane performed at 11,000 ft. and what the fuel endurance would be at that altitude. This test was needed to see if the plane had what it took for the three water crossings, each five to six hours, that would be part of the trip. The second test was to see what MY endurance would be for a journey with such long flying times!

The first part of the route for our trip included Dick, Helen, and me. It would begin at Boeing Field, my home airport, in Seattle and end at White Plains, New York, with fuel stops along the way. This would be done in what is known as VMC or Visual Meteorological Conditions. To fly VMC, you have to stay out of the clouds and fly with visual reference to the ground. This means each day's route depended on good weather.

Once we got to White Plains, the plan involved Dick leaving us to fly in a commercial airliner to Iceland, while Helen and I would get there by flying The Princess. First, in one day, we would travel from White Plains to Presque Isle, Maine, to fill up all our fuel tanks, including the tip tanks, then to Goose Bay, Labrador. The following day, we would begin a trip that would take at least 10 hours. The first leg of this trip to Narsarsuaq, Greenland, is over water, 674 nautical miles (nm) or 776 statute miles (sm), and takes five to six hours. After a quick fuel stop, we then fly to Reykjavik, Iceland, traveling 667 nm or 768 sm and another five to six hours. Helen and I practiced for this long day's flight on the West Coast beforehand.

———————

From Iceland, we planned that Helen and I in the Bonanza and Dick on a commercial plane would fly to Wick, Scotland, another 737 nm. Then, we would all fly in the Bonanza to London.

With full fuel tanks, the Bonanza has a range of 1,100 nm. That gave us a fuel endurance of seven to eight hours of flight time. The Bonanza held 114 gallons of fuel and burned about

10 gallons per hour (gph). With the leg distances and fuel stops we had planned, I knew our little plane could do it. No problem!

There is an interesting component of flying that I would like to explain. Airplane engines, like car engines, use a fuel/air mixture in the engine. When it comes to determining fuel endurance, you have to consider that at altitude, the air is less dense than at sea level. This means that you have to change the amount of fuel to work with the less dense air. To reduce the amount of fuel going into the engine, you perform a procedure called "leaning." To lean, you rotate the mixture control in the cockpit to reduce (or increase, when you descend) your fuel for the density of the air at your altitude to get the fuel/air mixture just right. If you overlook this important checklist item, your engine will start running rough and if you don't catch it, it can get to the point where your engine quits.

———————

Once we had our plan in place, it was time to prepare and test the readiness of plane and me for such a journey. Helen decided my first training flight would be from Boeing Field down to Monterey, California, which would be five hours of flight time. Dick came along and was able to visit his daughter, Leslie, who lives in the area. We flew down the coast on what is known as a Victor Airway. We specifically flew on V27 (Victor 27). This is a route in the sky for airplanes flying under IFR or Instrument Flight Rules. Victor Airways are for aircraft flying below 18,000 ft. We flew at 11,000 ft. to simulate the flight to Greenland. The V27 goes to Point Reyes, California, and then the airway turns southeast out over the ocean paralleling the California coast. As you look off to your left heading southeast, the Golden Gate Bridge and San Francisco presents a stunning view. The airway then takes you into Monterey Bay. When we landed in Monterey, it was exactly five hours later with no stops.

It was so exciting to fly that route and to know the airplane performed beautifully and that I was not too tired. But I got ahead of myself after we landed, when I began to worry about how I would accomplish 10 hours of flight time while wearing an immersion suit that I was told is very cumbersome and heavy. *One step at a time*, I told myself.

Dick, Helen, and I spent the night in Monterey and filed our flight plan back to Boeing Field coming up an inland route, Victor 23, which goes through the Sacramento Valley, by Mount Shasta, over Medford, Oregon, and into Seattle. We hit some weather by the volcano (Mount Shasta) and flew in what is known as IMC or Instrument Meteorological Conditions. This means you are flying in the clouds and all you can see are your instruments in the cockpit and nothing outside. My concerns on this leg were the freezing air temperatures and the fact that we were in moisture. The last thing I wanted was to pick up ice because my aircraft is not equipped or certified to fly in icing conditions. Thankfully, the plane stayed free of ice and we made it back home without any stops. Our first training flight was complete and Helen was pleased.

The second practice flight was just Helen and me going down to Salt Lake City, Utah, with an estimated flight time of five and a half hours each way. This flight was to be done in one day to simulate the long leg from Goose Bay to Greenland and on to Iceland. Our flight was beautiful, especially as we neared Salt Lake City. Part of my practice during this flight was getting familiar with communicating with a very busy air traffic control (ATC) agency at the Salt Lake City International Airport that wants small planes out of the way quickly so they can manage the coming and going of commercial planes.

After we landed, Helen's mother, Helena, picked us up and took us to lunch. As she drove us back to the airport, my fatigue started to set in. It was 95 degrees and 5:30 in the afternoon, and we still had to get home. Taking off out of Salt Lake was another new experience for me, since the airspace is so busy and the controllers work hard to separate small planes from the larger, faster aircraft. They had us fly directly over the airport and headed us north, and then we were on our way home. Flying back into the sun late in the day with these new experiences to process had me feeling excited in spite of my tiredness. Thank goodness for adrenaline. When we landed at Boeing Field, I now had a taste of a long day—11 hours of flight time! I was exhausted but knew it was possible.

---

Our plan was to leave in late July. Temperatures up in Greenland would be at their highest for the season, which we hoped would prevent us from encountering any bad weather or icing conditions. We planned on flying six hours a day to get across the United States. To build my endurance, I continued to fly on a regular basis and we started a very long check list of tasks to prepare for the crossing.

THE CHECK LIST

LOGISTICS AND PAPERWORK

Purchase insurance

> *Our insurance company would not insure the trip so we had to find a company that had a worldwide policy territory, European coverage for a total of 30 days, and the European Union Liability Limit.*

Contact customs in Wick, Scotland, to confirm customs entry into the UK

Order VFR (Visual Flight Rules) charts for Europe

> *These charts are mainly for when you are flying by reference to the ground and they are similar to topographical maps. We needed them to fly to Florennes, Belgium, (a plan that had to change once we got delayed so much in White Plains).*

Sign up for Rocket Route

> *This is a European flight planning program. You must sign up ahead of time or the European air traffic controllers won't let you fly! This was also related to our initial plan to fly to Florennes, Belgium.*

Collect fuel prices for all stops

Determine hangar fee for storing the plane overnight in
Wick, Scotland

*We ended up not making it to Wick. We had planned to drive
to London from there. Instead, we landed in Edinburgh, where
the hangar fees were $1,500 per night so "The Princess" had
to sleep outside for a week while we were there.*

Collect landing fees for all stops

Bring passport


TECHNOLOGY

Download the latest data cycle for the data card for the
Garmin 430 GPS

Download and update the data on ForeFlight for the US states on
our route (Washington to Montana)

*Foreflight is a navigation app on the iPad. It is imperative
that you have the most up-to-date information for the route
and weather before flying.*

Contact Jeppesen (the chart supplier) to get the proper coverage
for the data cards on the plane's GPS

*Jeppesen is the company that supplies all the chart data for
the Garmin GPS and all the paper instrument approaches to
land in bad weather.*

Test the GPS data cards in flight

Purchase power plug adapter for the iPad we will use in
the cockpit

*These days even commercial pilots use iPads for their
navigation charts. In the past, these pilots carried briefcases
full of papers. Our adapter plugged into the Bonanza's
cigarette lighter.*

Check the ELT (Emergency Locator Transmitter)

*If we were to crash, this device would emit a signal so we could be located and rescued. It is a requirement by the FAA to have this device.*

Purchase the Spotter GPS tracker

*This is an app that allows other parties to use a computer to track where our plane was on its route. This was how Dick and his son, Pierce, were able to keep track of us once Helen and I flew out from White Plains.*


SAFETY

Fill oxygen bottle

*Oxygen was used by Dick and me to make sure our oxygen levels were high enough. Oxygen helps to reduce fatigue and is a requirement if you are flying above 12,500 ft. for over 30 minutes and all the time for crew members flying over 14,000 ft. A regulator and a cannula are included so you can gauge the amount of oxygen that you breathe in.*

Purchase pulse oximeter

*This item indirectly measures your oxygen levels (which need to be at 90 to 95 percent) by attaching to your finger.*

Purchase a Personal Locator Beacon and register it with NOAA

*This is an item that is used by hikers and other adventurer types to deploy when they need to be aided or rescued.*
*We carried ours in the cockpit glove box.*

Reserve survival suits and life raft from Far North Aviation in Wick, Scotland, to be picked up in Goose Bay, Labrador

Do a weight and balance test for takeoff at maximum gross weight (3,400 pounds)

*Our first packing attempt found the plane to be 49 pounds over the limit because of my luggage so we had to take all the stuff out, lighten the load, and do a re-test!*

PERSONAL ITEMS

Purchase electrical outlet adapters for our electronic equipment for each country on our visit

Purchase en route navigation charts for the US

*These weren't necessary because we had a lot of technology on board, but I wanted to have the maps on hand to study them.*

Obtain the European contact phone numbers for my credit cards

Contact all my credit card companies to alert them that I would be traveling and purchasing fuel in Labrador, Greenland, Iceland, Scotland, and England

Convert some money to pounds and euros

Take a debit card for the ATMs

Make sure my father's rosary and my mother's St. Cabrini medal are in the plane

PLANE MAINTENANCE

Have the exhaust valve leak on the no. 5 cylinder repaired

Compression check

Oil change

Spark plugs checked or changed

Check the oil breather line for vent

PACK IN THE PLANE:

Five quarts of oil

Four spark plugs

Screwdriver

Wrench

Flashlight

Extra batteries

The Jeppensen Skybound G2 USB Adapter (the unit used to update the GPS data for our Garmin 430)

Satellite phone (for emergencies and it's a legal replacement for a high frequency radio that is needed over the North Atlantic)

CHECKLIST COMPLETE!

It is July 31st, our day of departure and I am wide awake at 4 a.m. I have only had a very light sleep. My first thought is, "What am I doing?!" As I look out my window, I can see the sun beginning to make its appearance over the Cascade Mountains where I grew up. Now thoughts of my dad and all those beautiful memories with him are flooding in. Will I ever see my mom again? My siblings? What will Dick do if I don't return?

I knew these thoughts were related to the butterflies in my stomach, but they were taking all of my energy and I needed to focus that energy elsewhere. I went to the window where I talk to my late dad and asked him to please take care of us.

Helen was buying her first home that morning so we three didn't take off until 11 a.m. When Helen saw the look of exhaustion on my face she reminded me that it would be "one nautical mile at a time." I had arrived at my first of too-many-to-count lessons of the trip.

Packed into our small plane and ready to go, it felt great to roll past the Blue Angels, who had just landed on Boeing Field. They are one of the reasons I have such a passion for flying. We got cleared for takeoff on Runway 31. *Advancing full throttle! We're off!* As air traffic control turned us east, I heard my friend, Nancy Auth, who was on the same frequency, wish us well. What a world this is, up in the air. It is filled with fun and friendships.

We arrived at our first stop, Glacier Park, Montana, and drove up to White Fish for lunch. We departed and encountered a thunderstorm cell that knocked us around until we landed at our next stop, Billings, Montana, where we spent the night.

We departed Billings for Mobridge, South Dakota. I looked down at the rough terrain and hoped my little engine would keep running. I had thoughts of my great grandmother, Annie Krug. On that prairieland below me, she had been left alone with two babies. I wished I had known her.

Mobridge was the prettiest airport I had ever seen — just a small airstrip surrounded by surprisingly beautiful green fields, compared to the dark terrain of the badlands we had been flying over. After we landed, we pulled up to the self-serve fuel spot and shut down the engine. As we got out of the airplane, a man came out and stared at us. I figured he was probably trying to make sense of what this older guy with one arm was doing with these two women pilots. He asked us where we were going. I replied, "The East Coast," but Helen promptly told him, "England." He lit up and said, "I flew the polar route 10 years ago to England!" I couldn't believe it! My next thoughts were, "If he can do it, we just might make it." We had lunch with him inside to escape the 105-degree day then took off and headed to Des Moines, Iowa. The temperature was the same there, but the air was much more humid. We found a nice hotel and had a great evening. The following morning was extremely humid as well. Our first leg for that day was from Des Moines to Rochester, Indiana, which took only three hours. Once we arrived, we used the self-service fuel again and got a crew car (the fixed base operators have these on hand to help pilots get around after landing) to drive to the Tweedlee D's restaurant for lunch.

This restaurant looked like something out of the 50s, complete with red carpet, red vinyl seats, and waitresses with beehive hairstyles. Adding to the interesting ambiance, the waitresses were vacuuming like madwomen while we were eating.

For the next leg of that day's trip, we filed an IFR (Instrument Flight Rules) flight plan over more flatlands to the Allegheny County Airport in Allegheny, Pennsylvania. The heat continued, making the plane hot for all of us, especially Dick who was in the back. He was a trouper— 88 years old, hooked up to a tank to maintain his oxygen levels at altitude, and having to get up earlier and earlier each day as we flew east through different time zones.

Heading to Allegheny, we needed to avoid the busy, Class B airspace that surrounds the Pittsburgh International Airport. As we did, an air traffic controller cleared me for the ILS approach. ILS stands for Instrument Landing System. If you are in the clouds, the ILS is a way for the aircraft to descend safely to an airport and land.

Forty miles later and safely past the international airport, I was on final approach for the Alleghany airport. When we opened the door of the plane after landing, 108-degree air welcomed us. While at dinner that night, Helen looked at the forecast and noticed it was good all the way to White Plains.

Since the trip to White Plains was going to be our shortest with only three hours of flight time, we decided to depart later in the day instead of getting an early start.

We learned a lesson due to that decision: it is important to take advantage of good weather when you have it! While pre-flighting, I noticed the air getting heavier by the minute. We took off and climbed up to 7,000 ft. Just as I leveled off, we started to hit some turbulence and within a few minutes we were in the clouds. A thunderstorm had formed rapidly. The air traffic controller we were in contact with had a heavy New York accent. He was extremely busy helping pilots get out of the storm. The turbulence got worse, so I took the plane off autopilot, slowed down, and hand-flew it so as to not exceed the maneuvering speed I needed. I had Helen tighten Dick's seatbelt to keep him from hitting his head on the roof of the plane when the turbulence was really rough. We asked the controller if we could descend. He said we couldn't due to the terrain, so we endured a rough ride for about an hour and a half. Finally, we were able to descend and get out of the storm. I remember looking to my right at Manhattan before crossing the Hudson River to turn toward the White Plains airport. After we landed, we got The Princess into a hangar as fast as we could, as we had been told another thunderstorm was coming.

We had made it to the East Coast! My sister, Maura, lived close by, so we had a visit with her and she was nice enough to take some laundry home to wash for us. We were now at a hotel. As Dick and I were getting settled, the thunderstorm arrived and affected the lights. My bigger concern, though, was Dick, who had come down with a medical issue that we had to call his doctor about. Our original plan was for Dick's son, Pierce, to fly and accompany him on a commercial flight to Iceland and then to Scotland to meet us as we arrived in each country. Mark, another of Dick's sons, was going to meet us in Iceland as well, and Dick's daughter, Leslie, and her partner, Kristine, would meet us in Scotland.

Everyone would then fly to London, where we would all meet up. I knew when this plan was getting arranged that all the stars would have to be lined up *exactly* for it to work. For example, Helen and I would have to have perfect weather and no mechanical issues — a tall order.

Dick's physician told us by phone that he could not leave New York until he was better, and she would only allow him to go to London, not Iceland or Scotland. All those flights and hotels now had to be cancelled and new ones arranged in London. As I looked at Dick, I remember thinking about "expect the unexpected."

Helen called to talk about when we could depart. The next morning promised to have a good weather window for departing White Plains and if we didn't leave then, it could be a wait of two to three days before the weather was good again.

In flying there is an acronym, IMSAFE, which stands for Illness, Medication, Stress, Alcohol, Fatigue, and Emotion. You are supposed to assess yourself as the pilot to consider any of these factors. I did that while I listened to Helen, and well, I knew I had four out of six of these concerns. Dick was sick, I was stressed out and emotional because I was worried about him, and I was exhausted. Up until this point, the only endurance flying I had done was the practice runs for this trip and those were on individual days and not back-to-back flights. I realized that flying long days in a row to get to the East Coast had exhausted me and I needed a break. My biggest worry, though, was about leaving

Dick, not only because he was ill but as I began to wonder, what if I never see him again?

I told Helen that I wanted to wait a few days. I saw the look of disappointment on her face. Being a ferry pilot, Helen knows she has to move when a weather window comes along, but I knew I couldn't leave Dick while he was ill, at least not right away.

------

After three days of some rest, and time with Dick, I finally felt I could fly again. Our first leg for this part of the journey would be from White Plains to Presque Isle, Maine, for fuel. From Presque Isle, we would fly to Goose Bay, Canada. It would be a total of six and a half hours of flight time. Dick, Pierce, and Maura were all at the hangar with Helen and me. I walked around my airplane at least six times. My stomach was in knots and every time I looked at Dick he gave me a huge smile.

I love my husband's smile; it's one of my favorite things about him. But I couldn't help thinking, what is wrong with him? Why doesn't he look worried? This is the last time he'll see me until we get to London . . . if we even get there! Dick has given me the world. He helped me fulfill my dream of flying, he gave me this airplane as well as a beautiful life, and, most of all, he has given me his love. How can I continue on this journey and fly away from him?

This moment in my life will never be forgotten; it was the hardest decision I made on the entire trip. Helen asked if I was ready. I glanced at Dick and there he was with that signature smile, the fuel for my soul. It was time.

Helen and I walked out to the airplane and climbed in. Dick was still waving as I looked back on climb out and my heart just sank. Helen saw my face and told me we didn't have to go, but I just kept flying.

------

Our flight up to Presque Isle was three and a half hours. We landed and fueled both the main and tip tanks. Because fuel in

Canada was more expensive, we got as much as we could at this stop. We took a short break and then took off for Goose Bay. This would be the first international leg of our trip. There had been a lot of preparation necessary for the international parts of our journey and Helen handled most of this planning. For example, we had to complete documentation for Canadian customs. We also had to call CANPASS, the Canadian Customs hotline, to advise them that we were coming. We had to make sure we called them at least two hours prior to our estimated time of arrival (ETA) in Goose Bay, give or take 15 minutes. Customs would meet us at Goose Bay and if we were late, we had to advise them of our new ETA. In addition, we had to have our personal documentation ready for them: passports and personal information, the aircraft owner's contact information, and the date of birth for all passengers and crew.

Eventually, we flew over the St. Lawrence River and were in contact with a French-accented air traffic controller. I asked Helen to take the radios, so I could look down at all that water. At that moment, I really wanted and missed Dick.

Then we started to fly over a massive amount of tundra. Helen could see that I was nervous and thought she'd talk about all the animals down below us like moose and bears. "Why don't we try to spot them?" she asked. All I could think of was, *This is not helping!* I finally had to let go of all the "what ifs" and just aim for Goose Bay. The airport is all by itself at the edge of the water. We did a straight-in approach, landed, and were welcomed by customs, who wanted to know if we were transporting any produce or meat. And, of course, they wanted to see our ID.

---

When we arrived in Goose Bay, we needed to pick up our immersion suits and life raft. We also needed to have our aircraft tail number handy because this information and our names would be marked on the suit and raft. For Helen and me, this was all arranged by a man named Andrew Bruce in Wick, Scotland, who works for Far North Aviation. Helen knew what to do to get the suits and raft. After landing, she found the building where these items were located and literally descended into a black hole, which I guess led to an underground basement storage area. Eventually, Helen emerged with our huge 13-pound suits and the raft. A question that I was becoming familiar with rang out in my head, "What am I doing?!"

We went to the Polar Hotel, which looked like barracks in the middle of nowhere, and checked into a very sparse room with bunks. Helen had me put on the immersion suit and we went over our emergency checklist of procedures to follow, should we have to ditch in the Atlantic.

In the cockpit you tie the sleeves of the immersion suit around your waist so you have the use of your hands to manage the controls and radios. In the event of an emergency, the procedure is to first get your arms in the sleeves of the suit and zip it up. You would then make a radio call followed by setting off your personal locator beacon and GPS spotter. I should say that flying the airplane is really the first priority, then this checklist. If you have to land in the water, you look at the water to position the plane so you can try to land parallel to the swells. If you successfully land on water, you open the door and tie the rope of the life raft to the control column, the T-shaped bar between the pilot and passenger's yokes (an airplane's version of steering wheels). This is important to do before throwing the raft into the water; otherwise, it will be taken away by wind if not secured to something inside the plane. Once safely in the life raft, you would hope to be rescued as soon as possible.

Helen and I headed for dinner to discuss the weather forecast. It looked as though there would be low ceilings and fog in Narsarsuaq the following day, but of course we would look at the weather in the morning, too. To make it to Greenland from Goose Bay, we needed to depart early, by 10 a.m., due to the time change in Greenland and because its airport closes at 4 p.m.

Unfortunately, I had a sleepless night. Helen and I met at 7 a.m. to discuss the weather and check out of the hotel. The weather in Narsarsuaq was currently a ceiling of 5,000 ft. broken, and the forecast for our time of arrival was 3,000 ft. broken. A broken layer of clouds means the sky in that area has a majority of cloud coverage but is not quite completely covered and you can see patches of the terrain while you are flying. Five thousand ft. and 3,000 ft. mean that the clouds are that high above the ground.

Helen looked concerned about the forecast, which worried me. We sat down to discuss all our options. Eventually, we decided to make the flight to the Narsarsuaq airport and file an alternative airport plan with ATC for Nuuk, which is about 100 nm north of Narsarsuaq. An alternate is a "plan B" airport that has, hopefully, better weather than your original destination. Nuuk's weather forecast was clear for the entire day. I want to point out here that the only reason I launched from Goose Bay with the weather the way it was in Narsarsuaq was because the weather at Nuuk was clear. Of course, when you choose your alternate airport, you must make sure that you have enough fuel to get there.

With our plan in place, Helen and I headed to the airport. After loading up the plane with the life raft and all our gear, we made our last pit stop and pulled on the big red immersion suits. You get into these suits fully-dressed, including shoes. Needless to say, they are very cumbersome and heavy.

I climbed into the plane and we talked to air traffic control to get our clearance to Narsarsuaq, taking off to the north at 9:30 a.m. local time and climbing up to 9,000 ft. At first, we were in contact with Gander Radio, the air traffic control radio contact for the Goose Bay area. After that, you are not in radio contact with anyone for about three hours, until you're far enough along to call Sonderstrom Radio, the air traffic control radio for Greenland.

Position reports are a requirement in a non-radar environment. A non-radar environment is when ATC can't see you on their radar screens. This usually happens in mountainous terrain, over large bodies of water, and in rural areas. Because they can't see you, they don't know exactly where you are and need you to tell them so they can keep tracking you. You tell them with a position report. To make a position report, you do the following: Call the air traffic control facility with your tail number and position. Give your current latitude and longitude (in other words, your position) and the current Greenwich Mean Time or Zulu Time. Zulu Time refers to the time at the zero meridian, also known as the prime meridian. "Zulu" is the Navy's phonetic way of saying "zero." Additional information that you need to provide includes your altitude, your next waypoint, estimated arrival time in Zulu, and the name of the following waypoint. You report about three waypoints in total. A waypoint is an antenna on the ground.

Our first and only report to Gander Radio was: "Gander Radio, Bonanza November Eight Eight Tango Juliet (N88TJ is our tail number). We are over Loach at 1100 Zulu, level at 11,000 ft., expecting (expecting to be at this location) 59 degrees North 50 degrees West at 1315 Zulu, next waypoint SI (Sierra India)."

When you can't reach air traffic control (ATC), you need to use higher flying aircraft in the vicinity to relay your information to ATC for you. To do this, you broadcast on air-to-air frequency 123.45 MHz. You want to keep in touch with the airliners so that in case of emergency, they will pass on your position report to the controlling agency. The agencies we used on this flight were Gander Radio in Goose Bay, Sonderstrom Radio in Greenland, Icelandic Radio, and Scottish Approach.

After I made this report to Gander Radio, everything was quiet. I absorbed the fact that we were no longer in radio contact and the next report would be a relay. We had been flying for four and a half hours in beautiful weather, but in the back of our minds, we were wondering what the weather at our destination was doing. When I got on the radio for the relay, I got a response from someone who called himself "Speedbird." I learned that was

British Airways. Through this contact, I was able to connect to Sonderstrom Radio and get the weather at Narsarsuaq Airport. They came back with wind being light out of the east, a visibility of four kilometers (2.5 sm), 700 ft. broken and 1,200 ft. broken ceilings, fog, and rain. My heart was racing a bit now because although we could see down through these broken cloud layers, we weren't sure if the visibility would get worse or better. We were still quite a way from Narsarsuaq.

---

As mentioned before, an instrument approach is a way to get down through clouds to land safely at an airport. Going in to Allegheny we flew an ILS approach that is the most precise approach that the instrumentation in our aircraft can fly. It can get you closer to the ground in low weather due to its precision. Narsarsuaq airport does not have that precise of an approach and can be a very challenging airport to fly into. It is surrounded by the Tunulliarfik Fjord and rising terrain. That is something to be aware of when you are in the clouds. When you can see outside, you can avoid terrain just by looking. But when you are flying in the clouds, you can't see the topography, so it's very important to stay at or above the altitudes listed on the charts to avoid terrain. The only instrument approaches at Narsarsuaq are "old school" NDBs. An NDB is an antenna that the pilot navigates toward or away from, using onboard instruments to get to the runway. At busier airports, there are more modern and easy-to-use systems to safely land a plane when the ceilings and visibilities are low.

For our NDB approach at Narsarsuaq, we would stay at 6,800 ft. and fly toward the NDB. We had to be at 6,800 ft. at this point because we were over an area of rising terrain that was the beginning of the Greenland Ice Cap. This is the altitude that has been deemed the lowest safe altitude in that area. Again, these altitudes are important to follow for safety reasons. After you cross the NDB, you proceed outbound (away from the airport) for one minute, staying at 6,800 ft. because you are flying toward higher terrain. This is so you can get in position safely to fly to the other side of the airport, where there is water and lower terrain, then descend and land. You begin a turn back to the NDB beacon at the airport descending to 5,800 ft. until you cross the beacon. Then you continue flying away from the airport on the side now with lower terrain and water, and start a descent down to 3,600 ft. Upon reaching 9 nm from the airport you begin your turn inbound (toward the airport) and descend to 3,100 ft. At 8 nm from the airport, you start your final descent to an altitude of 1,800 ft. You stay at this level until you get to 4 nm from the runway. If you do not have the airport in sight at 4 nm, you have to do what is known as a "Missed Approach," an immediate climbing left turn to 6,800 ft. toward the west to avoid the terrain. When you reach 6,800 ft., you turn back to the beacon at the airport to enter a holding pattern. A holding pattern is a delay tactic in aviation. It helps air traffic control (ATC) and you wait for the next opportunity and make a plan of action. If an opportunity doesn't present itself, you fly to the alternate airport you filed in your flight plan.

———————

Helen and I discussed our plan. We would start the instrument approach that would hopefully get us below the clouds and fly down to 1,800 ft. above sea level (about 800 ft. AGL or Above Ground Level). As I mentioned, this is the lowest altitude allowed, and if you don't see the runway from there you have to climb up and not land. If we saw any openings in the weather during that time, we would call the tower and break off from the instrument approach and fly in visually.

At this point in our route, heading east, we were almost at Greenland's shoreline and we could see the layer of clouds completely covering all of the landmass. I looked to the north, where the alternate airport was, and skies were clear. I wanted to divert toward that clear weather, but didn't say anything. As we came even closer to the shore, we made contact with Narsarsuaq's air traffic control tower. They asked us our intentions and we told them we would start down on the approach. The next 45 minutes of the shoreline-to-airport flight was another good example of why you should always keep in mind that you need to "expect the unexpected" when you fly.

We started our descent entering the clouds at 7,000 ft. We had what pilots call solid IMC (Instrument Meteorological Conditions), meaning we needed to rely entirely on our instruments because you couldn't see a thing out the window. I knew I just had to focus and I noticed that Helen now had her face smashed against her window looking for any sign of a hole that we could go down through and possibly out of these conditions so we could see the airport.

I was now on the approach and stayed at 6,800 ft., flying directly to the navigational beacon. I remember getting nervous and asking Helen if she could call out all of our altitudes, headings, and distances while I was flying, thinking that this would calm me down. In the back of my mind I was thinking, I can't believe we haven't broken out of this weather! The bright white reflection of the cloud in the cockpit was my reminder that we probably were not going to. Following the procedure for flying into Narsarsuaq Airport, we continued past the airport (that we couldn't see) and then came back over the airport again to start our descent down to 5,800 ft. with another eight miles to go before we could turn inbound for the airport. Frustratingly, we were still in solid IMC. I remember thinking and hoping that even though we were in the thick of it, somehow I thought we would break out. Helen was still calling out my headings, altitudes, and distances. I was now doing my turn inbound, starting my descent to 1,800 ft., which was the lowest we could go due to terrain underneath us. If we didn't have the airport in sight at 1,800 ft. or at 4 nm from the airport, we would not be getting in.

All of a sudden the tower called to give us the weather. It was a shocking "500 ft. overcast." We couldn't see a thing. Then the tower stated, "The airport is below minimums." That is another way of saying the airport is closed. As pilots, it is hard to process drastic changes in information like this. We had expected the weather to be good enough to get in (3,000 ft. overcast had been the forecast). Five hundred feet overcast is not good enough at all. In her effort to process this information and buy some time, Helen replied that we were proceeding to the Narsarsuaq Airport. We were still far enough away and had time to think about a backup plan.

At first, Helen didn't say anything to me, so I just kept flying and focusing on my altitude. She called out a five-mile final as a heads up that we were getting close to the 4 nm minimum distance out that we needed to determine if we could get in or not. I still thought we would get in.

Then Helen firmly called out, "Go Missed." In other words, "Get outta here!" I was still in complete denial as I added power and pitched up. She now was very firmly calling out, "Keep your left turn going, tighter, tighter." We were still in the clouds, and Helen was working on the GPS to enable us to see the terrain to avoid the mountain. We needed to be over the water on that tight turn, but all of sudden my airplane was shuddering. *What is that? Is that my engine?* Helen didn't seem concerned, but it was shaking hard. My thoughts were racing and in this order: *I'll never see Dick again! Why did I do this trip? Is this the end?* Other thoughts raced through my mind in a matter of seconds, most of them about Dick. Then I remembered when Helen called out the missed approach, I had brought my gear up but in the intensity of that turn, I forgot to bring up my flaps. I reached down to raise them and the shuddering disappeared. My airspeed in the turn and climb had exceeded the flap speed limitation.

We were still in the clouds climbing out, but when I reached 7,000 ft., there it was — the bright blue sky! I could breathe easy now, but only for a moment. I was leveling off and the tower called us to say, "State your intentions."

*I want to go home!* I thought.

We had filed the airport of Nuuk as our alternate, but Helen asked the tower for the identifier of an airport that she knew was closer. The tower told us it was BGPT, Paamiut Airport, Greenland, so she put it into the GPS. She quickly asked to change our flight plan and more importantly asked if this airport had fuel. The tower came back with an answer that they had 400 liters of fuel. I couldn't do any math at this point, but it was enough fuel for us, so we confirmed that we wanted that as our alternate destination. We were told it was closing in 30 minutes. Just as I finished my cruise checklist, I noticed my course needle was completely deflected to the left. That's when I realized we had an 82 knot crosswind! Then Helen said, "Bridget, we have to do another NDB approach."

And before I knew it, we had to enter the cloud layer again! I looked at this weather starting to close in on us and remembered that earlier, when I had looked to the north, it was clear. As I started my descent into the clouds, I looked out at my wing and saw a trace of ice. It was time for more intense focus. My mind seemed empty and I had no thoughts of anything except the next approach. We had to fly safely and get into the airport before it closed. Well, I have to say that I did have one distracting thought: *Why is everything closing around here?*

Once again, to calm myself and deal with the IMC conditions, I asked Helen if she would call out the altitudes and headings for me. I remember getting a little spatial disorientation on the procedure, and, at one point, I was convinced I was flying north when in fact I was flying south. I told Helen about it and she told me to ignore the feeling. All of a sudden, at 1,500 ft. we broke out of the clouds and there was this narrow runway surrounded by huge rock formations! I never put my gear and flaps down as fast as I did then and we landed successfully in Paamiut, Greenland. Just in time!

The place was deserted and the tower called to inform us the airport was now closed. Then they said "88 Tango Juliet, I have a message for you." My first thought was that we did something wrong. I said, "Go ahead." "Your husband knows you are here." I am embarrassed to say that I said to Helen, "Who?" That, in my book, is a sign of complete fatigue because I have a great, unforgettable husband!

Dick and Pierce had been watching the Spotter app on Dick's computer and had seen us divert from Narsarsuaq. To figure out why we had done that, Pierce found a phone number for the Narsarsuaq air traffic control tower and they told him where we were going. So then he called Paamiut, and that is how Dick was able to get a message to me after we landed.

———————

Looking back on the thread of events that led up to this flight on this day, it doesn't surprise me that I said that. Lack of sleep, worry about and missing my husband, launching from Goose Bay, holding my breath over the Atlantic, flying an unexpected approach, and then diverting to an alternate was a big day for me! My brain didn't have much extra space or energy left at that point.

We taxied off and shut The Princess down. *Good girl!*

When we emerged from the plane, the ground maintenance men were staring at us. I don't blame them. The sight of two women crawling out of a little plane with big red suits on must have been a surprise. My suit was now so stuck to me that I had to signal one guy to put his foot on my foot to get some leverage to get out of it. Helen told me to go up to the tower and she would unload. When I got up there, the controller, whose name was Brian, asked if I was okay. He thought I needed to sit down. I thought I'd had enough of sitting, but within minutes I took his advice. Brian told us he would drive us to a hotel, and we got in his truck. He gave us his cell phone number in case the weather was good enough to get out on the weekend, but he reminded us that the airport was closed during that time and we would have to pay $1,000 to open it. He mentioned that he would be caribou hunting but would be available if we needed him. As we were driving through the town, I felt far away from the world. Brian dropped us at the hotel and the owner came out to greet us in broken English. She got us to our rooms then told us she was closing and would see us in the morning. We asked where we could eat dinner and she suggested going over to the hard-to-miss blue building down the street very soon, since it was closing in 10 minutes. It was the grocery store. I was starting to get the impression these people don't mess around with closing times!

We soon found ourselves in the store with more people staring at us. We did look different. It took us awhile to figure out what to get since all the labels were in Dutch. We ended up with canned soup and bread. Fortunately, there was a can opener in the communal kitchen at the hostel-like hotel.

Before I left on the trip, my bank had suggested a debit card even though my credit card company said there would be no problem. As I got in line to pay, I looked around and realized, this is just like home, everyone is getting dinner at the end of the work day looking tired and bored. My credit card was not going through and now the line was growing. I remembered the debit card, and "approved" appeared on the screen. We headed back to our rooms. I had an unexpected surprise in the store the following day, when I walked around a corner and saw a tiny cold case holding something that made me feel I was still on the planet: a Starbucks® Caramel Macchiato!

In my room I received a phone call, the memory of which still brings a smile to my face. My instructor, who trained me for my instrument rating, called and asked if I needed to come in and do some approaches on the simulator. When I told him about the two approaches I just did, we had a big laugh. Thank you, Spence Campbell!

Helen obtained the weather briefer's universal phone number for Greenland and spent the next two days calling this guy and grilling him about the forecast so we could get out of there. I always listened in on the calls and took notes. I started to think Helen knew more than the briefer! For three days we had 100 ft. cloud ceilings. Finally on the fourth day, a Sunday, it was sunny—but if we wanted to get out it would cost us $1,000 to depart and another $1,000 to open the Narsarsuaq Airport to get our fuel for the flight to Iceland! Ultimately, the deciding factor to stay put was fog over the Greenland Ice Cap. So we spent Sunday morning walking around the village, which was mostly a collection of tiny shacks with non-English-speaking residents. Eventually, we found our way to the airport on foot to check on The Princess. When we got our weather briefing that afternoon, we got very excited, as clear skies were forecast for Monday all the way across the ice cap. Then there would be over a layer of clouds from the east side of Greenland to Iceland, and a warm front was forecast for 300 miles off of Iceland. The freezing levels were forecast to be at higher altitudes than we were flying, so ice shouldn't be an issue. We packed our bags and asked Brian to pick us up in the morning.

I had one more thing to do—call my husband to tell him we were getting out. When I reached Dick, he had some good news for me as well. He was cleared of his medical condition, and he and Pierce were booked on a United Airlines flight out of Newark for London at 10 a.m. on Monday morning. Dick had been in that hotel for seven days. I could hardly believe that we were both about to be on our way over the Atlantic. Actually, there was yet one more thing I had to do. I knew Dick had reserved a five-star hotel for our arrival to treat everyone. It was time to apply some blonde highlights in anticipation of being in London!

---

Brian picked us up Monday morning and we were the only ones at the airport. While loading up the airplane, the fuel we had reserved was being brought out to us. I had never seen a drum of fuel before and now I was nervous. *What if it was contaminated?* We took all they had, though. We said our goodbyes and the crew brought out the fire truck to escort us. It was very touching. As we departed to the south, I tipped my wing to the nice crew we would probably never see again.

Our flight down to Narsarsuaq was stunning. We flew at only 4,500 ft. right along the west side of Greenland heading south. I thought I saw a massive amount of fog off to my left then Helen explained that it was the ice cap. It took us 45 minutes to fly to Narsarsuaq. Coming in over the water to land, I now had a chance to look at the terrain that we never saw on our approach. It was very clear why we could only descend to 1,800 ft. to make a call on whether to go missed or not. There were mountains every-where as well as beautiful fjords! As we rounded the last set of peaks near the water on final approach to the east, there it was: the Narsarsuaq airport, surrounded by mountains on three sides and right at the edge of the water. I thought of all the men and women who came through here in WWII to fuel up on their way to England. I landed, and as I was taxiing I saw some very old, large concrete buildings that we found out later were used in the war. We went inside, but not before a fuel truck arrived to top us off. That fuel truck looked really good to me!

Upstairs in the flight center was the controller who had been in the tower three days earlier when we tried to get in. He was very curious about our flight and filed the flight plan to Iceland for us. There was also a ferry pilot up there who was delivering a plane to Russia. He said would be ahead of us and promised to talk to us in the air and let us know what he saw in regard to the weather. Our flight to Reykjavik was going to be five hours and most likely we would be over a layer at 11,000 ft. the entire way. We said our goodbyes and went down to The Princess. After putting on our immersions suits, we climbed into the plane, and taxied back to the runway for a west departure. We departed in the opposite direction of our arrival because the ice cap is so close to the airport; we had to depart away from the terrain and circle up to 11,000 ft. before turning east. With a more powerful airplane we could have climbed out to the east.

The scenery was stunning as we circled for a while. The water was such a beautiful blue, and it all seemed like a dream as I looked back down at the airport. When I leveled off and came upon the ice cap, reality became better than any dream. What a massive amount of raw beauty! I have always loved mountains and glaciers, but this was beyond anything I had ever seen. The ice went on for miles with sharp, rugged mountains protruding through the shade of steel blue. I quickly leveled off and put the plane on autopilot so I could grab my camera to capture the view. There was a part of me that thought, if the engine quits now and we have to do an emergency landing on that frozen landscape, we'll be sliding for miles. The controller was asking us to climb to 13,000 ft. but I just wanted to soak it all in. *Couldn't he just wait?* Before I knew it, it was time for a position report.

I got on the air-to-air frequency and asked if there was anyone who could relay my position to ATC. I was at 62 degrees North 40 degrees West at 11,000 ft. at 1530 Zulu Time. A Delta pilot came on and offered to take my report. I had just finished giving the report while glancing over at the beauty all around me when I realized that Dick was just farther down in latitude at this very moment, flying along at 41,000 ft. It was a shot in the dark, but I had to take it. I asked, "Sir, my husband is on United flight 18 from Newark to London. Is there any way to get a message to him that his wife is over the Greenland Ice Cap and all operations are good?"

"Well," he said, "I don't know who has the better deal, you or your husband!" This was the beginning of a conversation with four different airliners that had listened in and now they were asking us a barrage of questions. What color is your airplane? I told them it was silver so they named us the "silver bullet."

Why are you doing this trip? Where are you going? It was as though the very big world over the Atlantic had become small and intimate. It was a moment to remember forever.

The Delta pilot told me to stay on frequency and he would see what he could do. Not five minutes later he came back and told us that my husband's flight was delayed but that he contacted another United flight. They would try to raise Dick's flight once airborne and get back to us, but it would probably be another hour. I was so excited, I got tears in my eyes and just couldn't believe it all. Forty-five minutes later I heard,

"November Eight Eight Tango Juliet, are you on frequency?"

"Yes, go ahead."

"This is United flight 55. We have just sent a message to the captain of United flight 18 to relay to your husband that all ops are good."

---

Oh my goodness, I was beside myself! What were the chances of this happening? There's no way we could have planned that!

I looked back one last time at the beauty as we were now approaching the eastern shoreline of Greenland and ready to cross over to Iceland. Our weather was as forecast: we were over the cloud layer for five hours and then came into a warm front off Iceland. As we approached the shore, I thought it looked a lot like Puget Sound. I made a right turn toward the runway and touched down. As we exited the plane, customs came out and took our papers and left a good-looking stamp in my passport. I noticed I had a voicemail from Dick's son, Pierce. Pierce had been with Dick when the captain came back and delivered my message. He was very excited, and his message was fun to get. The captain had handed Dick a piece of paper with my position report on it, which we have treasured since.

Sometime after this adventure, my friend, Anne Simpson, who is a 747 captain for Delta figured out that the Delta flight we relayed with was one that goes from Amsterdam to Minneapolis.

```
ACARS BEGIN - 12/08/13 15:59:27 .N14121

12/08/13   15:59:10   VIEWED

DISP TO 0018/13
FI CO55/AN N34137
DT DDL YHO 131543 M46A
PLS PASS TO UA18 A RELAY FROM BONANZA 88TJ FOR
1ST CLASS PAX RICHARD COOLEY THAT WIFE IS ON
SCHEDULE AND OKAY..SHE WAS OVER GREENLAND AT
1500...62N40W-1530Z...AT 11000 FEET...63N30W-
1730Z..EMBLA..1815Z...LANDING AT BIRK 1900Z
UA18 SHOULD BE ABLE TO TALK TO 88TJ AROUND 30W
THANKS ... PLS LET US KNOW WHEN PASSED..



ACARS END
```

BRIDGET'S VIEW OF THE GREENLAND ICE CAP FROM THE COCKPIT AS
SHE GOT READY TO SEND A MESSAGE TO DICK, WHO WAS ON HIS WAY TO
LONDON ON A UNITED COMMERCIAL FLIGHT.

A SCAN OF THE NOTE DICK RECEIVED FROM THE
CAPTAIN OF HIS UNITED FLIGHT.

She was able to track down and tell the pilots who had helped us that we completed our trip safely and made it home. Again, one wonders at how small the world can seem sometimes! Thank you, Anne!

Dick's son, Mark, had planned to meet us in Reykjavik but due to all the weather delays, we didn't get to meet up with him there. He did find us a great taxi and tour guide who got us to our hotel. Once at the hotel, I felt like we were actually going to pull this off! Helen took a five-hour tour the following day and I did a smaller one and otherwise just sat outside a café taking it all in.

The weather for the final flight over to Scotland was bad enough to keep us waiting in Iceland for two days. Helen told me that waiting three days would be better, but she wanted to depart early because there were thunderstorms forecast coming from London toward Edinburgh. I told her I wasn't going to try to beat thunderstorms after flying across the Atlantic for six hours. That, for me, was too much of a risk after what we had been through already. I would go early only if there was an airport in Scotland that was clear and forecast to be clear through the day. Helen had an answer to that. Stornoway Airport at the north end of the Isle of Lewis fit my requirements. So we filed our flight plan.

We departed Reykjavik and climbed through a layer of clouds for about 80 miles. The freezing level was at the altitudes we were flying but, thankfully, we never picked up any ice. When we leveled off, Helen gave me a look of, "See? I told you so." There we were above the cloud layer in bright sunshine.

This flight took longer than planned due to air traffic control rerouting us. Helen thought it might have to do with the fact that we didn't have a high frequency radio. As we got closer to Scotland, it was fun to try to understand the controller's heavy Scottish accent. All of a sudden I saw a shoreline with a beautiful beach, and I was overwhelmed with emotion. I thought of all the pilots who had paved the way for us. They didn't have GPS or immersion suits and flew nonstop!

I had found out from my mother right before I left that my great-great-grandmother came over from Scotland. I thought how lucky am I at this moment to be doing this! As we came upon the Scottish Highlands, which were stunning, we encountered a head wind of 50 knots! This was due to the storm coming up from London, and when we looked to our right we could see numerous standing lenticular clouds forming. We took our time and added another hour onto our flight time. We were now in contact with Scottish Approach and preparing to fly an ILS approach into Edinburgh Airport. An ILS approach is much easier than an NBD approach!

The visibility was low and the sky had a purple hue. As we turned onto our final approach, we saw castles and aqueducts and—finally!—the lights for the runway. My mind couldn't believe we were actually here. Immediately after we landed, the tower told us to follow the border control car that came out on the runway so it could take us to customs. We shut down the plane and got out. As soon as we had taken off our immersion suits, the skies opened up and dumped everything they had on us! But we should have expected that. The forecast was exactly right.

The customs officer got us into the fixed based operator on the field, where private aircraft come in. A fixed base operator or FBO is an outfit that provides fuel and other services to private aircraft. We had to find a room for the night. At this point, Dick and his kids were all in London. Throughout this entire trip, Dick had watched our every move using the Spotter GPS tracking app on his laptop computer. Little did I know that two hours prior to our arrival, when Dick saw us make the shoreline of Scotland, he went down to the concierge in his hotel, ordered a car, and told his kids he had to find me. He was on his way on British Airways to fly to Edinburgh. Pierce had tried to stop him, but Dick just took off. So as Helen and I stood at the FBO counter still waiting for a room reservation, the phone rang. The woman helping us took the call and then told us in her heavy Scottish accent, "Your husband is coming up from London to surprise you!" All I could think of was how in the world would he find us? Then I realized Dick has been all over the world and knows how to navigate it.

The Edinburgh Arts Festival was going on, and Helen and I got the last two rooms in town at the Dakota hotel. We waited for Dick, and when the phone rang again, we told the lady to keep us a surprise and not tell him we were there. We climbed in a hotel van to go pick him up in the pouring rain, and as we approached the airport terminal there was my guy! I couldn't wait to jump out and surprise him. I caught him off guard and he grabbed me with tears in his eyes. The first thing he said was, "Will you fly back commercial with me?" I answered, "Yes!" Helen, Dick, and I got back to the hotel and walked straight into the dining room and had a celebration. It was the best evening ever!

Helen got us a flight for the following morning to London and I will always remember that morning. I went downstairs to find a double espresso, which they served with the thickest Scottish cream I've ever tasted. I was in heaven! And I was starting to soak it all in that I had successfully completed an amazing adventure.

———————

On the British Airways flight down to London, we were all three seated next to each other in the very back row. That position was such a contrast to being in the front seat with a mission that it made me laugh. But it was also a reminder: I hope I can always be in the front seat when I fly.

We arrived in London and all of Dick's children were standing at the entrance to that five-star hotel, holding flowers to welcome us. We enjoyed five days in London before coming home. I was caught off guard in London by feeling a little let down, which I'm sure is normal. It started with the fact that there was no way to plug in my hair dryer in the bathroom. It was really a change to go from being in control of a tiny airborne capsule with one focus in mind to the chaotic and hot summer tourist season in London.

On our flight home Dick treated me to first class, which had screens you could watch your flight on. I couldn't take my eyes off of my screen, thinking of our little plane flying all that way. When we finally arrived in Seattle and we drove up to our house, it felt surreal. Standing at the window in the kitchen doing dishes the next day really stopped me in my tracks. *How did I get here? Give me another mission!*

We hired Helen to fly the airplane back for us. She spent some time visiting her grandfather in Prague then she and her fiancé flew up to Edinburgh to fly The Princess home. She departed Edinburgh for Iceland and was in the clouds for the entire flight. When she landed in Iceland and looked under the cowling (the metal that covers the engine), she found oil every-where. She called us in the middle of the night to tell us. After consulting with our mechanic, she got the problem fixed then had to deal with the next obstacle: the weather that came in on her. She was in Iceland for four long days before the weather cleared. Her next legs were to Greenland and Goose Bay. Then another early morning phone call: were we willing to pay $1,000 to open up the Narsarsuaq Airport on a Sunday? Of course we were! *Just get that airplane home!*

So Helen flew to Narsarsuaq, did that crazy NDB approach, and fueled up. I watched the entire flight on the computer. When she landed, she texted me that she was departing for Goose Bay.

I still had the email contact info for the air traffic control tower in Paamiut, so I emailed and asked if they could let me know when Helen took off. I wanted to know because she had dropped off the computer and hadn't returned my text. Not a minute later he got back to me with "N88TJ just took off like a bat out of hell." I watched Helen for another five hours as she crossed over and landed in Goose Bay. I had wanted to meet her on the East Coast to bring the plane back, but there was weather everywhere. Due to all the delays and the fact that she also needed to get home, Helen started across Canada and flew from

Goose Bay to Spokane, Washington, in two days. I took a commercial flight to Spokane and flew The Princess with Helen and her fiancé into Boeing Field to complete our adventure.

The Princess flew 47 flight hours, 17 days, and her little engine turned 5,796,000 RPMs one way!

I wanted to be an astronaut in fourth grade and somehow that dream took flight in another way, and because of the generosity and love of Dick Cooley. He, too, was an adventurer on this trip. He is blessed with his faith and always does the right thing by the people he loves and cares for. He has been the launch pad for all of my aviation dreams and I am forever indebted to him for that and he has all my love.

Writing this, I see that it has taken years to absorb my experience and each memory gets sweeter with time. What did I learn? That it is never too late.

I carried this quotation with me in the cockpit, and it brought me great comfort:

"The will of God will never take you where the grace of God will not protect you."

A late-in-life highlight occurred in 2007, when Dick was one
of five recipients of the George H. W. Bush Lifetime of
Leadership Award at Yale. Here he is presented with a
commemorative vase by Richard C. Levin, President of Yale (center)
and Thomas A. Beckett, Director of Athletics.

# Return to Yale

I can see with some clarity that I began everything in my life too early. For some reason, I was always feeling the need to catch up. Things turned out well, but with less haste, the contributions I made and experiences I had could have been more meaningful. However, there is an order to my life, a bell curve-like course, from my Rye, New York, childhood to my present-day wonderful life in Seattle.

My bell curve has been influenced by both joy and tragedy. Being accepted at Yale at age 16 was exciting and challenging. While there I played varsity football as well as other sports, but I was still at the beginning of my ascent. The crash of my P-38 during World War II could have abruptly ended my climb, but while it altered my life it did not extinguish it. Who knows when I went over the top of the bell curve? I still experience moments of bliss, such as when I received the George H. W. Bush Lifetime of Leadership Award in 2007.

When the Yale Athletic Department commemorated the University's 2001 Tercentennial, it created the means for recognizing Yale's rich athletic heritage as an important component of the undergraduate educational experience. The development of a competitive temperament to ignite the trained intellect may explain many of the contributions that Yale has made to our planet's insatiable appetite for leadership during the last 300 years. The Yale Athletic Department established the George H. W. Bush Lifetime of Leadership Award to recognize and honor alumni athletes who, in their lives after Yale, made significant contributions in their worlds of governance, commerce, science, technology, education, public service, media, and the arts. The award was named in recognition of George Herbert Walker Bush, Yale class of 1948, who as an undergraduate played varsity baseball and served as team captain in his senior year, then went on to become the 41st president of the United States. He has spent his life as a leader, successfully and selflessly serving our country.

Alumni athletes nominated to receive the award were selected by a large and broadly representative alumni honors committee. The committee's selections were based on the candidates' participation as undergraduates in intercollegiate athletic competition and, more important, their lifetime contributions in their respective fields. President Bush gave his name to this award because there did not seem to be any recognition for Yale people who were non-academics. The honorees are selected every two years and the awards are presented during the Yale/Harvard football game weekend in New Haven. The 2007 awards were made at the Blue Leadership Ball, the fourth recognition dinner since the award's creation.

Every other year, five people are selected by the honors committee for the award. The head of the selection committee had called me in 2005 and asked if I would participate, and I told him no. At the time, life for Bridget and me was very complex, and it was not possible to make the journey to New Haven. I told him I was very sorry and that I knew I might be passing up something I would later regret. I also acknowledged that probably not too many people would say no.

I didn't say no twice. I felt humbled to be asked again. When I inquired about the award selection process, I was told there was a committee of 47 people.

I said, "What? How can you ever get anything done?"

"The selection committee," explained the committee person, "has to be that large because it has to make certain that all parties have their input and are represented." If you look at the five people who were selected for the 2007 awards, there was Anne F.

Keating, the managing director of Korn Ferry International; Kurt L. Schmoke, a former mayor of Baltimore and dean of Howard School of Law; James McNerney, the CEO and President of Boeing Corporation; Charles B. Johnson, the CEO of Franklin Resources Incorporated; and me. What the committee head said was that they have to consider all kinds of things. While Yale regards itself as a national university, it is a global university, so it has to look at the selection in terms of many varying factors.

Former President George H. W. Bush wrote a letter announcing those to be honored at the 2007 Blue Leadership Ball. It read in part:

*I have often said that any definition of a successful life must include service to others. We can all look to Richard Cooley, Charles Johnson, Anne Keating, James McNerney, and Kurt Schmoke as marvelous examples of selfless giving. They have made important contributions to their communities, their professions and, indeed, their country; and this tribute is fitting recognition of their efforts.*

*Richard P. Cooley, '44, fashioned an inspiring business career on the West Coast. A letter-winning varsity competitor in football, squash, and tennis, he left Yale in 1943 for military service during World War II. A plane crash cost him his right arm and all further Yale athletic competition, but did not prevent him from becoming a national squash champion — left-handed — in the mid-1950s.*

*Cooley joined the San Francisco-based Wells Fargo Bank in 1949. He rose to president and chief executive of the firm in 1966, becoming chairman and chief executive officer in 1978, and retired from Wells Fargo after 33 years in 1982. Almost immediately he was elected president, chairman, and chief executive of Seafirst Bank in Seattle, positions he held until his retirement in 1990.*

*In addition to his banking career, Cooley held directorships in such firms as United Airlines, Pacific Gas and Electric, and Egghead Software. In both San Francisco and Seattle he chaired the United Way; he has served on boards for opera and symphony orchestra organizations, museums, and hospitals. He also assisted educational institutions as an instructor, director, trustee, or member of the board of governors.*

*Charles B. Johnson, '54, has applied his economics studies at Yale to the investment and securities business. A varsity football player, Johnson spent three years in the U.S. Army before joining Franklin Distributors, Inc., as president and chief executive officer in 1957. Johnson helped spearhead the efforts of his class to restore the Yale Bowl as that landmark approached its centennial.*

*Anne F. Keating, '77, excels as a senior-level executive recruiter in the financial services and consumer sectors at the New York office of Korn Ferry International. A three-sport athlete and captain of field hockey, Keating earned nine varsity letters in field hockey training squad and the U.S. lacrosse team. Keating was the first recipient of the Nellie P. Elliot Award, given to the top Yale senior female athlete. In 1999, she was named to the Ivy League Field Hockey Silver Anniversary Honor Roll. Keating earned an MBA in marketing from the Wharton School, University of Pennsylvania. Keating is a founding member of Yale's WISER (Women's Intercollegiate Sports Endowment and Resource) Endowment and serves on the board of the U.S. Lacrosse Foundation. She is a trustee of Helen Keller International.*

*W. James McNerney, '71, has served several of the world's largest corporations at the highest levels of management. A baseball and ice hockey player at Yale, he earned his MBA from Harvard in 1975. He is the current chairman, president, and chief executive officer of the Boeing Company. He has worked at 3M, General Electric, and Procter & Gamble, where he is still a director. He is chair of the U.S.-China Business Council and The Business Council.*

*Kurt L. Schmoke, '71, distinguishes himself in the field of law, politics, and education. A lacrosse and football star while a history major at Yale, he attended Oxford University as a Rhodes Scholar before receiving his law degree from Harvard in 1976. After serving as assistant director of President Carter's White House domestic policy staff, Schmoke returned to his native Baltimore as Assistant United States Attorney, and was thereafter elected State's Attorney. In 1987 he was elected mayor of Baltimore. For 12 years he achieved outstanding success in programs to improve public housing and to enhance community economics development that won widespread praise. For his efforts in promoting adult literacy, President H. W. Bush, '48, awarded Schmoke the National Literacy Award in 1992. After retiring as mayor, Schmoke returned to the private practice of law with an international firm. In 2002 he was appointed dean of the Howard University School of Law.*

Bridget was ill and could not fly, but my daughter Sheila and her husband, Mark, joined me. Their son just happened to have an interview that day in New Haven, so he joined us as well. In all there were three of my five children, and two of my sisters, Ann and Helen. It was wonderful to have them there at such a pleasant family gathering. Seeing a lot of people and places that I had known as a young man brought back many memories that I had put behind me.

The event took place on November 16 in the Payne Whitney Gymnasium, which was newly renovated. It is one of the largest and most complete indoor facilities in the world. The building was given to the university by the Whitney family in honor of their son, Payne Whitney, class of 1898. The structure stands nine and a half stories tall, with a sports medicine center, training areas for each sport, and the Kiphuth Trophy Room, which displays all sorts of Yale memorabilia dating back to 1842. It is an enormous athletic complex that seemingly has been there forever.

The squash courts that I had played on had been dismantled, and in their place are 15 international-size squash courts and three exhibition courts, one of which is the only four-walled glass court in the country. You can have three or four hundred people watching the squash games now. It is very nice and I was really glad to see it. The new facility, which went from 21 courts to 15 because the new courts are bigger, was a gift from my old team-mate, Nick Brady.

The selection committee asked the honorees to come early in the day so they could spend time with some of the current team members, and I was asked to go to a luncheon with the men's and women's squash and tennis teams. There were probably 30 or 40 people there for lunch in Timothy Dwight, my old residential college, but aside from the dining area, the rest of the building was all locked up, so I couldn't see my old room. The dining hall had been renovated. We used to have waitresses come out and serve us, but now it is buffet-style, which is much more practical, and the food looked good. Next to the dining room was a meeting room with a long thin table, and there I sat down next to a squash player from Hong Kong. We talked while the rest of the teams filtered in. Dave Talbot, the squash coach, got up at the end of the lunch and gave my bio. He talked about my athletic career and then asked if I would say a few words.

Since he had already covered my sports history, I had to come up with some thoughts that could offer something of interest and maybe of use to these bright young athletes. I told them how I had returned from the war earlier than my peers because of a war injury and rushed through my final semester — only to graduate in uniform before going back to the hospital to finish the final work on my arm and learn how to use the prosthesis. In a sense, I told them, I missed my senior year with my classmates because of my sense of urgency. Most of my class had not rushed to finish up, but I had been in a hurry to graduate and get on with my life.

Although circumstances are different today, I asked them not to do the same, not to move so fast that they miss the moment. "You get more out of life if you address it with patience," I said. "Here I am at this point of my life, a man who attended Yale a long time ago, and I would like nothing better than to go back and study for four years. Do not rush through this place. Learn what you can and be glad for every moment you have the privilege to spend here. It's a big part of your life, so take your time and breathe it all in. In a way it is a little like playing squash or tennis. You have to be patient. You have rallies that go on forever, and you have to be able to wait it out in order to play your opponent the right way. Don't try to put the ball away immediately. Don't always go for the ace, because you may not make it and your opponent may have figured that out and it will cost you the point. Be patient with the point, with the game, and with life." The squash coach told me afterward that it was a good message for the students to hear.

---

After lunch I had an hour to kill before Yale's women's squash team was to play Stanford. It was the first game of the season for both.

With my free time I went looking for what we used to call the Yale Co-op, but it does not exist anymore. In its place is what is called the Yale Bookshop, which is run by Barnes & Noble. It is a much bigger place, right around the corner from where the Co-op used to be. It is big and beautiful, with two sides to the structure, one for textbooks and school supplies, and the other for clothes. It had very little similarity to the old place. Although it was bigger and better, it did not seem to have the same charm that I remembered.

I found that I recognized spots even though they were different in some ways and not so much in others, but buildings do not change. Buildings outlast people. In my time there were

10 residential colleges that were dormitories where we ate, slept, and maybe studied. Timothy Dwight was where I did all of that for about two years, and when I came back from the war I lived there again for my final semester at Yale. There were two new residential colleges that had been built closer to the gym, which was a little farther away from the heart of the campus. I found Yale's Anne T. & Robert M. Bass Library, which was built underneath the Cross Campus in 1971. The old campus was still there, and that's now where freshmen live before they go into a residential college. My freshman class was just over 1,000 students, but today's entering freshman class is about 1,300 students, so as things go, it has not grown that much. I am sure there are many more graduate students now. All in all, my wandering was bringing everything back, like I had been transported in time to my old neighborhood from the 1930s and '40s.

When I returned to the squash courts, there was a little ceremony before the match where I was introduced again as a former tennis and squash player. During the ceremony they gave me a picture of my 1942 team. You would never be able to pick me out if I showed you the photo; I was a totally callow youth. It was terrifying to see, and later when I showed the photo to Bridget, she did not recognize me. In November 2015, James Zug, a journalist who specializes in writing about squash, interviewed me and tweeted: "Magical morning spent in Seattle with inspirational Dick Cooley, finalist in 1942 intercollegiates @ BulldogSquash." Not bad for this old squash player!

At the match I saw the number-two woman play and it was terrific. The Yale woman was superior. In fact, she was so good I could hardly believe it. They hit the ball so hard! It was very high-level playing. That's when I learned why it is hard to be a three-letter person at Yale today: because when one gets on a team, there is training all year round. Plus there is a fall season and a spring season. Football always had spring training, but I never went to it because I had squash and tennis.

Today the physical training and the practice dominate what you do. It would be very hard to play more than one sport.

When I was at Yale you could do anything you liked. When I finally got on the varsity football team as a junior, I was playing on the left end of the line with two sophomores, Cottie Davidson, who was a guard, and Bolt Ellwell, who was also an end. Bolt Ellwell was a wonderful guy who died in the war the same year he had been elected the best athlete of the year. (I was number two.) He played football, basketball, and baseball. Today you could not do that. Each team would want you to spend more time working with them — and the coaches want to win, which means they want you to practice more. It is almost a full-time job. Even though the Ivy League schools are not considered to have first-class athletics, they still have their rules and compete feverishly with each other. They will never be in the same category as the Pac-12 or as big as Washington or California or even Stanford, but I am honored to have played for Yale.

---

After the squash match I went back to my room and put on my black tie for dinner. The reception was held in the Kiphuth Trophy Room, on the second floor of the gymnasium. There was a party there for all the awardees, the previous awardees, the generous donors, and many of the athletic department staff. One of the older men from the selection committee came up to me and said, "Well, I wanted to meet you. You turned us down last time." I told him it just did not work out for me, and he commented, "Glad you could make it this year." I think the idea of this award is good, but I knew it would be upsetting for me, and it was in a way. Just seeing a lot of people and places that I had known as a young man brought back many memories that I had put away in the past.

On the first floor was everyone who had paid to come to the dinner, about 600 people. There were over 800 in all at the event, including a photographer who took many great pictures.

There were two cocktail parties that were held from 6 until 7:30, and then the dinner program was supposed to start. A little after 7 p.m., the organizers started moving everyone from upstairs down to the basketball court. Initially, we were in a holding area with a big screen next to where we would be eating. There we had another cocktail area to keep up the momentum. Then they opened the curtain and we went in to find our table and discovered we had a nice one up front.

We had an excellent dinner and then the program began. The five awardees were seated on the left side of the podium, and on the right side sat the president of the university, the director of athletics, the master of ceremonies (Patrick Ruwe), the dinner chair, and the university chaplain. As we congregated, someone asked what order we should go in and it was determined that it should probably be alphabetically. I was the first in the alphabetical lineup and I was also the senior in the group. I sat next to my friend, Charlie Johnson, who was the only one I knew. He had his yellow pad with his written speech, which he had practiced. I said, "Geez, Charlie, I'm just going to wing it." He said, "Good for you, but I didn't have time to do that." I suppose he meant that winging it takes longer because you need more mental preparation.

There were several short talks, including a warm greeting from President Richard C. Levin, who welcomed the group, acknowledging the university's athletic philosophy, which emphasizes the enduring lessons that commitment to competitive athletics offers its students. "Learning how to strive to win, to compete with pride and honor, to make sacrifices, to persevere when all seems lost, and to develop a sense of obligation and responsibility for others are among the important lessons athletics teaches," he said.

Yale offers 35 varsity sports, as well as countless club, intramural, and recreational competitions, which President Levin observed, "provide camaraderie that often endures beyond the recollection of game statistics."

President Levin's speech recognized the quality of Yale alumni leadership in the world. The university recognizes its alumni who become leaders, and naturally they like leaders who stay closely connected to Yale. I felt I was a disappointment to the university because I am not closely connected to the school and have not kept in touch. In fact, this was the first time I had been at Yale in many years.

Thomas A. Beckett, director of athletics, was given a special award for all he had done for Yale in the last 13 years. It was a total surprise to him and was enormously popular with everyone at the dinner. In effect, he had been our gracious host and clearly deserved the warm acknowledgment.

Then it was time for me to speak.

*Good evening. I am really honored to have this award tonight. It means a tremendous amount to me. As someone who went through Yale as a "gentleman's C" type person and as an athlete, it is wonderful to see athletes get this type of recognition. I have three things I want to tell you tonight, or tell you about. One is my experience in the Yale-Harvard game in 1942, when I was playing on the Yale team and I started at left end. It was fortunate because that year we beat Harvard. We beat them 7 to 3, so you are getting the end of the story first.*

*There was one incident in that game that I will never forget. Game day was a gray, dark afternoon and the field was muddy. We were leading them by four points toward the end of the game, but Harvard was driving down on us hard and we were having a tough time stopping them. They got close to the goal line and all of a sudden there was a play that fooled us. The Harvard quarterback dropped back to pass to a wide-open receiver running across the field against the flow of the play. I could not get to him. Nobody could get to him. The ball sailed through the air for what seemed like an eternity, slightly behind the receiver hitting him in his midsection on his hip. I thought to myself, there goes the game. We did not have time to score and come back, but as it turned out, we did not need to. He dropped the ball, and we ended up beating Harvard 7-3. It was so wonderful! I can still remember that awful sinking feeling when that man ran across the goal line. But then he bobbled the ball! I don't know who he was, but it does not matter. The point is, we won the game and ended up beating Princeton as well, so Yale finished with a 5 and 3 season.*

*We were not terrific, but we beat Princeton and we beat Harvard and that made it a great success. This little gold football I received has both those game scores on it, and it is a treasure that I will have for my whole life. To be starting in both those games was a big thing for me. It was the biggest thing that happened to me at Yale as far as I can remember. A lot of wonderful things happened, but that was certainly the tops. That is the first thing I want to mention just to have you know as we play the Harvard game again tomorrow. Let's hope we win again. Looks like we have a good chance.*

*Secondly, I want to tell you about my arm. I was in the Army Air Corps and I lost my arm on a test flight. I was over in the 9th Air Force flying into Germany, and one day I had a test flight. I was flying over Northern France when something went wrong and the plane went in. I was lucky to get out of it, but without my arm. I did not come to until two or three days after the crash. I did not know I did not have my right arm because I still had those phantom feelings. I was in that hospital for a while and then another hospital for a while. It was the time of the Battle of the Bulge, and I ended up in a hospital just before Christmas in mid-France someplace, halfway between Paris and Le Havre. I do not know what caused it, but all of a sudden I knew I had lost my arm and it hit me. As I started to think about it, I realized that I was going to live and I was going to get home, but no matter what happened I would never be able to play football my senior year on the Yale football team. That was devastating. In fact, I get* teary-eyed thinking about it right now because that was when I cried. I cried and cried and cried because I could not have that one more year of playing football at Yale. And that is a true story.

Third thing I wanted to mention is what a great man we had here for many years, for over 40 years . . . a man named Johnny Skillman, who coached squash and tennis. I played for him all my time here. He was wonderful and I used to play well, but I could never beat him. I was always close to the top of the team on both squash and tennis with my right arm, and I came back and Johnny was still here, and he helped me and I started playing squash left-handed. Tennis not so much, because squash was easier and I got to play more. I was not as good because I had been a big hitter with my right arm and I did not have the strength or dexterity in my left arm to play the way I used to. With good coaching, the brains and the legs and the desire, I ran and got myself into the top level of squash. In 1953 I was very lucky. I had moved to San Francisco by then and with much help from a lot of people, starting with Johnny Skillman, I had learned to play the game again. I became a member of the Pacific Coast Squash team in 1953 that went to the Squash Nationals in Pittsburgh and won the national team championship. I have a picture of all of us who came out of the West to win this East Coast championship. It started at Yale with Johnny Skillman and the wonderful Yale squash courts, which have been upgraded to the magnificent squash facility it is today, thanks to Nick Brady's generosity and imagination.

It is great to be a part of this celebration. I am so grateful and so touched that the committee would think it was worth inviting me here tonight. What a privilege! I just cannot thank you all enough. If I had it to do again, I would.

———————

That was it, but it went over well, seemingly. My kids are prejudiced. They said, "You were the best, Dad!"

During the program the awardees received biographies written for the occasion, and commissioned oil paintings of each of us were unveiled that were to be hung in the trophy room. The committee also presented awardees with a recognition gift, a heavy crystal vase, so heavy in fact that I could not hold it up, so when I was being presented with it, I asked President Levin to hold it for me.

---

The next morning, Charlie Johnson and his class of 1954, who had done a tremendous fund-raising job to rehabilitate the whole Yale Bowl, were honored. Charlie rededicated the bowl in a ceremony that was held in the Coxe "Cage," a big enclosed building where the track team works out in the winter. It has been there forever. The organizers put on a brunch followed by a program that was basically to thank everyone for giving money to rebuild the bowl. The Yale Bowl is old. It's the first college bowl ever built and today it is still the largest university-owned college football stadium in the United States.

Yale's goal is to graduate a balanced person, one who is intellectually capable but also knows what teamwork is. Making businesses run is teamwork these days. In fact, many business schools right now emphasize being on a team because no one person can do it alone. Life has become too complicated and businesses are too complex, so it makes sense to construct a team that will get the job done. You get the right people on your executive team and you can do a lot of incredible things.

My dad told me that Yale was a good place for me. He went to UC Berkeley, but he worked in New York with Ivy League types. And the impression he got from his conversations with them was that Yale was a school where students can learn something.

I have to make a comment about the entire weekend because it made an impression on me. As I mentioned earlier, the dinner on Friday night was for 800 people. Although it was delicious, what really struck me was for that amount of people on a basketball court that was not exactly set up for such events, the organizers did an incredible job. The brunch the next day was another amazing meal, which was the result of another great effort. The place was decorated with an enormous picture of the renovated Yale Bowl on each side of this big building. There were tables, good silver, thousands of servers . . . it was done really well. Then when it was over, we were all trundled off to the game. At halftime they got us all out on the field with Charlie Johnson. The five honorees stood in front. I was standing next to President Levin as Yale songs were sung.

We were each introduced and given a brief acknowledgment. The exciting thing for me was that it was the first time I had been on the Yale football field in 65 years. The last time had been when the Harvard player dropped the pass. Sixty-five years ago! It was still the same place with real grass, albeit pretty soggy. People were falling down and slipping in the mud because it had rained. It brought back a lot of memories that I had not thought about in a very long time. It was sad that Bridget was not able to attend because I wanted her to see it and experience this moment with me. She felt horrible that she could not be there, but she was ill and it was very cold that weekend. Besides, I had my two sisters and my kids to take care of. It was my job to make sure they enjoyed themselves because I had brought them into something they had never participated in. It was their first chance to see Yale, and I felt responsible for them.

One thing that hit me was walking on that turf again and realizing what a lucky person I am! How many people get to experience something full circle like that? The fact that I could walk on a field that had meant so much to me as a teenager and experience it once more this many decades later was truly satisfying. It reminds me again how God has kept me going. When He decides it is over, well, that will be it. But in the meantime I am thankful for all the people who have helped me keep going, and that includes the people at Yale.

The weekend brought back a lot of emotions for me. As I told you, I like to look forward and not go back. When I look back, it gets me riled up. I am not saying that it is bad, but when I move forward in life, it is an escape from the past. However, working on this memoir has forced me to go over things that I have not reviewed in a long time. It is difficult to take a hard look at what was good and what was not so good, what was satisfying and what I could have done better. Some things make me sad, and there are other things I wish I had not done. The event at Yale was a little bit like that in that I recognized so many things it was almost as if I had never been away. I felt so glad and privileged that Yale had been a part of my life.

The only awful thing about that weekend was that Harvard creamed us. At the dinner on Friday night everyone was saying, "Go Yale! We will be the next Ivy League champions!" But the game just blew up in our face! We were supposed to beat Harvard, but when I left, we were behind 37 to 0. I think Yale got a touchdown in the last minutes after we left, but it was too little too late. Harvard looked like a well-coached team.

After the game, my sister and my son and I went to church. Later the five of us who were left went to dinner in the hotel. It was a nice close to a great weekend. The next day we got up early, caught all our connections, and after a full day of travel returned home. It was a long day, and I was really tired. It was a drain on my psyche. I was glad I went, but when I returned, it was like a window in my life had opened for a while and brought me back to my early days. It was warming and nostalgic and reminded me again of how lucky my life has been. I had a wonderful time visiting Yale, but now it was time to remember that life has moved on and there was still much to be done at home in Seattle. After a weekend of being the center of attention, it's good to be reminded to get back to your daily life, plug back into the routine of things, and accept that the past is the past. It is hard, even strange, to do, but I am comfortable and happy with that.

The 2007 recipients of Yale's George H. W. Bush Lifetime of
Leadership Award from left to right, Kurk Schmoke, James McNeary,
Anne Keating, Charles Johnson, and Dick.

Dick's five kids at Leslie's home on Donner Lake. From left to right:
Pierce, Sheila, Leslie, Mark, and Sean.

# Fatherhood

In thinking back to the days when we lived in San Francisco, there are many things that come to mind. Earlier in these pages I commented on my propensity to rush ahead to do the next "thing" instead of enjoying and absorbing the place and situation I was currently in. That pattern of going ahead through life affected much more than just my business career.

When my oldest three children were young and in playpens and cribs, I did my best to do my share of baby care. Like many fathers, I had some unforgettable experiences. One time I was left alone and in charge of all three children. I realized this was clearly a mistake as soon as the youngest of my little darlings required a diaper change.

She was bouncing around in her crib with little on but her soiled diaper. Getting her out and laying her down quietly on the changing table was a challenging task for most young fathers, particularly for one with only one arm. Think about it. I had a hold of her and the diaper came off and there she was, just as perfect as God made her. As I adjusted my grip on her, another exciting thing started happening, and there was no stopping a brown deposit from nature depositing itself in my hand. What a mess! I was appalled. And there was little I could do about it.

There is no point in trying to describe the next half hour in detail. It was completely memorable and an experience I will never forget . . . or wish repeat in this life. Cleaning up my little daughter and everything else — the crib inside and out, the changing table, my arm and upper torso, and my sweat suit — was a job that I barely got done before my wife got back from the store. It was a great lesson, which I was not able to discuss with anyone for a long, long time. After that a golden rule of mine was to never be caught with my three youngsters alone in our home or anyplace else. What a MESS! And what a smell!

As I look back, I realize that being a scoutmaster or a Little League coach may not have been a solution to the problems Sheila and I had, but those activities would have given me more time with my family. Having those experiences would no doubt have been better for me and very possibly for the children. They were all in good schools and taken on interesting trips, but our day-to-day family life could have been closer. Today they are all scattered about and communications are sparse. All my children have done well, but I am not involved in their daily lives as much as I could or would like to be. Their closeness with their own children's activities is a much fuller experience than mine was. In recent years that gap has closed a bit for me and that has been a pleasure. Following what they (and their children) are doing is fun and sometimes I am able to participate. With one child in Rhode Island, one in Sacramento, one in San Francisco, one in Carmel, and one in Heaven, it is not easy to go out for coffee at the drop of a hat. Still, we are able to visit and communicate much more often than in those early days.

My five wonderful children from my first marriage to Sheila are Leslie, Pierce, Sheila, Sean, and Mark. And from having been married to Mary Alice, I have six more children. Their names are Karin, Susan, Michael, Jim, Anne-Marie, and Bruce. I pray for them daily and for their families.

DICK'S STEPCHILDREN AT HIS 85TH BIRTHDAY CELEBRATION.
FROM LEFT TO RIGHT: KARIN, DICK, SUSAN, ANNE-MARIE, MICHAEL,
BRUCE, AND JIM.

Losing Sean has been hard. I can hardly believe he is gone.
I felt the emotional impact strongest and most suddenly when the
immediate family was gathered together on the Monterey shore
when we were putting his ashes adrift in the swirling white surf
as he had requested. It was then that I knew he had truly moved
on to his next life, and the first tears really came. There was so
much love and sadness at losing him so early in his life. His
children, Bridget and Sean Jr., were very brave. It will be hard for
them to fill that empty spot in their lives.

Looking back there is probably much more I could say about
being a dad, but I'm not going to do that now. It has been a
privilege and a joy, mixed in with times of great worry and
sorrow. God has blessed us in so many ways that gratitude is
what I feel most at this moment — to Him and to all the people
in our ever-expanding community who have shared themselves
so fully. We live and depend on all those around us.

Just as the family was learning about Sean's illness, I had my
90th birthday party planned. The timing of this terrible news and
this joyous occasion was not what we ever would have wanted.
But with the party about to happen, we all decided to go ahead.
This meant Sean and his brother Mark were not at my party. The
family pulled together. Sheila traveled far by plane to make it to
the party and make her dad happy. Leslie and Pierce gave tributes
to me on behalf of all the family using their own words. Their
toasts below are just two from that day, which was bittersweet
because of Sean's and Mark's absence.

———

Leslie's toast:
*When I was a small girl, before I could tie my shoes, I watched
my father tie his shoes with one hand. It didn't occur to me that
he was doing anything unusual. I had watched as he carefully
tied his shoes countless times. When I tried it myself, he gave me
directions that included using two hands. I didn't think anything
about it. It was just my dad. It also never occurred to me that*

there was anything extraordinary about Dad's ability to swing a tennis racket or a squash racket or a golf club with his left arm. I knew he had been an accomplished college athlete, but I didn't tune into the fact that he had been right-handed and was now playing all these sports with his left. He became nationally ranked and among the top 10 in squash with his left arm and was on the team that won the national squash championship in 1953, beating those smug East Coast rivals, but all of that was over my head at the age of 10.

After I learned to play tennis, I occasionally played with my dad. Several times we entered the parent-child tennis tournament at our club. Dad maintained his enthusiasm even when I double-faulted and gave calm, encouraging directions. After several attempts, in 1963 we actually won the tournament. If it was hard for him to play with a thirteen-year-old of mediocre talent, it wasn't obvious. When the mean team on the other side of the net tried drop shots on me, Dad was all over it. He was literally all over the court. I thought we were an amazing team. He even let me hit the ball once in a while. Dad was probably glad when Sheila and Pierce got old enough to play tennis because they were really good at it. He didn't have to be all over the court and he let them hit the ball more often. We could all see that Dad wanted to win. That was our dad.

As a young person, it didn't strike me as unusual that my father went to church every day. It was just something he did. At some point, I decided to tag along. It was a big deal, but not for the reasons you might think. Going to church early on a weekday morning with Dad meant you had him to yourself for a few minutes, but you had to be willing to endure his near terrifying strategy for getting there. You had to be brave. From the top of a hill in San Francisco where we lived, Dad took on the task of driving to church as though brakes were an inconvenience and stoplights were not to be reckoned with. His only goal in getting to church was to make all the lights. This involved times when we *slowed to a crawl and other times when we scorched the asphalt as he propelled the Ford Mustang forward.*

*Since he was usually driving a manual transmission — get it?— he did the steering with his leg while he shifted and then tied his tie. In this little competition with lights, sometimes he won, sometimes he lost, but the game was endlessly entertaining to him. That's our dad. Later in life, Dad put words to something I had observed, but never fully appreciated. He said, "You need to have a system for everything you do." This applies to parking a car in the garage where the fit is tight or an airplane in a hanger where the space is just large enough to accommodate a wingspan. In garages, he has tennis balls dangling from the ceiling in precisely the right spot. If you pull the car or the airplane into the prescribed spot, just enough the graze the tennis ball, you win. And you can win a lot. You can win every day. It was Dad's system.*

*Some of the best conversations we had with Dad occurred on a ski lift or in an airplane. I guess it was something about being suspended in air that made him reflective. From a young age, he impressed upon us the importance of making a contribution . . . to family, to community, to church. He said we have been blessed with many advantages and it is important to give back. It took a while for me to understand what he was talking about, but as a teenager, I certainly got that it was a deeply held value. A value he has spent a lifetime quietly demonstrating. That's our dad.*

*There are other values we have observed and absorbed over a lifetime and perhaps the most important is also the simplest. It's about love. Love. A quality Dad has in abundance. There are eleven kids, eleven partners, and many grandkids. Dad, or Dick as he is to some, has had many opportunities to test just how far he could stretch that love. He has loved us even when he doesn't understand what we're up to. His approach to the twists and turns of life in this very large family has been to love more and pray harder. I suspect there are times when he has kept us all afloat by sheer will and fortitude. As Dad knows all too well, some of the worst decisions make for the very best stories.*

*So, putting this all together, I think it comes down to what I'll call life lessons from Dick or Dad. The first is this. Patience is essential — especially with yourself. Competition is exciting. Always have a system. And if you didn't make the lights today, there will be another chance tomorrow. Keep learning and stay curious. Cultivate vitality. Put boundless energy into the people in your life who you love. Pray and have a list so you don't forget anyone. Eat lots of tuna fish, and laugh every day, laugh every chance you get. Never let your daughters call you dad in an elevator. Share anything except your ice cream cone and never admit your age until you finally find yourself trapped at your own ninetieth birthday party.*

---

Pierce's toast:

*Very wonderful, Leslie.*

*I remember the first time I met my father. We were driving. I imagine there had been many drives before, but this one called "morning drive" that comes to my mind is unique. This is my first memory. There was nothing before this. I'm a passenger. I'm in the front seat and we are moving. I look forward to my feet and it's like I woke up in this position and life starts. It's cold. I'm bouncing around a little bit and I look over and there's Dad. We are going down a tree-covered street and from earlier experience, not remembered, I somehow figure out that we are headed to church.*

*Dad is quiet and I'm not sure if I could even talk. I slide over next to him, maybe for some warmth. He is wearing a polo shirt and the stub of his arm sticks out beneath his sleeve. I move closer. I take it and I press it to my face. It was cold and soft and wonderful and felt so good and comforting.*

*When I took his arm, I could feel and connect to things I now have valued about Dad my whole life. His love, of course, but it was his strength, protection, and warmth. His generosity of self, gratitude for the moment, and his humble bearing as he was driving with me to commune with God.*

*He taught me these things through his touch and grace. In that moment, I would begin my lifelong effort to emulate this great man, my father. And since that morning when we went to Mass, if we talk on the phone or we spend our precious time together, I feel these things. Dad's love is constant and obvious to me every day since that first cold morning memory. What I felt when I pressed that stub of his arm to my face and cheek . . . this has never faded and remains a true constant in my life.*

*There was another drive. Drives were always wonderful with Dad, as Leslie told you. Yeah, it was a time we had together, and a place where I couldn't run away and he had control of me. In this particular situation, we were driving to the airport in San Francisco and he was putting me on a plane, by myself, to fly east to spend a month with my aunt Peggy, in Southampton with all of my cousins. I think I must have been about eleven or twelve years old and this whole adventure so far away from mom and dad and my family was really scary for me. Three thousand miles away and I really didn't know these people very well. I must have been panicked. Anyway, I think this must have been very difficult for Dad as well because he was quiet most of the drive. And then, as if he was thinking, it came. Dad told me that he had something he needed to tell me.*

*I was thinking maybe I'm in big trouble. It didn't turn out to be that way. He was quiet a little longer and then he spoke. And I kind of moved towards the door and I hunched over.*

*And he said, "I have something to tell you about women." I knew this must be really, really bad because there was a lot of quiet. Whenever he did these kinds of talks, it was usually in my* room and I was in trouble. He told me, "I want you to know this before you go back east. A week or so during a month, a woman . . . well . . . most women get cranky."

He said, "I just really want you to know it's not your fault." Okay. This was like lifting a weight off my end. I felt so good, and it answered so many questions. It wasn't really that bad, but I realized that I just had the sex talk. I did, you know?

I remember kissing him goodbye, boarding the plane with some tears, and I took his words with me. The amazing takeaway from this simple, awkward, mysterious, open-ended, and short conversation helped me to shape my mind and my heart in relationships with women. Anyway, I knew that I must dig in and stick to it with my female relationships, especially when I was confused by the amazing brains that women have. I am grateful for this early lesson. It's one that I learn from every day.

Another time when I was little, I was skiing with Dad at a place called Sugar Bowl. It's a place where we learned to ski in the morning in classes and then in the afternoon, we free skied. The free skiing was easy with Mom or Dad or the three of us, Sheila and Leslie and me. This one particular day, Dad and I were skiing. It was a pretty stormy day. We went up one of the long lifts. On the top, it was pretty much a white-out and blowing like crazy. It was cold. When we got off the lift, we skied down to Mogul Ridge and we skied through the trees. It was beautiful. When we came out on Christmas Tree Ridge, it was a total white-out. Couldn't see anything.

The ice was blowing in our faces and we got separated. I felt lost and cold. I didn't think I was going to be able to make it. So, I think I just hunched over and Dad skied up and put me between his legs and took off his glove. He got the snow out of my face and kind of cleaned me up and stood me up and prompted me on. From that moment on, I've never been cold and not known what to do. He taught me what to do.

*I'm not quite as prepared as my sister, Leslie, but that's my job in the family. There are a couple of things that I share with Dad from the first time we went to church together. Those things that I experienced from those early days are things that I feel every time I'm with him. We spent time together the year before last when Bridget flew across the Atlantic Ocean. While we waited, and we waited in different places, what was constant was early morning Mass and the feeling that he gave me in that first memory. It is still my guide, my compass rose.*

*It's as if holding that little arm was like being plugged into him. It's like a hard wire and I am everything because of that moment. I am grateful because he has given me such a strong model of what is right and what courage is and what service is. Actually, the biggest thing my father has given me is faith. And I believe that the second you think you can control something, you've lost faith. I don't spend much time trying to control anything. I should have spent a lot more time on this, but the biggest thing is faith. In closing, I just want to say that Dad gave me many beautiful things. On the other end of it, while I have some of his athletic abilities, I also have the bad knees that come after if you abuse your body.*

*And at one point in time, we had melanoma in the same year. Faith. I called him one time and I said, "Dad, you know, I've had this, and I've had this, and now I get to have another knee surgery." He laughed at me and said, "Oh, my little boy is becoming a man." "Dad, I really don't care about any of that stuff," I said.*

*Dad, your life is a roadmap of mine. I love you and you're one heck of a man.*

Dick standing near Bird Creek in Anchorage, Alaska, June 2012.

DICK HAVING A DISCUSSION WITH FATHER RYAN, PASTOR OF ST. JAMES
CATHEDRAL PARISH IN DOWNTOWN SEATTLE.

Chapter 17

# Faith and My Catholic Fiber

*Having faith was number one for Dick. It was something that ran through him; it was part of his "fiber." But Dick was the first to admit that he had to work on it. This is why he went to Mass every day. Dick's thoughts on his faith are organized under the different headings in this chapter.* —Bridget Cooley

## FAITH

I am always praying for more faith. I cannot explain it to anyone. I hope my belief in God never goes away. It is a gift to believe, but it is not logical. It does not fit inside your mind easily in a secular society. God has let me choose and let me go my own way. God witnesses terrible things, but He still loves everyone. There is no understanding of the awful things people do to each other, but I believe these things happen because the outside self becomes more important than the inside self. The outside self is what we show to others — worldly stuff, desire, power, and authority — and it becomes more important than the inside self where God resides in your soul.

## FAITH IS A GIFT

There are temptations that stand in the way of faith. Faith is a gift. You cannot buy or sell it. There is no book that can tell you how to find it. Some people do not have it, which is sad. I feel very fortunate to have faith. I have not seen anything that has shaken my faith in the church. I can distinguish between what I consider to be some of the poor behavior of the hierarchy and the good behavior of so many more. Going to Mass is the same in the general sense of the word, no matter where in the world you pray. Christ is with you everywhere.

HOW THE LOSS OF MY ARM AFFECTED ME

My desire to do good certainly came out of my accident. I have a need to thank God for keeping me going and helping me as He has my whole life. Mostly, I am appreciative of what I have been given. I want to thank the hundreds of incredible people who have contributed and helped me along the way. I have had a good life and I am comfortable. And, as I have said before, I have been very lucky. Although there are some things I have failed to do, I have been able to do some positive things along the way. Trying to become a better person is an endless task.

CONFESSION

In the old days when there were many priests, there were large churches in New York every 10 or 15 blocks. Confessions were heard every day in the morning around Mass times, and sometimes in the afternoon. If you had been naughty, you could rush down and confess right away. The idea with confession is that you promise not to do it again. In other words, you say, "I promise, God, that I've done this sin and I won't do it again." But everyone does it again. Even Jesus said that in the Scriptures when Peter asked him, "Lord, how often should I forgive my brother when he does something wrong? Seven times?" And Jesus said, "No, 70 times seven times." In other words, Christ knew that we are human and that we would make the same mistakes again, even if we did not want to.

PENANCE AND CHANGING TIMES IN THE CHURCH

Our humanity comes up and we forget our promise. So you can go to confession. Today we rarely have a confession. I hardly ever go. I want to go once in a while because early in my life it became a ritual. Today there is a scheduled time on a Saturday afternoon for a half hour at an inconvenient moment, or you can make an appointment. There are not enough priests to sit around waiting for penitents, and it does not seem to be the practice in the Catholic Church any longer.

Penance seems to have gone away, but it is still a sacrament of the Catholic Church. No one said it is not real, and no one said that God will not forgive you for your sins without it. The point is that, somehow, like a lot of things in the church, even though the rules did not change, the practice has shifted a bit. People have gone on to other ways of observing Christ's laws. It is not the same as it was. I think the current Pope is trying to bring back penance a little bit. The act of penance includes saying your own Act of Contrition then excusing yourself to God. You tell Him you are really sorry and that you will not do it again.

The last part of the Act of Contrition that we recite says, "I promise to confess my sins, to do penance, and to amend my life. Amen." The basic thing here is "amend my life." In other words, do not make a habit of committing the same sin over and over again. I'm older now. The nature of my sins has changed, as has their frequency, but I still feel the need to amend my life.

## FAITH SHOULD NOT COME FROM FEAR

It is hard for some people to understand, but the church that I grew up in dominated people by fear. You were afraid to go to hell and you wanted to go to heaven. Many of the old-world Irish priests who populated the churches in America would talk fire and brimstone. They would get up in the pulpit and say, "You can't do this! You will go to hell!" Although I believe there is lots of truth in that, the way it is presented makes a difference. If you are trying to bludgeon the faithful into good behavior, that is not good. I think it colored a lot of the things I used to do. You should do the right things because you love God and want to please Him, not because you feel the threat of eternal damnation.

## FAITH CAN HELP OVERCOME FEAR

Making the varsity football team at Yale was a personal victory over my fears. It was physical fear—being seen as cowardly, not standing up for myself. I never thought I was good enough to be a martyr. On the other hand, if you point a gun at me and say, "Christ is not good, and if you believe in him I will shoot you," then I hope I would say I believe in Christ, so shoot me. Then I am a martyr. That kind of bravery comes with great faith, and you have to believe in whatever you are doing.

## BELIEVE STRONGLY AND TAKE A STAND

Whatever you believe in, you must believe strongly enough to take a stand, or determine how much you will listen to someone before you compromise. Because when you compromise your beliefs yet still believe in a life of eternity, it is not a very good bargain. What I pray for all the time is faith. I hope I have the strength to keep my faith and it will never desert me. Faith is not this little thing we do when we go to church. It is very different, and it is deep inside you. My mother thought I had a remarkable faith. She had faith, but was not confident that she believed enough and was worried about her position before God at the end of her life. She was afraid to die, yet watching her struggle at the end, I could never think of any time she had ever displeased her God. So faith remains a gift from God, and those who have it are truly fortunate. There are Buddhists, Jews, and many other religious persons who believe in what they do. They have their faith just as much as the Christians, and for them it is just as vital.

## DOING THE RIGHT THING

While reading this memoir, you've no doubt been aware that I'm pretty big on going to church. Why? Because I find that going to church makes me think about doing the right thing. It is a big basis for my existence and, in a way, cushions everything. This is not to suggest that I am tremendously spiritual or mystical; it is not that at all. It is that I need to go every day because I need that sort of structure. I need the reminder of who I am. I need to know that there is someone up there running the show and not me.

## HUMILITY

For me, the biggest things in life are humility and love. And church is humbling. I need to understand that I am just one of seven billion people and God is keeping track of all of us. He loves you and He loves me.

## THE INFLUENCE OF THE BENEDICTINES

I learned when I went to Portsmouth Priory that the Benedictines were about work and love. You love God and you work. Benedictines work and pray and try to stay in the background. I do not like to be in the front. I can be in the front and am happy to do that when necessary, but I prefer to be behind the scenes and work hard to be sure that whatever the project, it will work out the best it can for everyone.

## HAVING A DAILY PRACTICE

Religion keeps me in balance. I used to be afraid that if I did not go to church every day, I would get out of the habit of going, and then I might never go again. Now I go every day that I can because I love God. It is an act of devotion that helps me love everyone else the right way, too. We can all benefit from that reminder every day. Going to church holds me together. It is a part of my DNA, so to speak. I am third on my prayer list. I pray that I will be humble and full of love. I pray that I will be gentle and kind, that I will be patient and understanding, and that I will be wise, even though these goals may seem to be almost unreachable. I pray that I will overcome my selfishness and pride and that I will do God's will each day.

## TITHING AND USING YOUR GIFTS TO HELP OTHERS

Age tends to make a person more thoughtful and possibly more mature, hopefully less selfish and self-centered. We all fight that. We all take care of ourselves first. I have learned in life that you have to change and adapt. When you give money away to those in need, you will not go broke. It is that little extra boost that may help someone who is having a hard time. In the last couple of decades I have tried to tithe, but I could have given away much more and not perished. How much more? It is difficult to say because at what point are you really showing your love for your fellow man? How far should you go? Spiritually, that is a big moral and ethical question, and it is a question that each one of us must answer on our own. I think about it a lot because, to me, the needs always appear to be greater than my gifts.

## GOD LOVES EVERYONE

Every single person helping would make a difference, even if the difference is inside you, because you have overcome your own selfishness. I walk by homeless men and women on the street every day. I always try to give something and not make judgments. It is not fair to judge others because how do we ever really know their plight? They want something, so I give them something because if that were Christ, I would not want to walk by Him because He died for me and helped me get along in life so I could overcome my sinfulness. He has given me direction and someplace to go, so I feel that I need to help those people somehow. We all have just as much right to be here and, as far as I'm concerned, God loves all of us and we would not be alive without His love. What might be hard to imagine is that God loves the homeless just as much as anyone else; and maybe He loves them even more than those of us who are more fortunate. He does not choose one person over another, so if that is the case, then it is our job to help those who are less fortunate and not be judgmental ourselves.

God loves everybody, so the two big commandments in my life that I try to follow are love thy God and love thy neighbor. The homeless are our neighbors, and we have to love them and do what we can for them. There is always the thought that there is nothing you can do to change their lives and maybe you can never give enough, but I don't believe that is true, so I give what I can whenever I can.

### Mentoring

I enjoy mentoring MBA students. Having one or two of them each quarter gives me a chance to keep up with what the current generation is doing and to participate modestly in their activities. Sometimes I am amazed by how they approach opportunity, and sometimes my advice, though old-fashioned, helps them get ahead.

### Wanting things

At times when I get busy and involved in the daily pressure of living, this is harder to remember. Right now I do not want anything badly: I have gotten past wanting things. I do not want to be rich. I do not want to own a Picasso. I would like to have enough money to live easily, which so far I have.

### Helping others

During my remaining years I want to help people. That gives me something to look forward to every day. I am not sure how it works, but through the church I can trust. I can feel that if I stick with the Ten Commandments and the rules of the church that are God inspired, then I will be okay. I will do what He wants because no one can do it all on their own. I have been able to feel that way all during my lifetime.

ON DEATH

When I die, I hope that God will decide the day and that it will not be unpleasant. I just hope that it will not be today, but that God will decide the right time and I can die happily with the hope that I will be going to heaven.

My faith is strong enough that I do not have doubts. That is where I am now, anyway. When you get to the end of your life, which is where I certainly am, you begin to think: When I die what is going to happen? Where will I go? Who am I going to see? What is heaven? What are the joys of heaven? What do you have at the end of your life? You have your mind, your heart, and your soul. And you have the ability to love people and the ability to help people. I do not want to be without love for all eternity. I would like to be with love, and I think that is where heaven is. Whether there is a time in between that is truly a purgatory, a time to be purified before you can enter the place of love, no one knows. It is clearly a mystery, a big one. But I have faith in my final destination.

Ecclesiastes 3: 1-8
THERE IS A TIME FOR EVERYTHING

A reading from the book of Ecclesiastes.

*There is an appointed time for everything,*
*and a time for every affair under the heavens.*
*A time to be born, and a time to die;*
*a time to plant, and a time to uproot the plant.*
*A time to kill, and a time to heal;*
*a time to tear down, and a time to build.*
*A time to weep, and a time to laugh;*
*a time to mourn, and a time to dance.*
*A time to scatter stones, and a time to gather them;*
*a time to embrace, and a time to be far from embraces.*
*A time to seek, and a time to lose;*
*a time to keep, and a time to cast away.*
*A time to rend, and a time to sew;*
*a time to be silent, and a time to speak.*
*A time to love, and a time to hate;*
*a time of war, and a time of peace.*

*The word of the Lord.*

AMONG MANY OTHER COMMON INTERESTS, DICK AND BRIDGET

SHARE A LOVE OF FLYING.

The closer I come to the end of my bell curve, the more aware I become of my dependence on other people. Ailments meet me each morning. My fingers do not work the way they once did, and my bones are sore. I am not able to control bodily functions as well. As the years stockpile, I have learned to accept help from others and be grateful for it.

Bridget and I have become closer and closer, and she worries about keeping me alive and vital. It is understandable, as there is more than 30 years' difference in our ages. It may be a hard time for her when I go, but I tell her that it will be okay. I've lost loved ones. I know God will take care of her, I tell her, as He has taken care of me. Besides, you can never tell what might happen in 16 years. I cannot handle this for her, much as I would like to, but my faith is strong, and I know God will look after her.

The other day I told her about the bell curve and that she had better be nice to me because she may have many more years to worry about me. My mother reached 98 and my dad died at 93, so maybe I will reach 100. It might not be a pretty sight, but on the other hand, my warm heart will be there to keep her happy. We have longevity in our family and I try not to worry about it, but it is in the genes. My sisters do not want to live that long. As of the summer of 2016, Ann has passed away and her twin sister, Kay, celebrates her 88nd birthday this year in November. Helen, my youngest sister, is now 84 (but I just missed calling her on her birthday). If I can just keep going and keep Bridget going the way she is, all will be fine.

It's a documented fact that people are living longer. Younger people do not understand that changes come over your body, but not over your mind. Your mind tells you that you can do almost anything, but the body wonders "how?" When people get older, their problems change. It is not about retirement anymore. If you are 65 and retired, you are not going to be able to play golf for more than another decade, or certainly not as well as you once did. One gets stiff and loses muscle tone. You cannot hit the ball as far. I found that started happening to my golf stroke when I got to be around 60.

My memory is not the same as it used to be, either. I forget things and do things like leave my wallet in the car. I have to worry about my watch, my wallet, and my glasses. Those are things I have to remember when I leave the house every day. You cannot rely on your memory. I can go down to the kitchen for something and forget what I went down there for. Forgetfulness adds to my day, so it is nice to remember and avoid some of those trips. I do not think people are planning for those things or thinking about developing systems for aging. We are all getting older, lasting longer. We all have memory problems. Everything is not as tight as it used to be. But it is okay. It is perfectly normal, but how do we help people deal with it? There is no point in getting mad or frustrated by the process of life.

As you get older you need to develop systems so you can live the same way you have always lived, and that is made easier if you find ways to ease the aging process. Sometimes people try to commiserate and say that they forget things too, and although they are trying to be nice, it does not help the people who are forgetful. For instance, I write on my calendar the things I need to do each day, and during the day I check them off. That is probably one of the reasons people retire — so there is more time to deal with this kind of thing! Because we are living longer, it is important to be positive about it.

Over the years, I've had a lot of operations. It started when I had a torn cartilage in my knee at age 16. I fell on a rock while skiing in Vermont. That year there was not enough snow and it was easy to hit something. The knee operation is most likely the reason I did not get into the Navy Air Corps during WWII. They said my knees would not hold up, but I played varsity football for two years and those knees held up fine.

The army was not as particular and it took me, bad knee and all. I had the cartilage repaired on the other knee after the war in 1953. I had fallen on a tennis court.

An arm weighs about six pounds, and the loss of it changed my balance. Many of the operations I have had in my life had something to do with the P-38 accident. There were many skin grafts. As I get older I have had melanoma and prostate cancer surgery — and nerve operations for different things, not to mention the knee and hip replacements. When I go to a medical office and have to fill out the form stating all of my operations, I write, "Too numerous to mention." I cannot remember all that stuff. It is strange because I know I have probably had lots of operations in comparison to most people, but they have all been good. After all, if I had not had them, I probably would not be here.

One of the things I want anyone who reads this book to take away is that I feel good about myself and the course my life has taken. I appreciate what I have been given. I have no complaints, and I feel good about where I am right now. There are no burning desires that need to be filled.

Eight years ago, I wrote the first version of this book, called *Searching Through My Prayer List*. I did that after some family urging and with help from writer and editor, Ann Boreson. *Searching* was my first attempt at a hardcover book recounting many of the occasions which made my life interesting and fun. As are many first efforts of this kind, different items were left out that could have added to its depth and fullness. With this new effort I am hoping to fill in some of those holes. Also, since the first book, some very extraordinary events have happened in my life.

First and most heartrending and difficult was the death of Sean, my second son. He died a year ago after fighting pancreatic cancer for 16 months. He was only 54 years old, in great shape, and did everything he could to conquer the disease. He was good and kind and an able contributor to all his family and friends.

Another event was that I turned 90 and had a large party that gave my family an opportunity to come together. I am now 92 and my aging body needs more and more care.

Eight years ago, my family-inherited arthritis was hardly visible. My body was limber, loose and able to turn on a dime to swing a tennis or squash racquet with ease. My golf swing, though only with the left arm, was smooth and productive.

But gradually the joints began to stiffen and my 200-yard drive became 100. The rhythm and the continuity disappeared along with my golf game. When your arm cannot go higher than your shoulder, your days of Saturday golf seem ended.

Although you need something to hold onto, riding a bike becomes a challenge that you avoid.

I have multiple myeloma cancer. One of the problems with this disease is that an abnormal protein, an amyloid, is made by the plasma cells in the bone marrow. The production of this protein is continuous and it infiltrates and destroys normal tissue like the heart, kidneys, and nerves. I am taking strong chemotherapy medications to try to slow down the growth of the protein. Additionally, I take daily diuretic pills to reduce the fluid that accumulates in my body due to heart failure. As a result, I have had to learn to spend lots of time in the bathroom.

As my normal activities go away, there is much more time for additional reading and other less active pursuits.

These days I have my wife, Bridget, and three extraordinary caregivers to take care of me. One caregiver is with me during the weekdays, one comes in at night and one covers weekend evenings. My own driving is cut to the bone and we have had to learn to adjust to the fact that I need a driver to get around. Our social life is minimized and so is my cocktail hour. Drinking only happens on rare (and big) occasions. My weight has gone down to 160 –163 pounds, with walking limited and slow. Bridget watches and helps with my daily shower. She helps me dress and get out of the house in time for Mass. Our wonderful caregiver takes me to church and brings me home for breakfast. After that it is either physical therapy or off to the office to keep track of my bills with Mahal (my daytime caregiver), who pays constant attention to see that nothing bad or unexpected happens to me.

I'm not wearing dress shirts to the office very often these days. It's mostly sweaters and a jacket for colder weather. I haven't bought a new suit in over twenty years. By 4 p.m., most of my energy has seeped away and it is time to head for home — and hopefully a nap. I usually do some form of spiritual reading in my bedroom chair, but shortly the eyes get heavy and dreamland beckons. If Bridget is home, we often have some of our best talks before dinner. Then she makes the dinner and washes up the dishes, while I do the drying and putting away. Unless there is a TV program we really want to see, it is up the stairs and time to read. Bridget gets me ready for bed.

During the week I put in two days of PT in an effort to maintain my strength. There are also innumerable doctor visits to keep track of my medical numbers. As mentioned before, walking is not my cup of tea, even though my doctor thinks it would be good for me. Having lunch with old or new friends is a big plus, which does not happen often enough. Lunch is usually a good time to catch up on my reading. Dinner with friends is also fun and something Bridget and I both would like to do more often.

While running Wells Fargo there was constant travel; it was almost too much. Yet having settled down in Seattle, I began to miss it, though the treatment for my amyloid protein makes going out of town difficult. Bridget is not too keen on the idea, considering all the things that go with taking care of me during travel. Having been retired since 1990, the expense of personal trips has become more of a consideration. Like my father, everything I earned was from salary and a healthy retirement program, which does not survive the end of my life. It is important for me to save and be sure that there will be ample funds to keep Bridget going after I am gone. I have resigned from several clubs and found other ways to keep the cash flow under control.

When you are in your 90s the simpler life can be quite appealing. Pulling back into your family makes considerable sense and can be personally quite rewarding. Spending more time at home turns out to be a plus and not a problem.

While Bridget continues to fly and work at improving her skills, I have had to let my flying go, as it would be difficult (if not impossible) to pass the physical right now.

It is like golf. I really miss it but it is not in the cards at the moment. Instead, I take pleasure in seeing that Bridget is doing well with her golf swing and is beginning to learn how to fly a jet.

That gives me a lot of excitement and much to think about.

Physical therapy helps in many ways but does not seem to increase my energy and stamina. On most days I feel tired and out of energy much of the time. You cannot help wondering how many years (or months) lie ahead. Too much of that kind of ruminating is not uplifting and makes a positive attitude hard to hold. People I see comment on how well I look, but I find it hard to believe.

Sleeping through the night does not happen often and I wish it did; I need more sleep. Lying in bed tossing around early in the morning has never been much fun, particularly when there seems to be so much uncertainty ahead. Trusting in God and relying on my faith has always been my way of coping. I think about Him a lot and I know He loves me and everyone else. But when you are approaching the end of the line, you need a lot of help. Your faith is there to protect you and so is your God. It is the time you give yourself totally to Him and trust it will all work out. That is the best and only thing you can and should do, but it is not easy. Our Pope is asking for our prayers and I am asking for his.

The amyloid protein problem is unrelenting and to date has no clear cure. Slowing down its growth is the present way of trying to deal with it. There are approved chemotherapies that I take at the start of each month. Depending on how they work, my heart will continue until the load becomes too heavy.

Each case is different, making it hard to know exactly where you are on the longevity scale. In my mind it is normal to try to prepare for one's trip to the next world, but it is not easy. After four months of trying to get a handle on what lay ahead, I visited with my four principal doctors. The prostate specialist told me the cancer was under control and that I would not die from it. She then told me that at the age of 92, I could die at any time and should have my life organized to cope with the eventuality because I was clearly at risk. Going to sleep at night and passing on was possible at any time. It was not predictable and Bridget and I should have our affairs in order while still thinking clearly and not under stress. That was a lot to think about.

The heart specialist thought I was doing quite well and that nothing disastrous seemed indicated. He wanted to see me again in three months.

My regular doctor and kidney specialist told me that all my numbers were good and that she was sure I could count on three more years of life and possibly more. All of this was a lot to absorb for me and for Bridget. The amyloid specialist told me that, as of November 2015, the protein blood numbers showed a slight improvement but he had no comment on the future trend. Sticking with my God and leaving it up to Him remains the only answer and that I will try to do. It still leaves much for Bridget and me to think about.

Recently, I have had to confront the fact that being an amputee means you have no "spare" to work with and when the remaining arm goes, you are really in trouble. Due to an ongoing issue with carpel tunnel and being weak from a recent infection, my reliable left arm is no longer working, and I now need help with everything that requires a hand or an arm. To support me and Bridget, I now have 24/7 care, and a man has been added to my care staff to help lift me. The other night, I was so weak that I needed constant help through the night and Bridget only got an hour of sleep. My doctor called for immediate tests to see if I'd had a stroke. I spent a whole day getting tests and scans. All of those showed that I am fine. The only issue they came up with was that I have a hardened artery. Happy with these results for now, I requested ice cream and got a double scoop with the crew — Bridget and my caregivers. Mahal, one of my caregivers, helped me turn my cone so that I could enjoy it and not spill too much on myself. That's life right now for me. And there doesn't seem to be any quick fix around the corner. The surgeon who performed my recent carpel tunnel surgery on my left lower arm says that it will take six to 12 months for my arm to get better. It's all a little scary. The stress of the unknown builds up more than I know sometimes.

But as long as I continue to have medical appointments every three months or so, I feel encouraged. Nevertheless, all of these events have shown that significant preparation is needed for when I am not here. Bridget and I have talked out many details that we had so far evaded. We have seen our financial advisors, our key medical persons, and our attorney. We have a start on setting up a meeting with members of my immediate family to discuss the intimate details of what they all feel about my passing on to the next world. At the end of his life, Sean had a meeting like that which was considered very helpful to all who came.

II Corinthians 9: 6-9
GOD LOVES A CHEERFUL GIVER

A reading from the second letter of Saint Paul
to the Corinthians.

*Consider this, brothers and sisters:*
*whoever sows sparingly will also reap sparingly,*
*and whoever sows bountifully*
*will also reap bountifully.*

*Each must do as already determined,*
*without sadness or compulsion,*
*for God loves a cheerful giver.*

*Moreover, God is able to make every grace*
*abundant for you,*
*so that in all things, always having all you need,*
*you may have an abundance for every good work.*

*As it is written: "He scatters abroad,*
*he gives to the poor;*
*his righteousness endures forever."*

*The word of the Lord.*

Dick in the cockpit of his Beechcraft Bonanza.

# Desire and the Unknown

*My LORD GOD, I have no idea where I am going. I do not see the road ahead of me. I cannot know for certain where it will end. Nor do I really know myself, and the fact that I think that I am following your will does not mean that I am actually doing so. But I believe that the desire to please you does in fact please you. And I hope I have that desire in all that I am doing. I hope that I will never do anything apart from that desire. And I know that if I do this you will lead me by the right road though I may know nothing about it. Therefore will I trust you always though I may seem to be lost and in the shadow of death. I will not fear, for you are ever with me, and you will never leave me to face my perils alone.*

Thomas Merton
*Thoughts in Solitude*

I have this desire to do good. It certainly came out of my accident. A need to thank God for keeping me going and helping me as much as He has my whole life. I want to do good, and in that exists a concern about things I have not done or that I could have done but didn't, because I was afraid to make a mistake or would look different from my contemporaries. I am not talking at all about my strengths or my weaknesses. I am concerned about that, but I have to be honest: I am who I am.

The stories that make up this memoir reveal the events that have shaped my life as a person, a husband, a father, a banker, and an educator. Its purpose is to describe and honor the people who have been seminal to my life so that my family and friends might better understand my driving forces. Writing it has also provided me with a perspective I might not have achieved without the soul-searching that an honest autobiography demands.

The relationship to my God and my church has been paramount, and from my earliest years until now in my early 90s, this has been a constant as well as the foundation for my actions, hopes, and prayers.

When I started this memoir project in 2008, it was not totally clear to me why we were doing it. Bridget wanted me to write about many of the happenings and events that had taken place in my life, because she thought the thread of my faith followed me clearly in almost everything I have done or that happened to me over the years. That fact was important to her in deciding to marry me. She also thought the story would be interesting to many people. The first edition of my story, *Searching Through My Prayer List*, came out in 2010. In the summer of 2015, I decided to update that book because I had more to say and more had happened to me. This book, *Level Best*, is the result of this second effort to tell my life story.

A few months ago, Father Ryan at St. James Cathedral in Seattle preached a fine homily on what Saint Paul said about average Catholics and Christians. Saint Paul believed that all the faithful should be missionaries, not just highly motivated saints and heroic, well-known missionaries in difficult parts of the world. Every one of us has the duty to share the good news of Christ's life and teaching. All of us can become true missionaries in our own backyards, without having to travel to the deepest part of Africa or Asia. As I thought about that homily, it began to dawn on me that this memoir might give me an opportunity to share some of my beliefs about my faith that could help some people understand what Christianity is about, and by example, how it has affected my life. If I did that, maybe Saint Paul might think I was doing my part, however small it may be.

If you have come this far with me, I hope that you think this is true, and I hope that you have enjoyed the ride. I also hope that some of the lessons I have learned will be helpful to you as you pursue your own future. As we have gone along, that hope has been one of the main drivers to complete this project.

Another driver has been my need to tell you about my faith and what it means to me. As a matter of principle, it is important to stand up for what you believe and share it with your family and friends. If it helps your life in even the smallest way, then the effort and time were more than worth the price. Thank you for sharing my life experiences with me. The opportunity to think about them and put them down on paper has been interesting and personally rewarding.

# My Prayer List

My prayer list started many years ago. It's hard to remember exactly when it began or what prompted its creation, but this list has become an integral part of who I am. My closest recollection is that I started it after I got married and had a family, and long after I lost my arm. I was always frantic — trying to make ends meet; get along with my wife, Sheila; take care of the kids; deal with all the expectations and disappointments of life; and still do things that I wanted to do. I was working hard but did not yet have any specific goal besides doing well. I was very involved in the business of banking and trying to be a good person, so I would be surprised if the prayer list started before I was 40.

So from the time I was in my forties, I have recited my prayer list regularly like a mantra. Each name on it represents a time in my life. The list links together those who have given me love, friendship, opportunity, and understanding, as well as those who have asked that I pray for them in their time of need.

The names on my list extend back into my early childhood and adulthood. For example, the lifelong friends I made a Portsmouth Priory (Peter Flanigan, Jerry Dwyer, and Gordon McShane). My mother, Helen Cooley, was Peter's mother's godmother. Peter's mom was not Catholic by birth, but Peter's dad was, and their four children were raised in the Church. Mrs. Flanigan remained independent until the day she decided to become a Catholic. That's when my mother became her godmother and, like Peter, these two mothers have a prominent place on my prayer list.

At Yale, my Catholic roommate was Jim Buckley. My deep regard for him has lasted and grown through the years as our paths have continued to cross with his marriage to my sister, Ann.

After she was involved in a serious automobile accident and Jim's subsequent exceptional care of her during her recovery, he earned a top place of honor on my prayer list.

Over the years, I've been named the godfather to many children of my friends. But I'm a bad godfather because I've forgotten who they all are, other than they are children of the Phlegers, the Millers, the Kilduffs, the Willoughbys, and others. I became a godfather because a lot of people we knew were Catholic but did not move in Catholic circles. In a sense, I became a link to the church. There were not that many people they could ask to be a Catholic godfather for their children. I think this is one way I got to have so many, because some of the families I became involved with as a godfather were not that close. I understand the situation; we had the same problem when looking for godfathers for some of our children. If a person wasn't Catholic, he or she couldn't be a godparent. I pray for my godchildren each day. I pray that they know God and love God and that God gives them the gift of faith and blesses them in their lives.

I think about all the people who have been wonderful to me, the people I care about, those who have been instrumental in so many important incidents that have happened to me, and I want you to know them, too. There are also those who made a fantastic impression on me; it may have been one time only, but the effect on my life was huge. I have found it impossible to add each one of these people to my prayer list because there are so many to whom I owe a debt of gratitude.

Each day I pray in bits and pieces, often while I am in the car. Lately it is becoming increasingly hard to recite the list, not because I have any less affection for those who have made my life rich, but because the list is long and covers so many years. Along with the regular list, there are others I pray for spontaneously on special occasions. I do not want to miss anyone, but each day I ask God to please cover the ones I may have forgotten.

I am always adding to my prayer list because either I meet someone I want to pray for, someone asks me to pray for them, or they know someone who is in need. I don't know why people ask me to pray. Maybe it's just because they know that I do.

I suppose praying is a little like giving alms. It is important to not blow a trumpet so that everyone knows your good deeds. Pray quietly and your heavenly father will see and reward you later on. You should be humble and full of love. I have always been sort of a secret Catholic. I have never promoted or paraded my faith around and have generally lived in a non-Catholic social world. I think some people who know me and my faith might hold me to a higher standard of responsibility. My faith certainly holds me to a higher standard. I know that if I do something wrong, I will disappoint those for whom I may have been a force for good. Everyone is affected by what you do, so you have a responsibility to do the right thing and serve as a good example to others. You never know how many people are depending on you. There is good in everyone. Sometimes you have to dig a little deeper to find it, but it is there.

So here is my prayer list. If you look at these names and you see why each person is on the prayer list, you will get another viewpoint about the things that have happened to me in these 92 years of life. Bridget is first because she is my wife, my love, and the person who is so incredibly important to me in what I am doing each day.

Dick standing behind his sisters in Sun Valley. Shown from left are
Kay, Ann, and Helen.

## FAMILY

### Bridget McIntyre Cooley

We were married in July 2003. Bridget is important to me and important in my whole life, whether in this world or the next. I will be forever grateful to her. I have learned so much from Bridget that it would take another book to describe all the ways in which our relationship has prospered and been fully rewarding. It was she to whom the first version of this book, *Searching Through My Prayer List,* is dedicated because she encouraged me to write down my experiences. She is the saint who keeps me alive.

### My unnamed savior

This is the man who saved my life after my P-38 crash in 1944. I pray for this man and I hope that his kindness has been repaid many times over. I just wish I had been able to thank him in person.

### Richard P. Cooley

Husband, father, retired bank chief executive officer, and teacher. I pray that I will be humble and full of love. I pray that I will be gentle and kind. That I will be patient and understanding and that I will be wise. I hope that I will overcome my selfishness and my pride. I pray that I will do God's will each day.

### Sheila McDonnell Collins

My first wife and the mother of my children. We enjoyed travel and golf. After we parted company, she went on to become the first woman granted membership at Cypress Point. On that course she made two holes in one, and they were both on the same hole, number 15. She was a very good athlete.

After 20 years of marriage, Sheila and I went in different directions. I became head of the Wells Fargo Bank and was busy with that. During our marriage, I found it hard to meet expectations both at home and at work. The combination of the two things was very difficult. When it got to be too much, or when I thought it was too much, I decided to leave the marriage. It was not a good decision for our family. I should not have forced this divorce. Sheila died in 2008. I never had the opportunity to tell her how, in retrospect, I felt about our marriage and that for all those intervening years she has been a part of my prayers. I pray for Sheila every day, hoping that she has found peace in heaven.

## My Children

I pray for my five children and Mary Alice's six children. Mary Alice's children have lost their fathers, and with her passing, they have lost their mother. While I am not able to see them all the time, I consider them to be my children. I want to be the best stepfather I can be. Three of her children live in Los Angeles, one in San Francisco, one in Alabama, and one in Seattle.

## Leslie Cooley

My oldest daughter and a college professor. Leslie thrived while growing up. She was born with a quick wit and has become quite successful. She began college at Scripps, and later graduated from Stanford with a degree in psychology, after which she became a counselor for the Davis School District in California. She continued her education, and a decade later she received her Ph.D. Along the way she married her college boyfriend, but the union failed. Her education and life experience led her to an unconventional relationship, and she announced that her choice as a life partner would be Kristine Jensen. Kristine has fit well into our family. Leslie joined the faculty of Sacramento State University and earned tenure before she turned 45.

## Miles Cooley

My grandson and Leslie's son, an attorney. While in Davis, California, Leslie in her work met Miles, a young African-American boy for whom she cared a great deal. She became deeply involved in his troubled life, and when he turned 18 she adopted him. He is my oldest grandchild and is an outstanding young man who is now a litigation partner in a Los Angeles law firm.

## Kristine Jensen

Leslie Cooley's life partner, an experienced psychologist who specialized in difficult, complicated cases.

## Richard Pierce Cooley Jr.

My firstborn son, who is a natural athlete and who also has incredible mechanical skills. His first marriage was to Laurie who was from Woodland, California. They had two children, Richard Pierce Cooley II and Ann Cooley. At an early point in his life, Pierce had trouble with alcohol. I tried to get him to go into a treatment home, but this did not work the first and second times. The third time, he decided to do it on his own and went to a treatment facility in Sun Valley, stayed the course, and came out clean. He joined AA and for the next 15 years did not have a drink.

I was always proud of him for that accomplishment. He is now married to Christie Lane. She is smart, quiet, easygoing, and she really loves him. One never knows if he is actually going to stick with it, but I think that his wife would get in touch with me if help is needed. This is an answer to a lot of prayers.

LAURIE TENHUNFELD COOLEY
Pierce's first wife and the mother of Pierce III and Ann

RICHARD PIERCE COOLEY III
My grandson, Pierce and Laurie's son

ANNE COOLEY
My granddaughter, Pierce and Laurie's daughter

CHRISTIE LANE COOLEY
Pierce's wife

SHEILA COOLEY
My second daughter, family law attorney. She is capable and thoughtful, and she has made a fine resume of her life — and done it all on her own. Her legal practice includes wills, family law, guardianships and such, and she does a large amount of pro bono work.

Sheila has a full life with her family and her law practice. My father would say to me, "That Sheila, she's a great piece of work." She loves her husband, Mark Gagan, and their three children, and that is what it is all about for her.

MARK FAGAN
Sheila's husband and a Brown Medical School researcher, instructor, and administrator

KATHERINE FAGAN
Sheila and Mark's oldest daughter

DYLAN FAGAN
Sheila and Mark's son

CHARLOTTE FAGAN
Sheila and Mark's youngest daughter

SEAN COOLEY

Fourth child for Sheila and me and a commercial real estate businessman. People liked him, they trusted him, and he was smart. His first marriage did not work out, but he and his first wife, Brenda, did have two children, Bridget and Sean Jr. Sometime later, Sean met Jean Kayser and they were married in Sun Valley. Jean graduated from the Wharton Business School, but decided that she wanted to be a doctor rather than a businesswoman. She went back to school and eight years later became an obstetrician/gynecologist and went to work at the Kaiser Foundation in Oakland, California.

As a couple they liked to travel, play golf, and ski and were totally attentive to Sean's children, spending much time with them. Sadly, Sean passed away in April 2015. This memoir is dedicated to him.

BRENDA PAYNE COOLEY

Mother of my grandchildren, Bridget and Sean Jr.

BRIDGET COOLEY

My granddaughter and Sean's daughter

SEAN COOLEY JR.

My grandson and Sean's firstborn son

JEAN KAYSER

Sean's second wife, obstetrician/gynecologist at the Kaiser Foundation in Walnut Creek, California

MARK COOLEY

My youngest son. He has become the family entrepreneur. Undeterred after a failed attempt to start a smoothie business, he and two friends bought an organic foods company in South San Francisco. He learned a lot in his first business venture, but learned again that you have to have sufficient capital to sustain a business. Mark and his partners have built the business to a small profit and are hoping for further increases. Whatever Mark does he does well, and with no children so far, he has turned into an exceptional support person and caregiver in our family.

## Joan D'Ambrosio

Mark's wife and an attorney. Mark married Joan D'Ambrosio, a smart woman he had known since high school. While he was slugging it out in the food business, she went through law school, joined a San Francisco law firm, and became a full partner there before she was 40. She and Mark have good common sense. They work hard and travel extensively.

## Mary Alice Clark Cooley

We were married from 1983 until her death in 1999. While we did not live together before she moved to Seattle in 1983, we saw a lot of each other, and it was an experience not to be equaled. When I pray for Mary Alice, I pray that she will be full of love and close to God in heaven. She was an extraordinary mom and a wonderful wife. She contributed to everyone she ever met in her life.

Mary Alice was widowed three times. Four of her six children (Karin, Susan, Michael, and Jim) were the product of her first marriage. Anne-Marie and Bruce were the children of her second marriage, to Bruce Cordingly.

## Karin Costa

Mary Alice's oldest daughter, an animal lover and sales manager. Karin was married to a Hollywood stuntman and was in the midst of a divorce when I met her. At the time, she was working in the movie business as the personal assistant to the well-known director John Carpenter. Then she worked for eight years for Weight Watchers and managed the Southern California sales district for three years. She loves dogs, horses, and people. She is fun and interesting, and everyone likes her a lot.

## Susan Janneck

Mary Alice's second-oldest daughter, a travel agent. Susan was married to John Janneck, an accountant and investor. They lived in the Hollywood Hills a few miles from Mary Alice. Susan worked as a travel agent at a company in Brentwood. I am always amazed and inspired that she has stuck with it and done so well in such a vast and changing industry. Her marriage to John did not last, but she has a nice home in the San Fernando Valley and an incredible son who is working as an investment banker in Southern California. He is handsome and smart, a tremendous golfer, and someone she can be enormously proud of.

MICHAEL BURNAP

Mary Alice's oldest son, banker. Michael worked on an oil rig in Southeast Asia. He had gone to Taiwan during his third year of college and married a Taiwanese woman. After a year working out of Singapore, he came back to California and graduated from the business school at the University of Southern California. For a time he worked for Seafirst but left the bank when it was sold. He and his first wife were divorced and he married a Japanese woman, Irene Tanabe, who did pro bono legal work and eventually decided to become an Episcopal minister. She has a small parish in Hawaii and Michael works for a bank that is owned and operated by people in Birmingham, Alabama. They manage to keep their marriage going over this distance. Michael is smart, great fun, and a person you can count on. I enjoy his company immensely. He has two fine children.

JIM BURNAP

Mary Alice's son, a commercial real estate businessman. Jim was living with Mary Alice in Beverly Hills, and as she prepared to move to Seattle, he moved out to a local apartment. He was seeing a friend, Sarah, from the University of the Pacific in Stockton, and two years later they were married. Sarah is a smart, capable woman who is in media sales. They have two sons who are growing up to be quite the young gentlemen and people with good futures ahead of them.

ANNE-MARIE CORDINGLY

Mary Alice's youngest daughter, a teacher. With her second husband, Bruce Cordingly, Mary Alice had two children, Anne-Marie and Bruce. Anne-Marie lives in San Francisco. She was a teacher at the Town School for Boys for a time and taught Latin to fourth and sixth graders. She is a gifted athlete. How she gets done everything she does amazes me. When you see pictures of her, she is the mirror image of her mother at the same age. She is a delight and someone who is cherished and respected by all.

BRUCE CORDINGLY

Mary Alice's youngest son, a writer and documentary film producer. Bruce was going into the 10th grade and at the last minute was accepted at Lakeside School in Seattle, which turned out to be fortuitous. Since we had no close relatives or friends in the area, the three of us became a small nuclear family for a time. Through our business connections, Mary Alice and I began to get acquainted around the town, but it was harder for Bruce.

School started in September and he did not know one person at Lakeside. His first personal phone call to do something outside school came the following March. He turned out for Lakeside's football team and also played racquetball. However slow the start, 20 years later the closest friends he has are those he met at Lakeside.

Bruce writes and produces television documentaries. He has been through a lot of school and done many things. He did publicity work for a Japanese trading company, and through his many business dealings, has still managed to keep in touch with the whole family, particularly Sheila. He has found a wonderful young woman who wanted to move back to Seattle, where her family lives. They were married in 2009 and had their first child, Eliot, in 2010.

### HENRY AND HELEN CLARK

Henry was a self-made man, GM executive, and Mary Alice's father. I never met Helen, but I did know Henry. He had to go to work when he was 14 or 15 to support his family, which he was able to do. He had a long career at General Motors and ended up running their big Los Angeles plant. For a long time he worked in Detroit as the assistant to the chairman. He was a remarkable man. He did not have a lot of schooling, but he taught himself through reading and hard work. He was conservative with his money. He was not a born Catholic, but converted, and eventually became well known to the Cardinal in Los Angeles. He was a Knight of Malta and an erudite, bright man. Henry loved Mary Alice. She was his little girl, and he took great care of her.

### HENRY FORD II

Sheila's sister's husband, our brother-in-law. He was tremendously pressured, and sometimes criticized for his lifestyle, but I always thought he was terrific and appreciated his giving ways, spirit, and kindness to all of us. Praying for him every day is the biggest thank you I can give him, and I will never stop. Also, I always buy Ford cars, and that is something I will always continue to do.

### JUDY CHASE LUDWIG

My second wife and mother to Jessica and Coco. Judy's first husband had worked for Saks, and through him Judy was well acquainted with all the names in the fashion industry. She was interested in colors and decorations and knew clearly the kind of home she wished to have. As a family group we seemed to get along fine. There was no friction like in my first marriage, but I was unhappy. Judy tried hard to make the marriage work. She was a good person and a good wife. The problems were in my head. Even though our marriage did not last, I pray daily for the two girls as well as Judy.

DICK COLLINS
Sheila's second husband, an equestrian. My two youngest boys went with Sheila to Pebble Beach and lived there with Dick as their stepfather. He taught them about horses, polo, and work. In fact, they both became accomplished polo players. Sean became the captain of the University of California Davis polo team that won the national championship four years in a row. Mark also played on the team but not as long as Sean.

JAMES MCDONNELL, SHEILA'S FATHER, a stockbroker
MRS. MURRAY MCDONNELL, Sheila's mother and the family organizer
CHARLOTTE MCDONNELL, Sheila's older sister, the fourth of the McDonnell children
BASIL HARRIS, Father of Basil Jr. and Dick
MARY HARRIS, Mother of Basil Jr. and Dick, and my unofficial godmother
BASIL HARRIS JR., Childhood friend in Rye, New York
DICK HARRIS, Basil's brother and later Sheila's brother-in-law

MURRAY MCDONNELL
Sheila's older brother, a stockbroker, and the father of Peggy Vance. Murray McDonnell was Sheila McDonnell Collins's older brother. He was fifth in line of the 14 McDonnells. Murray was the one who took over the family brokerage, had trouble with it, and eventually lost it. He married Peter Flanigan's only sister, Peggy, and they had nine children together.

GEORGE AND HELEN COOLEY
Uncle George was my father's youngest brother
HAROLD AND HELEN PIERCE
Uncle Harold was my mother's younger brother.

I pray for these uncles and aunts for no particular reason other than I liked them and I think someone should be praying for them.

JIM AND ANN COOLEY BUCKLEY

Ann was my sister and one of the twins. She was the wife of Jim Buckley, my old roommate at Yale. They lived in Sharon, Connecticut. Each day I pray for my family, and that includes my three sisters, but especially I pray for Annie and Jim. After Annie had an automobile accident that resulted in her being paralyzed, their whole world was turned upside down. Annie endured her situation with incredible courage and grace, setting a fine example of how one accepts God's will. Jim handled it like a saint and a star. They got along as well as anyone could under those circumstances. They were always dear to my heart. Annie passed away several years ago. Jim still lives in Sharon.

JIM PIERCE

My oldest cousin from my mother's side of the family and the son of my mother's oldest brother. Jim's brother, Jack, and I hung out together when my parents I and took summer trips to California. Jim, who was eight years older than I, was a good man who took care of everyone, particularly my mother. I pray for Jim as sort of a catchall because I have so many family and friends who have died over the years. There are so many gone that I cannot name them all, so I have this category in which I pray for cousin Jim and all close family and friends who have died.

JIM COOLEY

Uncle George Cooley's only son. Uncle George Cooley was my father's youngest brother. Jim is his only son. I pray for them daily. Jim is one of my two first cousins who are still living. I see him occasionally and we correspond. He has kept in touch with my sisters and is a good man. He did not go into business like his father but worked in the post office his whole life. He is comfortable, he travels a great deal, has a partner, and I don't know much more about his life than that.

HELEN PIERCE COOLEY, my mother
VICTOR E. COOLEY, my father

STEPHANIE CHASE MCCALL

Stephanie is the younger sister of Judy Chase Ludwig, my second wife. She is a fine lady and has two children. Her husband used to work in the bank. He's from Rhode Island and is independently wealthy. They live in San Francisco.

HELEN COOLEY REILLY

Helen Reilly is my youngest sister. Her husband, Miles, was a wonderful man who has passed away. She told me not too long ago that she is coming out of the grieving period. I told her to allow herself at least three years, and she's just about there. She seems to be holding up well. She has women friends and I think they have been a big support to her. She just came back from a trip to Peru to see the sights of Machu Picchu, and she is beginning to do a lot of things she did before. She was overwhelmed by the situation for a long time. It's nice to see her coming back and getting on her feet again. She is an active woman, a contributor to the community in many ways, and she has a full and meaningful life. The fact that her daughter, Megan, lives relatively close in North Carolina is a boon to her. She has two grandchildren, and I think Helen makes them a big part of her life. Megan and her husband, Steve, have been very helpful to her, enormously caring and supportive.

MEGAN AND STEVE BUSER, Helen Cooley Reilly's youngest daughter and my niece. Steve is Megan's husband.

KAY COOLEY

My sister, Kay, lives in New Jersey in a Quaker residence home. She has her own apartment and is very much involved in the activities that go on at that center. The place is called Medford Leas. She started something that she calls the Medford Leas University where she invites different speakers to talk to the residents from the various colleges in the area. It has been successful and she has done it all on her own. She is constantly planning and trying to figure out who she can get to come speak and how to keep people interested. She holds the position of secretary to the board of directors who run the place. She has a full life although at times she can be lonesome, but she has managed to keep herself active, which is wonderful when you consider that she spent many years in quite a different life, as a nun.

MY GODCHILDREN

I'm a bad godfather because I've forgotten who they all are. I know that one of them is Peter Phleger and one is Doug Miller, one is a Kilduff and one is a Willoughby, but I can't come up with all six. I pray for them as a group each day. I pray that they know God and love God and that God gives them the gift of faith and blesses them in their lives.

## CAREER FRIENDS AND ASSOCIATES

RANSOM COOK, My boss, mentor, and predecessor at Wells Fargo
STEPHEN CHASE, Former chairman of Wells Fargo
MARY CHASE, Stephen's wife

### ERNIE AND KITTY ARBUCKLE

Ernie was my friend, adviser, and also the chairman of Wells Fargo from 1968 to 1977. He stuck to his retirement principles and retired from the bank at the age of 65.

### ROBERT WATT MILLER

Director of Wells Fargo and head of the San Francisco Opera. Bob ran the San Francisco Opera for 40 years and was known as a very distinguished gentleman in the Bay Area. His father had been chairman of the American Trust Company. He was an influential member of the bank's board. What sticks in my mind about him was that for all his aura and dignity and elevated standing, when you talked with him one-on-one he was warm and down to earth. Bob had four children. I knew them all, liked them all, but I was particularly close to his youngest son, Dick Miller.

### LUKE AND GAIL HELMS

Luke was the Seafirst chief executive following my retirement. He was at Seafirst when I came to Seattle in 1983 and was one of the top managers, running all the national business. He is a personable, smart man. I tried to hire him once at Wells Fargo in Beverly Hills, but it did not work out for him or us. However, when I came to Seattle, he was a friend and someone I respected. Luke is very creative.

I was chairman of the executive committee of Seafirst for a few years after Luke took over as chairman and CEO. He did a good job of running the bank. In fact, he did such a good job that Dick Rosenberg took him down to San Francisco to do media and marketing for Bank of America Corporation. After a year or two he resigned and went out on his own. In Seattle, Luke was well regarded and known by all in the Seafirst Corporation and in the community.

Luke is into new ideas and thoughts. I pray for Luke and his family — his wife, Gail, and their three boys — who were close to us and important to my time in Seattle.

## SEAFIRST BANK

There are three banks I pray for. Seafirst is the first, and next on my list is the Bank of America Corporation and the people I worked with there — Dick Rosenberg, Sam Armacost, and all the people who took us over when Seafirst was going broke in 1983. Bank of America bought the stock of Seafirst and saved us from bankruptcy, then gave us time and the capital to get back on our feet, which we did. We became an outstanding investment for the Bank of America Corporation, one that was important to their survival when they had their difficulties in the mid to late 1980s.

## BANK OF AMERICA

Sam Armacost was in charge of Bank of America Corporation when it bought Seafirst. When Bank of America had its troubles, Sam lost his job and the directors brought back Tom Clausen. He stayed there for five years. He had already retired from the World Bank when he made the decision to return to run Bank of America. In the meantime, I hired Dick Rosenberg to come up and take my place when he was working for the Crocker Bank in San Francisco as the number-two person. He wanted to run his own bank and I told him that if he came to Seattle he could run Seafirst, but he did not stay long enough to do that. He was in Seattle for about a year and a half. He was so impressive that Tom Clausen could not leave him in Seattle. He went to San Francisco to take over the top second or third job at Bank of America then succeeded Clausen when he retired for the second time.

I pray for DICK ROSENBERG, former chairman and chief executive officer of Bank of America; SAM ARMACOST, Bank of America chairman who in 1983 agreed to purchase Seafirst; and TOM CLAUSEN, Bank of America chief following Sam Armacost.

## CARL REICHARDT

Wells Fargo chief following my retirement in 1982. As well as Carl Reichardt, I pray for all the Wells Fargo people I worked with from 1949 through 1982. That was my primary career. Ernie Arbuckle and I hired Carl from the Union Bank in Los Angeles. We brought him to Wells Fargo to run one of our holding company subsidiaries. He did such a good job, there was no question that he was the person to take over for me when I retired. He brought in some very good people and he brought a wonderful sense of how to make money for Wells Fargo. Carl was an outstanding banker and an excellent credit man and someone who was bound to be successful. We were lucky to have him.

## WELLS FARGO BANK

The third bank I pray for. I always thought of myself as a Wells Fargo person. That has changed now because I have been in Seattle almost as long as I was in San Francisco. Wells has since been sold to a company in Minneapolis. When that sale occurred, the Minneapolis people, as part of the arrangement, moved their headquarters to San Francisco and took over the management of the bank while retaining the name Wells Fargo.

## MIGUEL DE LA MADRID

Former president of Mexico. Miguel de la Madrid was the president of Mexico for six years. I got to know him through Wells Fargo when he was head of the credit department of the Mexican national bank. I liked him and we got along well. After he was president I didn't see him very often, but he was someone I wanted to pray for.

## UAL, INC.

I pray for Harry and Judy Mullikin and Eddie Carlson and the United Airlines people I worked with. When I went on the board of United Airlines in the early 1970s, there was a fracture in the management and the existing CEO was asked to resign. Eddie Carlson was running Western Hotels at the time and was asked to come in and take over the chairman and CEO position of UAL, Inc. and United Airlines. UAL, Inc. was the holding company, and it had purchased Western Hotels the previous year.

When Eddie went to Chicago to take over United, Lynn Himmelman stepped up to be chairman and chief executive of Western Hotels. He kept the job until he retired and was replaced by Harry Mullikin, who was also put on the UAL and United boards. Eddie was my sponsor when I first came to Seattle. Lynn Himmelman helped a great deal as well, but I was closer to Eddie. I began praying for him and then I combined it with Harry and Judy because they were a big part of my life when I moved to Seattle. Harry Mullikin was the head of the search committee for Seafirst in 1982 and was the person I negotiated with to get the job of running Seafirst in 1983.

HARRY MULLIKIN, Board member at UAL and Seafirst
JUDY MULLIKIN, Harry's wife and close friend to Mary Alice
EDDIE CARLSON, UAL chairman and friend
LYNN HIMMELMAN, UAL director and chairman of Westin

CALTECH
I pray for the Caltech people I worked with to help maintain the institute's vision, research, and leadership. I was on that board for more than 30 years.

KAISER FAMILY FOUNDATION, Its purpose and contributions
to humanity
RAND CORPORATION, Its work for America and its leaders
DON RICE, Chief executive officer of RAND for 17 years
JIM THOMPSON, Chief executive officer of RAND following Don Rice

SEATTLE SYMPHONY ORCHESTRA
For its contribution to my city. When I came to Seattle after leaving Los Angeles in 1983, I was president of the Los Angeles Philharmonic board. After I was in Seattle for a while I was asked to join the SSO board, which I was happy to do, but I did not want to be active in the management or take on any large fund-raising job. I had to get the bank under control and get through the United Way campaign. After that I did spend more time with the symphony and ultimately became president. I joined it with a man named Sam Strom, who was one of my big supporters and directors at the bank. He was chairman and I was president of the symphony for two or three years. He got slightly ill and tired of it, so I became chairman of the symphony board. I did that for a couple more years, until it got to be too much and I found a replacement, which turned out to be an unhappy choice. I left under conditions that were not absolutely wonderful, but the symphony has been doing much better lately. They almost went under once or twice, but mostly through Sam's efforts, it came together. We have a new hall thanks to Jack Benaroya, who was never on the board but gave a really large contribution to the symphony's hall, which now bears his name and that of his wife, Becky.

SAM STROM, Seafirst board member and Seattle Symphony
Orchestra chairman

SEATTLE ART MUSEUM
A cultural gift to Seattle, the Seattle Art Museum came to me shortly after I moved here in the mid-1980s. I told them I did not want to be on the board. I had been on the Los Angeles County Museum board, and I did not want to take that on in Seattle because I did not think I would have enough time.

However, a friend of mine and some other people said that the museum did not have much business participation and they wanted me to join. Along with three other business contemporaries in town, I joined. I went to the meetings and, although I did not participate as much, they soon had me running the operations committee. From then on, it was not too long before they asked me to be chairman of the board of the museum, which I did for a couple of years.

I was chairman of the board when Mary Alice died, and if I had not had that organization to worry about and deal with, life would have been much harder. It gave me something to do when my life was bereft and empty. I have maintained my connection with the museum ever since in sort of a senior advisory capacity. In my opinion, it is the best nonprofit board in Seattle. In addition to the downtown museum, there is an Asian Art Museum. Part of the recent expansion was to build a sculpture park near Elliott Bay, which has proved to be an enormous boon to the city. Situated on a nine-acre plot of land that could have been more condos, the space was acquired by the Art Museum and the board committed to raising the money to build a sculpture park. Over a million people went through it the first year and it is growing in popularity. The Art Museum is an enormous factor in town culturally. The people you meet on that board are well positioned as leaders in the community and deserve a lot of respect for their efforts.

UNIVERSITY OF WASHINGTON, My MBA and EMBA students
SEATTLE UNIVERSITY, My MBA students
When I retired from the MBA program at the University of Washington after 10 years, my class was one of the school's most popular. I think we were able to get the message out to the students about the "real world" experience. We have covered my teaching subjects at UW and SU earlier. It is important to pray for each of them.

FRANK MELCHER, United Way chief of staff in Seattle

MICHAEL MELCHER
Frank Melcher's son. After Wells Fargo, my list includes the United Way people and a young man named Michael Melcher. I spent five years working with the United Way in San Francisco, and when I came to Seattle they asked me to get re-involved, which I did. In every campaign there is always a chief staff person who runs it, does all the work, and manages the volunteers. When I became chairman of the campaign in 1996, there was a man

named Frank Melcher who was the United Way of Seattle's chief person. He was the one I depended on the most when I was running that campaign. He was a nice man as well as knowledgeable and experienced in the organization. He and his wife had a child, Michael, who was born deaf and blind. When I pray for the United Way people, I always pray for Michael Melcher. His father, Frank, is still active in United Way but in different cities.

## Mark Pigott

PACCAR chairman and CEO, contributor to both my MBA and EMBA classes. My educational bent after I retired from the bank was supported by Mark Pigott and PACCAR, Inc. I was on the board at PACCAR for a while, and when Charles Pigott retired his son, Mark, was made chairman and CEO. The board has 10 members, mostly outside members, and Mark has run the company for more than 10 years. His record has been extraordinary. The stock has done better than most tech stocks or almost any other stock around. They have done a super job of creating high-quality truck transportation for this country and around the world. They bought a company in The Netherlands (DAF) that was in financial difficulty, developed it, and now they are going like gangbusters in Europe. In fact, one of their officials told me the other day that if you want to get a PACCAR truck in Europe, you have to get on a list, and it takes about a year to buy it. In the United States today, with our slowed-down economy, it takes about three weeks, which gives you an idea of the balance they have with the company in Europe. The products over there are a lot different from the products here, but they have many commonalities. The Europeans tend to leverage one company against another, with almost no debt, and it works well. Mark has handled that and he has taken technology to the highest level ever in a trucking company. He calls PACCAR a technology company.

Mark has taught at both Seattle University and the University of Washington. He has been a fabulous teacher and a tremendous supporter of the program. Mark is good on his feet; he comes in with slides and videos and trucker's hats for the class, and they love it. He is firm and strong and there is no doubt about what he thinks and where he is going.

When I retired from teaching in the spring of 2015, the schools were able to find successors in both programs at Seattle U and the University of Washington. Mark insisted that he be maintained as a guest speaker in both programs. He remains committed to teaching students and enjoys fielding the questions. He has sponsored the program financially, both through the company and personally.

# FRIENDS

## Jerry and Jane Dwyer

Jerry was my tennis partner at Portsmouth Priory and a lifelong friend. He was also a bachelor most of his life and finally started going out with Jane, who was 20 years younger. She told him when he was in his late fifties that if they were not married before he turned 60, it was over. They did get married. I think he was 59. They have had a wonderful marriage.

Peter Flanigan , Portsmouth Priory classmate and lifelong friend
Thea Flanigan, Peter's second wife
Horace Flanigan, Peter's father and a New York City banker
Mrs. Horace Flanigan, Mother of Peter and John and my mother's close friend and godchild
Peggy Flanigan McDonnell, Peter's sister and Sheila's sister-in-law and mother of nine children
Brigid Flanigan, Peter's first wife, who passed away eight years ago

## John and Nancy Flanigan

John was Peter Flanigan's brother. John and Nancy had a fine relationship. I did not see John as much through the years. John eventually left Los Angeles and moved to Reno and lived there until he died. His second wife, Nancy, is a star. She has been a good wife to him, a good mother to his children, and is a warm, self-sufficient, interesting, and can-do-anything person.

## Carl and Jean Livingston

Lifelong friends from San Francisco, one of the first couples Sheila and I met. We had the unique experience of sharing the same baby nurse when we were having our children. Carl's family had a dry goods store in downtown San Francisco that his father ran until he died and Carl took over.

Gordon McShane, Classmate with Peter, Jerry, and me at Portsmouth
Gordie was married to three women who were all widows. He outlived the first two, but with his recent marriage he was not as fortunate. He died of a massive heart attack while they were on a trip. I still pray for Gordie, and I pray for his family and his kids, hoping they are all doing well.

Cal Knudson, Seattle entrepreneur, Seattle Art Museum board member, and friend

JULIA LEE KNUDSON
Friend to Mary Alice when we first moved to Seattle. Julia Lee was the wife of Cal Knudson, whom we met through Peter Flanigan, my friend in New York. Cal and Julia Lee were down on the Oregon shore on a weekend when she suddenly died in her rocking chair. It was a shock. She had a brain tumor and no one could have seen that coming. I have been praying for her ever since.

JACK AND DIANE LAMEY
Jack was a Seattle doctor and a golfing friend. Diane was a friend of both Mary Alice and mine. As with Julia Lee Knudson, Diane suddenly developed a brain tumor. We went to see her in Swedish Hospital, but she did not survive for long. It was a terrible shock. She had been one of Mary Alice's earliest friends in Seattle. I pray for both Diane and Julia because they were kind, good women who died too early and so unexpectedly.

HERMAN PHLEGER, My father's best friend through life
ATHERTON PHLEGER, Herman Phleger's son and a good friend

CYRUS VANCE JR. AND PEGGY FLANIGAN VANCE
Cyrus was a former Seattle attorney and the son of President Carter's secretary of state. Peggy and Cy have two children, and Cy did an outstanding job with his Seattle law firm. He was a Democrat and interested in politics, which he must have inherited from his father. He moved to New York City and was elected Attorney General. Peggy was Peter Flanigan's niece. One day I was talking to Peggy at a social function. We got talking about the family and somehow the subject of her father (Murray McDonnell) came up. It was after he died and the business had gone south. She defended him, and defended him well, I might add. She said that a lot of people criticized him inside and outside the family about the way he ran the business and the fact that it was not successful, but she told me that he was a good father. "He would call us all at least once a week. He always kept in touch, and we always knew he was there for us," she said. After that talk with Peggy, even though I had not felt close to Murray, I thought that I should pray for him, so I put him on the list and he's been there ever since.

SALLY MAILLIARD
Daughter of my mother's best friend, Miriam Van Sicklin. Aunt Miriam Van
Sicklin was my godmother. I had always known Sally even though she was
somewhat younger than I. When we moved to San Francisco I got to know
her better. We moved in the same circles as Sally and her husband, Jim. Sally
was a strong lady. She had five children, which she appeared to have had
with great ease. Jimmy died of cancer and Sally died almost a year later of
the same thing. In each case it was unexpected and much too early in their
lifespan. I like thinking about them and I like to pray for them every day.


JIMMY MAILLIARD
Jim was from an old San Francisco family and we used to do one thing a
year together — we partnered in the Pacific-Union Club Domino
Tournament. It is a big tournament that happens annually and, as everyone
knows in San Francisco, it takes nearly a year to complete. Jimmy was a
good domino player and played a lot, whereas I was an average player and
did not play that much. Jim felt it was one way that we would make sure we
saw each other, so he always signed us up to play together.


TOMMY AND AMY-ANN SULLIVAN
San Francisco friends. Tommy was a real estate broker and he and his wife,
Amy-Ann, were social friends of Sheila and me. We saw them a lot at
parties in San Francisco and Burlingame. Tommy died young, and
Amy-Ann remarried, but she also died at an early age, within four or five
years of Tommy. I wasn't that close to either one of them, but for some
reason I started to pray for them and I just decided to keep doing it. There
is no reason in the world to quit. They were nice to us in many ways when
we lived in San Francisco and I hope that they are doing well in heaven.


DICK AND ANN MILLER
Robert Watt Miller's son and my close friend in San Francisco. Dick and
Ann had 12 children. Ann became a Carmelite nun after Dick passed away.


BEVEN BRADBURY
Australian friend with a wonderful singing voice. Beven Bradbury was a
friend I met on business trips to Australia. The first time I went there, he
said, "Dick, come back. Come back at Christmastime. It's a lovely time of
year." I wrote to Beven and told him we were coming with our youngest
son, Bruce, and his friend. Beven said how happy he was when we arrived

back in the county. He came and picked us up the next day for lunch, which was Christmas Day. That was a pretty big offer. I felt guilty about it, but I couldn't say no because I really wanted to do it. Beven came to the hotel and said, "Dick, your letter just arrived. It's a J.I.T. (Just in Time). We got your letter yesterday." In effect, he had one day's notice that we were coming for Christmas. He stepped up and was as kind as he always was.

We went to his house for a wonderful Christmas luncheon. It was tremendous. They had all their children and grandchildren, and everyone sat around one table. It was the kind of thing that you would hope to have happen in another country because you'd like to see how others celebrate. One of the remarkable things Beven did was sing a long song at the end of the lunch. It was a dirge about Australia's beginnings. It described all those early years when all the convicts were sent to Australia and how they made the country what it is today. It was mournful but wonderful. It was a tradition each year. Clarisse was his wife and she had presents for all of us. What an outpouring of friendship and love. Just what you would hope for. Beven died a few years later.

SHERM SIBLEY, Friend and chief executive of Pacific Gas and Electric

WILLIE CANNON
Hawaiian friend and Bank of Hawaii's chief executive officer. Willie Cannon was Hawaiian. I met him through the Bank of Hawaii in Honolulu. One of Willie's children was in school with my daughter Leslie. Willie smoked too much and got lung cancer. I was in Hawaii when he died. I was on another island and flew to Honolulu. I went by the hospital to see him and there was no one around. He was wheezing, but sedated. There was no one there, so I stayed with him and prayed. I will always remember him in that bed, hours before he died, and breathing out his life. It didn't seem right that he was alone at that time. Leslie came with me to the funeral.

EDWARD GILLETTE
California born insurance man and Bohemian Club member. My old friend Ed Gillette was from San Francisco and in the insurance business. My connection with him was the Bohemian Club. We entered the club about the same time and stayed in the open camp for new members. Two years later we joined the Mandalay Camp together. For the first 10 years at Mandalay, we roomed together. Those were the years when I was going up three weekends in a row during the month of July. We would act in the

plays or do whatever they asked you to do. Ed was a character. He was a golfer, and we played some together. He'd been through the Naval Academy in the war and grew up in Santa Monica. Our time together was mostly at the Bohemian Grove, and there we saw a lot of each other. Always a friend, he was upbeat and willing to help you any way he could. He died many years after Sherm Sibley, but he died similarly in a fishing accident and drowned in a river.

### DICK AND MARGIE ALDEN
Dick was a prominent Los Angeles attorney and a newer friend. He was married to one of Mary Alice's closest friends. When we lived in Los Angeles we saw a lot of them. There was a group of eight or 10 of us who spent time together socially, and they were a part of that group. Dick did very well. He eventually got out of the law firm to work with Hughes Medical, became a businessman, and made himself a small fortune. He was also a lawyer for the Irvine Estate, where he advised Don Bren, the owner. Dick and Margie were a wonderful couple. They lived well and traveled a lot. Dick died after a long bout with cancer. It was somewhat similar to what happened to Mary Alice's third husband. It went on for a year or so and was very hard on him and on Margie. Both of them had been married before and had children by other partners. They had a house in Sun Valley where they would put us up until we bought our own house. They thought the world of Mary Alice, and I guess they accepted me as we went along.

### EVA GARZA LAGÜERA AND HER FAMILY.
Eva is the wife of Eugenio Garza Lagüera, a business friend from Monterrey, Mexico, whom I knew from Wells Fargo. I used to go to Mexico at least once a year because we had lots of business going back and forth and hoped to get more. Eugenio was one of the movers-and-shakers in the town of Monterrey, which is sort of like Chicago, a big manufacturing area. We became social friends as well as business acquaintances. One day we must have been talking about religion or at least a subject that could make an easy transition because Eva said to me, "Will you pray for me?" I said, "Sure, I'll pray for you and your family. I'd be happy to do that." She asked me over 30 years ago in the 1980s and I am still praying for her every day. Eva was a bright star. She was a good mother, personable, and smart. Eugenio has passed on, but I hope all is well with the family and I pray that they are safe.

# FAITH CONNECTIONS

FATHER EGON, Woodside Priory founder

One of the things that I look back on with pride during my time on the West Coast is my affiliation with Woodside Priory School, a Benedictine boarding school. The Benedictine monks at Portsmouth Priory gave me such a tremendous education and spiritual backbone that I am grateful they are able to continue their mission.

Woodside Priory was founded some 50 years ago after eight Hungarian Benedictine monks escaped from behind the Iron Curtain in the late 1940s and made their way to Canada, then to the East Coast of the United States, and eventually settled in the San Francisco area. I was living in San Francisco at the time, and one of the monks put in charge of securing a location for a school contacted me for help. A location was found in Woodside, in the hills behind Stanford University in the Portola Valley, and the Priory was opened in 1957. One of the Hungarian monks and Father Egon Javor were two of the school's founders. I came to know Father Egon well during my years as a banker in San Francisco. I think about him a lot and I will always miss him. I am glad he was my friend.

The Priory continues to thrive, and although it has changed to primarily a day school, it remains a high-level college preparatory school for more than 300 students, including boarders from South America and Asia. People have welcomed and supported this school with incredible influence and generosity. It has become an intellectual center.

When Father Egon died in 2008, he was 91. My oldest son, Pierce, and I went to his funeral. He was laid out in the school's chapel and he was beautiful. His face looked rested and as though he was at peace.

ARCHBISHOP'S OFFICE

I pray for their guidance and sacrifice. I put it that way because in raising money or being involved in some of the efforts that the archbishop wants to see happen in the community, you do not always deal with the archbishop personally but often with someone who has been appointed to do the job. In my case, the archbishop's office has supported the Fulcrum Foundation, and during my time in Seattle, I have known three archbishops.

The Seattle Archdiocese went through a lot of problems with Archbishop Hunthausen, who had strong ideas about government and what was the right moral thing to do in certain situations. He was rather liberal, and there were many conservative Catholics in town who objected to his views on life. He was more accepting of the gay population, and he had his own ideas. He did not like nuclear arms, and he did not like the fact that nuclear bombs were in this state or that Trident submarines were 30 miles away from downtown Seattle. One year I think he refused to pay half his taxes in protest against the nuclear presence here. In any event, the church hierarchy in Rome and in Washington, D.C., got after him and tried to make him resign. His chancellor, Father Michael Ryan, defended him well enough that he was not forced to resign until he was 75 years old, when all bishops must retire.

While that was going on, they sent an auxiliary bishop out to be his backup. Apparently the Vatican people in Rome told the auxiliary bishop one thing but neglected to tell the archbishop of Seattle what the new bishop's powers would be. There was a political brouhaha in the church, and the first backup was sent to Pittsburgh. He was Archbishop Wuerl and he has done well since he left Seattle.

After that another bishop, Archbishop Murphy, was sent out from Montana. He stayed and when Archbishop Hunthausen retired, Archbishop Murphy took over. Archbishop Murphy was popular, but unfortunately he became ill and died in office after he had been in the job for only a few years. He was replaced by Archbishop Brunett, (also from Montana). Archbishop Brunett is 75 and had to submit his resignation. The Vatican does not have to accept it, but he had to make the gesture. Whether we have a change coming up in the near future, I do not know, but it is amazing to me that I have known three archbishops here in the 25 short years I have been in town.

Over the years I have worked with the archbishop's office on many occasions. I have contributed to the level of my ability, which is not tremendous. A lot of the people who work around the archbishop have become fine friends to me, and I feel fortunate to have met them.

The biggest thing for me that came from working with the archbishop's office was the Fulcrum Foundation. It is an organization set up to provide scholarships and help for the parochial school system. The church school systems all over the country are in dire need of funding and support, just as the public school programs are. It turns out that many of the Catholic schools struggle to make it. They do not have the income from the parish they once did and cannot charge the students enough to keep the schools running.

The archbishop needed an organization devoted to raising money and keeping the school system going. That is what the Fulcrum Foundation has done. It has been going for eleven years, but its first drive was for

$40 million. They did more than make their goal and have raised more money for this group of Seattle schools than has ever been raised before. The foundation has one fund for giving scholarships. They are not big scholarships; it used to be $500 per person per year, but now it's up to $650 a person. It is just a partial scholarship, because it costs $2,300 on up to go to a parochial school these days. Other private schools in the area charge upward of $15,000 a year. Parochial schools provide a solid education and impart the values of the Catholic church. Keeping them going is probably one of the most important things that a Catholic can do in any part of the United States. Father Rowan was the chairman, the initiator appointed by the archbishop to do this job. He was succeeded by Father Ryan when Father Rowan moved to Portland to be dean of humanities at the University of Portland. I was the vice chairman and there were three or four other founding directors on the board. The board has been expanded to 20 people or so, and it is an organization that in its short eleven years has gained considerable respect.

All over the country Catholic dioceses are having the same problem with schools. Everyone is looking for a solution. There is not one solution, but they can learn from each other. I think our success in Seattle has been an inspiration to many other dioceses that are trying to solve the problem of funding a good education for children.

FULCRUM FOUNDATION, Care and keeping of our community and Catholic education
ARCHBISHOP HUNTHAUSEN, A humble man of God with strongly held opinions
FATHER MICHAEL RYAN, Pastor of St. James Cathedral Parish and chairman of the Fulcrum Foundation
ARCHBISHOP BRUNETT, The former head of the Church in the Pacific Northwest
FATHER ROWAN, Founding chairman of the Fulcrum Foundation

SEATTLE PREP
I pray for the people at Seattle Prep, which is the oldest private school in the city of Seattle and run by the Jesuits. I was on that board for four years, during which time they got into terrible trouble. The school was running a campaign and had a disaster with the president, who had to be relieved and replaced. They had a board of 12 to 15 people. It was interesting, but at the same time it was frustrating. It was impossible to get anything done

without lengthy discussions including all sectors of the community, with many of them represented on the board. It was a debating society. Meetings would go on for four hours without fail, covering matters that on other boards could have been dealt with in an hour or less. There was a lot of discussion, and everyone had a chance to say what they thought. Needless to say, it was interesting and I learned a lot. After four years of bickering, I got off the board. Mary Alice was getting worse and I could not spend all the time the board required to function.

The school has done well. Gradually they got through the weak spots. They had a successful fund-raising drive early on when I was on the board. Since I have been off, they have had another successful fund drive. It is seemingly an Irish Catholic enclave, and they have not been able to solve the problem of diversity in the school. The faculty of about 70 members has been there longer than anybody, and it is hard to move them around. I was able to help them a little bit with their finances. More parents and capable people have come on board since, which has caused a rejuvenation over the last five to 10 years. They have a new president who was president of one of the biggest high schools in the diocese, Blanchet. There is a good intellectual quality there and they are tied in with Seattle University, which is also run by the Jesuits.

St. James Parish

An attentive Seattle Catholic institution. St. James Cathedral Parish and the Immaculate Conception Parish are different but I lump both parishes together. St. James is the one I go to almost exclusively. I occasionally go to Mass at other places, but my principal support goes to St. James, where Father Michael Ryan has been the rector for over 20 years. He is an outstanding person, loved by everyone, and has done an enormously productive job for the community, not only for the Catholics but for everyone else as well.

Immaculate Conception

A parish of color and commitment to its community. The Immaculate Conception Parish is the oldest parish church in Seattle. The church was supposed to be a cathedral 100 years ago, but the bishop wanted to move the cathedral farther downtown, so the Immaculate Conception Parish remained on 18th Avenue, and St. James is on 9th Avenue, closer to downtown. I support them both. At Immaculate I am not active, but I have helped them with some of their drives and things they have needed.

### The Pigott Family

For their contributions to education and our Church. The Pigott family has generously supported education and the needs of the Catholic Church since William and Ada Pigott established their family in Seattle in 1895.

### The Lee Family

For their support of Catholic education and our Church. The Lee family generosity supports Catholic education and the Church. They are an extraordinary and well-liked family.

### The Stamper Family

The Stampers' specific support for the elementary grades in reading and training in the ethical values of life through books has been successful countrywide.

### Pope Francis

For the strength he must possess to lead the Church. Then I pray for the Archbishops Brunett and Hunthausen and all the bishops of the Catholic Church that they may be humble and full of love. That they may run the Church the way Christ intended. That Catholics and all other Christians may be recognized by the love they have for each other.

### The Medical Community

For their efforts over my life that have helped me survive. I pray for the doctors and nurses and all the others who have helped me survive thus far. There are so many of these extraordinary people that I am not going to list them separately, even though my gratitude and debt to each one is huge. Without their lifelong support system, my life would have been entirely different and probably would have ended many years ago.

———————

# Father Ryan's Homily

I think that if Dick were to have his say, he would tell me to be brief and to the point this afternoon, and not to make a big deal about him. Dick Cooley was a "big deal," of course, but he was also a very humble man. He may have been larger than life — a "captain of industry" who reached the pinnacle of his profession, a leader in this community who walked easily among the great and the near great, but he was remarkably humble. With Dick, it was always more about you than about him. The title of the first edition of his book makes that clear: *Searching Through My Prayer List*. The focus of so much in that book is on others, not him. So I'm thinking that, from his place with God, Dick may be surprised that so many are here today. But I'm sure he's delighted that the people in life he loved the most have gathered to remember and pray for him in this Cathedral that was an important place along his journey of faith.

I'm not going to tell Dick's life story this afternoon. Dick did that very well in his book. And I'm not going to eulogize him, either, or canonize him. (Although it does happen to be All Saints Day — draw your own conclusions!) No, all I want to do is acknowledge what we all know: that Dick Cooley was one extraordinary man and that we were very blessed to know him and call him friend!

Bridget, my heart goes out to you. What a wonderful companion, friend, and soul mate you were for Dick and he for you. He adored you, and you him. You were so good for each other. Magic. Your love was sweet, beautiful, and strong. One of the great joys of my life was witnessing your vows back in 2003. And renewing them with you and Dick just a couple months ago was a great joy, too. The smiles in the photos we took tell the story of a day I will always remember.

My heart also goes out to each of you in Dick's family as you give your father and grandfather back to God. Your loss is great and the fact that you knew it was coming and had time to prepare for it doesn't remove the sting.

Let me get down to business now — Dick would want that! — and reflect on the readings (Ecclesiastes 3:1-8, II Corinthians 9:6-9,* and Luke 7:1-10) we just heard. Each of them was a little window onto Dick, each of them found an echo in his life. The passage from Ecclesiastes reflected for me Dick's no nonsense, down-to-earth, considered, philosophical way of looking at life. No one knew better than Dick that life has its rhythms — happy rhythms, sad rhythms, sprightly rhythms, slow rhythms, dances, dirges, jigs and jazz, and everything in-between. "There is an appointed time for everything: a time to be born and a time to die . . . a time to weep and a time to laugh, a time to mourn and a time to dance . . . a time to embrace and a time to be far from embraces…a time to be silent and a time to speak . . .."

With his ever so keen mind and sharp wit, Dick knew all that. And he lived it. As much of an "in charge" guy as he was, Dick knew that this world was ultimately God's world and that it unfolded according to God's plan, not his, and he willingly and generously put himself at the service of that plan. Dick was blessed with many gifts but two I would single out were patience and perspective. Dick had great patience. Think of the way he put his shattered life back together when a lesser person would have folded. It was nothing short of amazing. For all his drive, he was a remarkably patient man — with a patience born of wisdom and experience. And he had perspective on things. He knew what was important and what wasn't, and he had no inflated sense of where he fit into the grand scheme of things. During a recent conversation, Dick spoke calmly and frankly with me about his coming death, and as he did, he smiled and said, "It won't be the end of the world."

That was Dick. He had perspective on things and a lot of wisdom. And, while he had good reason to take himself seriously, he didn't take himself too seriously. He was too humble for that, too aware of God. And I'm quite sure that Dick's commitment to starting — or ending — every day with Mass had more than a little to do with all that. It's where he gained perspective and it's where he learned humility. And it's what prepared him to die with grace and gratitude.

Listen to some of his own words from his book: "I go to church every day not because I'm a 'holy roller' and not because I'm tremendously spiritual or mystical; it is not that at all. I go every day because I…need the reminder of who I am. I need to know that there is someone up there running the show and not me…. This is where humility comes in. The biggest things in life are humility and love." What could I possibly add to that?

The reading from Second Corinthians was all about giving. But not just any giving. Cheerful giving. There are a lot of givers in this world, as you know, but some of them, frankly, give giving a bad name, so painful do they make it look, and so grudgingly do they do it. Not Dick Cooley. Giving was in Dick's DNA. Cheerful giving, generous giving. Dick gave generously of his means and was equally generous in the way he shared his experience, gifts, and talents. There are many fortunate individuals in this community, too many to count — and many important institutions and organizations — in business, education, healthcare, the church, and the arts with Dick Cooley's fingerprints all over them. They bear the mark of his genius, his vision, his leadership, and his sterling, uncompromising ethics. We here today are not the only ones who have lost Dick Cooley. Seattle has lost him. But his contributions live on and our loss is heaven's gain because how can the God who loves a cheerful giver not have welcomed Dick Cooley home!

I chose the gospel story of the Centurion whose servant was ill because the Centurion reminded me of Dick. The Centurion was the big man in town, the one with power and influence, but he refused to play the power game. He wouldn't even approach Jesus himself; instead, he depended on others to go on his behalf. And when he learned that Jesus was actually on his way to visit him, he sent word to him not to trouble himself because he didn't feel worthy to have him enter his house. A word from a distance would suffice. And it did, of course.

Dick had the humility of that Centurion. Like the Centurion, his concern was not for himself but for others. And Dick had the faith of the Centurion, too. With every fiber of his being, he believed in Jesus — in his love, his power, his mercy. He never considered himself worthy of any of it, of course, but he believed nonetheless.

And there is another reason why I chose that passage. The words of the Centurion are words Dick spoke every time over the years that he received the Eucharist. Words full of humility, words full of faith, words of deep conviction: "Lord, I am not worthy to receive you. Say but the word and I shall be healed." Like the Centurion, Dick knew what it meant to give orders and for people to snap to, but that was never what it was about for him. It wasn't really about power, it was about service. I'm reminded of a conversation we had years ago in which he told me of his admiration for our retired Archbishop, Raymond Hunthausen, a humble servant leader if ever there was one. Dick liked that about him — liked his humility, his courage, his strong yet gentle leadership. "Hunthausen," he said to me, "he's the real thing." I would say the same about Dick. He was the real thing.

———

Enough! No matter how long I talked I wouldn't say enough, so I think it's time simply to thank God for Dick — for his great soul, his keen mind, his humble ways, his good humor, and for all the ways he touched our lives. It's time to thank God for him and to commend him to the God who was so good in giving him to us. Time, too, to ask God that Dick's mantle might fall over all of us in some way — especially over you, Bridget, and over each of Dick's children, stepchildren, grandchildren and great-grandchildren — as you continue your journey of life. As you do, you will do well to take a chapter from Dick's book — holding on to faith as he did, speaking the truth as he did, caring for others as he did, and making a difference as he did. I can think of no better way to honor his memory.

I'm going to give Dick the last word. From his book: "When you get to the end of your life, which is where I certainly am, you begin to think. When I die, what is going to happen? Where will I go? Who will I see? What are the joys of heaven? When it comes down to it you have your mind, your heart, and your soul. And you have the ability to love people and to help people. I would like to be with love for all eternity and I think that is what heaven is… It's clearly a mystery but I have faith in my final destination."

Dick, so do we! And with good reason. When I think of you, I think of those immortal words from the Prophet Micah: "You have been told, O man, what is good and what the Lord requires of you: only to do the right, to love justice, and to walk humbly with your God." That was you, Dick Cooley. In every way. And we are better people because of it, and our world is a better place. Rest in peace, dear friend. Be with the God you served so faithfully, the God who is love!

Father Michael G. Ryan
*St. James Cathedral*
*November 1, 2016*

* *These readings can be found on page 305 and 315, respectively.*

Dick at Sun Valley, Idaho.

BRIDGET AND DICK RENEW THEIR WEDDING VOWS ON JULY 5, 2016.

# Reflections by Bridget

As I look back on my life with Dick I am flooded with memories of a loving, selfless, generous man who only wanted the best for others. His beautiful spirit is what stood out for me.

After first meeting him, I appreciated his humility and kindness. While helping others, he always had a soft delivery and yet remained a leader. In his own world, he was driven but never pressed others to be the same. Rather, he would give you a gentle shove to show you how to trust yourself so that you might soar. For me and many who looked up to him, he provided these gentle shoves. But I also considered him my launch pad from which my dreams became real and took flight.

He was a gentle giant. It takes a big man to be in the background.

Dick came out of left field. I believe those are the best relationships. The ones you don't plan or expect. My relationship with Dick snuck up on me and caught me off guard. My years with him were the best of my life.

The memories that stand out the strongest are his faith and how he walked the walk by attending Mass seven days a week no matter where he was in the world. When he prayed, a look of complete devotion would come over his face. Nothing else existed at that moment.

Every day, Dick got on his knees to thank the Lord for a second chance. And when Dick stood up, he spent every moment helping all of us and touching all of our lives.

There was a humility about him, which, as I began to find out about all of his accomplishments, caught my attention even more. He never talked about his World War II experience and the powerful airplane he flew, the crash of which resulted in the loss of his right arm. "It was just something I did," he would say.

That he took up flying forty years later in a high-performance aircraft is nothing short of a miracle.

A defining moment was the first time I watched him tie the laces of his shoe. I remember he wanted to show me after I had asked about it. Looking back now, I think of all the systems he had to develop to survive with one arm. I would say this particular one, along with tying his tie, were the hardest he had to accomplish. He carefully laid one lace over the other, looping it through to create the bow and tighten. This took quite a few minutes. I couldn't stop the tear that fell from my eye onto the lace of the shoe. And I knew then how much I admired this man and wanted to be with him.

As I started to spend time with Dick, I was in awe not just with the day-to-day tasks he had to face but the added joys of his life that most people take for granted or don't even get to do. He flew a high performance airplane, he hit a golf ball 200 yards, he skied in Sun Valley from the top at 10,000 ft., he could smash a squash or a tennis ball, he worked out and rode a bike, he ran two banks, and he traveled all over the world.

I developed a respect and an admiration early on that far outweighed any concerns about our age difference. So when the day came that he told me his intentions were to marry me, there was no hesitation. Even the way he made that statement was attractive. I found Dick Cooley fascinating in every way.

Every move he made fascinated me because as I stood next to him and watched him, I realized that he had to work a hundred times harder than me just to get the same thing done. Not once in all the years I was with him did he ever complain. His bigger fear was losing the function of his left hand. He did not want to have to depend on anyone. The week he completed the last chapter of this book, his hand went numb and he was very concerned. Two months later, he couldn't use it. It was the first time I saw him cry. A few months after that, he lost all feeling in his legs and even then he was only concerned about his hand. The hand that shared and gave everything to all of us.

Dick showed a grace and strength through the last two years of his life that confirmed again who he was: loving, patient, trusting, kind, and gentle. As his body changed, he graciously accepted what was happening and kept thanking the Lord for his wonderful life.

Dick's curiosity about life was one of his best traits. He wanted to know how everything worked. He didn't have any fear. He would be curious about something, study it, then go after it. Dick Cooley knew how to execute. He knew how to take action and get it done. If something didn't work out, he just went down a different road.

If I had to come up with one word about Dick, it would be love. When we arrived home from our honeymoon, he looked me straight in the eye and said, "The honeymoon is just beginning." He wasn't kidding. If Dick Cooley cared about you, he poured himself into you. He was quiet about it and completely committed. I was the luckiest girl in the world. It brings me great comfort to know that he is buried next to his parents and was given full military honors at his memorial service in Santa Clara.

Dick Cooley was a giant, but he was also just my cute little guy. Though there was nothing little about Dick Cooley. Dick always wanted to do the right thing and do his best. He was the finest example of a human being I have ever encountered. It was a privilege to be with him. God is the lucky one now.

I am who I am because of the Lord. I am who I've become because of Dick Cooley.

Dick at a black-tie function with Bridget.

UPPER: BRIDGET AND DICK ON THE FAIRWAY AT
AUGUSTA NATIONAL GOLF COURSE, 2007.

LOWER: NEIL ARMSTRONG WITH BRIDGET AND DICK.

*"On the surface it seems like a conflict: the drive to be self-reliant vs. self-awareness of one's limitations. But to Dick, both could be harmoniously achieved as long as you have a positive attitude. That attitude was Dick's most treasured system, and a lasting inspiration."*

— Will Guyman, November 1, 2016

# *Index*

*time flies...*